Britain's Pensions Crisis: History and Policy

British Academy Occasional Paper · 7

Britain's Pensions Crisis: History and Policy

Edited by

Hugh Pemberton, Pat Thane,
& Noel Whiteside

Published for THE BRITISH ACADEMY
by OXFORD UNIVERSITY PRESS

Oxford University Press, Great Clarendon Street, Oxford OX2 6DP
Oxford New York

Auckland Cape Town Dar es Salaam Hong Kong Karachi
Kuala Lumpur Madrid Melbourne Mexico City Nairobi
New Delhi Shanghai Taipei Toronto

With offices in
Argentina Austria Brazil Chile Czech Republic France Greece
Guatemala Hungary Italy Japan Poland Portugal Singapore
South Korea Switzerland Thailand Turkey Ukraine Vietnam

Published in the United States
by Oxford University Press Inc., New York

First published 2006

British Library Cataloguing in Publication Data
Data available

Library of Congress Cataloging in Publication Data
Data available

Typeset by
J&L Composition, Filey, North Yorkshire
Printed in Great Britain
on acid-free paper by
Antony Rowe Limited
Chippenham, Wiltshire

ISBN 0–19–726385–2 978–0–19–726385–3

Contents

Notes on Contributors

Gordon L. Clark is Halford Mackinder Professor of Geography at the University of Oxford. He is affiliated with the Institute of Ageing at Oxford and has been Director of the Saïd Business School's executive education programme on pension reform. His recent books include *Pension Fund Capitalism* (2000), *European Pensions and Global Finance* (2003), and the *Oxford Handbook of Pensions and Retirement Income* (2006).

Maurizio Ferrera is Professor of Social Policy at the State University of Milan. He also directs the Center for Comparative Political Studies (Poleis) at the Bocconi University of Milan and the Research Unit of European Governance (URGE) at the Collegio Carlo Alberto, Turin. He has recently published *Welfare State Reform in Southern Europe* (2005) and *Rescued by Europe? Social and Labour Market Reforms in Italy from Maastricht to Berlusconi* (2004).

Frank Field was Minister for Welfare Reform between May 1997 and July 1998. He was elected to Parliament in 1979 as Member for Birkenhead and was previously Director of the Child Poverty Action Group. A former Chairman of the Social Security Select Committee, he is the author of numerous works on welfare, low pay, and social issues. He is currently Chairman of the Pensions Reform Group.

Jay Ginn is a Visiting Professor at the University of Surrey. She has published widely on pensions, especially on how pension system design and reform affects the degree of gender inequality of pension income. Recent books include *Women, Work and Pensions* (co-edited with D. Street and S. Arber, 2001) and *Gender, Pensions and the Lifecourse: How Pensions Need to Adapt to Changing Family Forms* (2003).

Howard Glennerster is Professor Emeritus at the London School of Economics. He is the author of *British Social Policy since 1945* (2nd edn, 2000), *Understanding the Finance of Welfare* (2003), and, with John Hills, David Piachaud, and Jo Webb, *One Hundred Years of Poverty and Policy* (2004).

Jose Harris is Professor of Modern History at the University of Oxford. She is the author of *William Beveridge: A Biography* (1977; 2nd edn, 1997), and of numerous other works on the history of social thought and social policy. Her most recent book is *Civil Society in British History: Ideas, Institutions, Identities* (2003; pbk edn, 2004).

John Hills is Professor of Social Policy and Director of the ESRC Research Centre for Analysis of Social Exclusion (CASE) at the London School of Economics and was a member of the Pensions Commission. His most recent publications are *A More Equal Society? New Labour, Poverty, Inequality and Exclusion* (co-editor, 2005), *Inequality and the State* (2004), and *One Hundred Years of Poverty and Policy* (co-author, 2004).

Karl Hinrichs is Senior Research Associate at the University of Bremen's Centre for Social Policy Research and Professor of Political Science at Humboldt University, Berlin. His present research interests focus on the German welfare state in comparative perspective.

Patricia Hollis (Baroness Hollis of Heigham) was, between 1997 and 2005, Minister in the House of Lords for the Department of Work and Pensions (formerly the Department of Social Security). Previously she had been Reader in Modern History and Dean of the School of English and American Studies at the University of East Anglia, as well as Leader of Norwich City Council. Her publications include *Ladies Elect: Women in English Local Government 1865–1914* (1987) and *Jennie Lee: A Life* (1997).

Paul Johnson is Deputy Director of the London School of Economics and Professor of Economic History. He has written widely on the economics of ageing and pensions and, most recently, co-edited *The Cambridge Economic History of Modern Britain* (3 vols, 2004).

Katharina Müller is a Research Officer at the German Development Institute (GDI), Bonn. Her published work on social policy and economic issues in Latin America, Eastern Europe, and Central Asia has been widely translated and her book *The Political Economy of Pension Reform in Central and Eastern Europe* (1999) won prizes from both the European Association for Comparative Economic Studies and the American Association for the Advancement of Slavic Studies.

Hugh Pemberton is Lecturer in Modern British History at the University of Bristol. He is the author of *Policy Learning and British Governance in the 1960s* (2004) and a number of other works on post-war British economic policy. Prior to his academic career he worked for a number of years as a business analyst in the life and pensions sector.

Steven Sass is Associate Director for Research at the Center for Retirement Research (CRR) at Boston College. Sass was previously an economist at the Federal Reserve Bank of Boston and was the founding editor of the Bank's *Regional Review*. He co-edited *Social Security Reform: Links to Saving, Investment, and Growth* (1997). Other publications include *The Promise of Private Pensions* (1997), the CRR *Global Issues in Brief* on the reform of the US, UK, and Australian retirement income systems, and, with Alicia Munnell, *Social Security and Stocks* (forthcoming).

Pat Thane is Professor of Contemporary British History and Director of the Centre for Contemporary British History at the Institute of Historical Research, University of London. Her publications include *The Foundations of the Welfare State* (1982; 2nd edn, 1996), *Old Age in English History: Past Experiences, Present Issues* (2000), and, most recently, *The Long History of Old Age* (2005).

Noel Whiteside is Professor of Comparative Public Policy and Senior Fellow at the Institute of Governance and Public Management at Warwick University. Her publications include *Pension Security in the 21st Century* (edited with Gordon Clark, 2003).

Acknowledgements

This book is the product of a conference held at the British Academy in June 2005. This was generously co-sponsored by Zurich Financial Services (UK) and B & CE Benefit Schemes. The editors would like to extend their profound thanks to the Academy and to our sponsors for making both the event and the book possible. We also wish to thank Professor Howard Glennerster, FBA for supporting our proposal that the British Academy host the conference, Angela Pusey for her extremely efficient organization of the conference, and Lord Hunt for offering a stimulating introduction to the issues it covered.

1.
Introduction

HUGH PEMBERTON, PAT THANE, AND
NOEL WHITESIDE

Creating a socially just and financially viable pensions system for the aged is one of the most urgent political issues in Britain today. The Pensions Commission, set up by the Labour government to examine the problem, observed in its first report that 'the UK state pension system is among the least generous in the developed world' and that private-sector alternatives were 'in serious decline'.[1] In its second report, the Commission recently concluded that 'major reform of the UK pension system is needed to create a new settlement for the 21st century'.[2] The final nature of that settlement remains unclear, but few doubt that it is needed. If we are to create such a settlement, however, we need to understand why the capacity of our pension system to deliver old-age security is so poor.

As the Pensions Commission noted in its first report, 'The problems of the British pension system today reflect the cumulative impact of decisions and commitments made, and of policies rejected, often with unintended consequences, by governments over several decades.'[3] Plainly, the history of pensions policy through these decades matters because it is hard to devise a lasting solution to a crisis whose origins we do not understand. The consequences of past decisions may constrain options for change. Past successes and failures hold lessons for policy-makers today. For similar reasons, we should understand the historical development of systems elsewhere. How come some offer better pension security than that in the UK? How do they cope with similar pressures?

This volume corrects the neglect of history in the pensions debate. The product of a conference at the British Academy in June 2005, it combines

[1] Pensions Commission, *Pensions: Challenges and Choices. The First Report of the Pensions Commission* (London, 2004), pp. 58 and 80.
[2] Pensions Commission, *A New Pensions Settlement for the Twenty-first Century. The Second Report of the Pensions Commission* (London, 2005).
[3] Pensions Commission, *First Report*, p. vi.

the work of British historians, policy analysts, and activists with that of overseas experts to examine both the roots of the present crisis and how best to solve it.

The Roots of Britain's Pensions Crisis

At the end of 2005, on the eve of the Pensions Commission's second report, John Hutton, Secretary of State for Work and Pensions, noted that old-age security was 'without doubt, one of the most important public policy challenges facing the country'.[4] He set out five tests for any lasting settlement: it must promote personal responsibility and be fair, affordable, simple, and sustainable. At present Britain's system of pensions is failing on all counts.

That the system was, and is, in crisis is not universally accepted. Tim Congdon, for example, denies that aggregate pension savings are inadequate.[5] The Institute for Fiscal Studies argues that, taking all sources of wealth and entitlement to Pension Credit into account, only 11.3 per cent of retirees would have an income below two-thirds of current net earnings.[6] Phil Mullan claims that future costs can easily be met through economic growth and appropriate redistribution.[7] The Pensions Commission itself, perhaps diplomatically, has framed its definition of the crisis in terms of the future rather than the past, despite noting that a solution requires 'adjustments to public policy and/or individual behaviour which ideally should have been started in the last 20–30 years'.[8] The government points out that in real terms the average pensioner has never been better off.[9] This can be read as a comment on the undoubted long-run inadequacy of British pensions, though this was not, of course, the government's intention.

Nevertheless, despite such reminders about the relatively attractive retirement prospects for some, not everyone has been so fortunate as the 'average' pensioner. The median income of the poorest fifth of pensioner

[4] J. Hutton, 'Securing Our Future: The Pensions Challenge', speech to the Institute for Public Policy Research, London, 24 November 2005, www.ipr.org.uk.

[5] T. Congdon, *Providing for Pensions: Savings in a Free Society* (London, 2005).

[6] J. Banks., C. Emmerson, Z. Oldfield, and G. Tetlow, *Prepared for Retirement* (London, 2005).

[7] P. Mullan, *The Imaginary Time Bomb: Why an Ageing Population Is Not a Social Problem* (London, 2000); P. Mullan, 'Ageing and the Pensions Crisis', *Spiked*, 8 December 2005, www.spiked-online.com/articles/0000000CA4E3.htm.

[8] Pensions Commission, *First Report*, p. 1.

[9] See, for example, H. M. Treasury, *Pre-Budget Report, 2000: Building Long-term Prosperity for All* (London, 2000).

couples, for example, grew by only 34 per cent in real terms between 1979 and 1996/7, compared with an average increase of 54 per cent and an increase of over 80 per cent for the richest quintile.[10] Such growing disparities reflect the problems of a pension policy that has relied primarily on fostering voluntary savings, either under occupational pension schemes or as personal pension plans. Since its election in 1997 the Labour government has sought to deal with this, targeting additional pension expenditure on the poorest pensioners (who are disproportionately female) by introducing the Minimum Income Guarantee and Pension Credit. Yet, still, in 2001/2 the median income of women aged 65 and over was only 57 per cent of that of men of the same age.[11]

Indeed, the idea that Britain's pension system, both public and private, is in trouble has gained hold over the past decade. In 2002 the government announced the establishment of a Pensions Commission to 'report on how the current voluntarist approach is developing'.[12] The Commission interpreted its brief more broadly. It noted: 'Pension reform has too often in the past proceeded on the basis of analysis of specific isolated issues.' It wisely concluded that it was impossible to analyse part of the system without considering the whole.[13] The conclusions of the Commission's first report (which was widely welcomed) were blunt: there was an impending pensions crisis; and that crisis could be solved only if the country accepted the need to work longer, save more, pay higher taxes, or adopt some combination of these. The Commission's second report has also been widely praised. Many have echoed Peter Riddell's judgement that the Commission has succeeded in changing the terms of the debate: the focus having shifted from whether reform was needed to what that reform should be.[14]

What exactly is the nature of Britain's pensions crisis? Its components include:

- demographic change arising from changes in both fertility and longevity;
- changing patterns of labour force participation;

[10] Department of Work and Pensions, *Simplicity, Security and Choice: Working and Saving for Retirement* (London, 2002), pp. 19–20; Office for National Statistics (ONS), *Pension Trends*, 1 (London, 2005), 25.

[11] S. Arber and J. Ginn, 'Ageing and Gender: Diversity and Change', *Social Trends*, 34 (London, 2004), 1–14.

[12] Department of Work and Pensions, *Simplicity*, p. 10.

[13] Pensions Commission, *First Report*, p. v.

[14] P. Riddell, 'Debate is Now about How, Not Whether, to Reform', *The Times*, 1 December 2005.

- the inadequacy of the basic state pension;
- the failure to provide adequate pensions for women, the majority of pensioners, who are ill-served by a system based on lifetime employment;
- the inadequacy of voluntary provision via personal saving, a tendency reinforced by:
  - the complexity of the system
  - a widespread lack of trust in the pensions industry;
- the decline of traditional defined-benefit occupational schemes, and their replacement by defined-contribution schemes exacerbated by:
  - the collapse of global financial markets in 2000–3
  - the introduction of international accounting standards rendering company pension fund deficits more transparent.

All these components have their roots in the past, and those roots are often deep.

The so-called 'demographic time-bomb', for example, has two dimensions. First, the birth rate, which rose after 1945 with the 'baby boom', began to fall in the late 1960s, declining below replacement level in the 1970s. It has remained below replacement ever since. So, as Paul Johnson points out in Chapter 11 of this volume, it has been clear for more than thirty years that provision would have to be made for more pensioners. At the same time, an unprecedented increase in life expectancy, the product of post-war advances in living standards and in medicine, has raised average male life expectancy at 65 from twelve years in 1950 to an estimated nineteen today and female life expectancy from fifteen to twenty-two years over the same period. Between 1971 and 2004 the median age of the UK population increased from 34.1 to 38.6.[15] Average male life expectancy at 65 is projected to rise further to twenty-one years by 2030, and to 21.7 by 2050; female life expectancy at 65 to twenty-three and 24.5 respectively.[16] Yet, while the rate of increase has been particularly fast of late, and while forecasting life expectancy is fraught with difficulties, as John Hills argues in Chapter 12, the actuarial profession has reacted far too slowly to what is in fact a long-term trend stretching back over more than a century.

A low birth rate and increased longevity have both tended to increase the numbers of those not working relative to those who are (the depend-

[15] ONS, *Population Trends*, 122 (London, 2005).

[16] Pensions Commission, *First Report*, p. 2.

ency ratio). This increase has been compounded by two important post-war social changes. First, successive governments since the 1960s have encouraged increasing numbers of young people to study at university, thereby delaying their entry into paid work. Second, despite increasing longevity, there has been a tendency to early retirement, not necessarily voluntarily.[17] In 2003/4, UK employment rates of men and women aged between 50 and state pension age were 72 per cent and 67 per cent respectively, and this was an increase on the even lower rates of the 1990s.[18] Hence pensions have been stretched in two ways by demographic and social changes: they have had to last for longer while years of contribution have been reduced.

These pressures on pensions have been partly offset by the increase in female labour force participation since the 1960s, which raised contribution income, though at the cost of future increased liabilities. Immigration also has helped to postpone the crisis, and may continue to do so. Ultimately, however, pension ages will have to rise to reflect the welcome rise in longevity over the past century. Indeed, this is already happening. The trend to early retirement is currently declining and employment rates of older people are rising.

Working longer offers one solution, but the inadequacy not only of future but of existing pensions presents greater problems; problems that are also inherited from the past. The continuing problems of women, highlighted by Pat Thane and Jay Ginn in this volume, stem from the post-war decision to base the state pension on a contributory system. As Thane explains, the extensive relative poverty of older women was exacerbated by the shift from non-contributory to contributory state pensions in the early twentieth century. She also notes that Beveridge's own initial, preferred, proposals sought to build into the state social insurance system provision for the needs of women who were not in continuous paid employment. These, like his proposal to build in incentives to delayed retirement to cope with the future ageing of the population which he and others at the time anticipated, were rejected by the Treasury and the post-war Labour government. Had more attention been paid to Beveridge, the post-war British pension system would still have been

[17] The role of age discrimination in inducing early retirement was stressed by the House of Lords Select Committee on Economic Affairs, *Aspects of the Economics of an Ageing Population*, vol. 1 (November 2003), pp. 29–33. As Clark makes clear in this volume, employers also found early retirement a useful means of restructuring firms in the 1980s and 1990s.

[18] ONS, 'Focus on Older People', May 2004, www.statistics.gov.uk/CCI/nugget.asp?ID=878&Pos=1&ColRank=2&Rank=224. UK labour market participation rates for the over-fifties are higher than those in most EU member states.

imperfect, but it would have better adapted to respond to subsequent social and demographic change and, in particular, to the needs of women. Today, the Department of Work and Pensions notes that only 23 per cent of women retiring in 2004 were entitled to a full basic state pension, and only 17 per cent received this on the basis of their own contributions. Of the 3.3 million receiving Pension Credit, 2.18 million are women.[19]

Not that the post-war pension settlement was ever generous. Beveridge aimed at state provision for subsistence in old age, not at generosity. If people sought 'higher standards' in old age, he expected them to save for it, ideally through non-profit institutions, such as friendly societies.[20] Yet even a subsistence pension proved unacceptable to the Treasury, as Jose Harris reminds us in Chapter 2. Thus, ever since 1946, the poorest pensioners have been dependent on means-tested supplementation. During the past quarter-century the Treasury has sought, with considerable success, actually to reduce further state pension commitments, for example by index-linking the basic state pension to prices rather than earnings from 1980.[21] The result has been a steady fall in the basic state pension from about 20 per cent of average earnings in 1977/8 to about 15 per cent in 1997.[22] While Labour subsequently introduced some ad hoc increases which raised its value to 15.6 per cent of average earnings in 2005/6, in the longer term retaining price indexation would progressively reduce the state pension to 11.6 per cent of earnings by 2025/6, the lowest in the western world.[23]

In parallel with this withering of an already inadequate state basic pension, state earnings-related pensions have also been subject to long-term attrition. As Hugh Pemberton (Chapter 3) and Noel Whiteside (Chapter 8) demonstrate, the Treasury has never willingly accepted generous earnings-related state guaranteed pensions like those developed in continental Europe since the Second World War. Labour's planned state earnings-related pension was blocked throughout the late-1950s and 1960s. Since Labour's proposal for a National Superannuation Scheme strongly resembles the Pensions Commission's proposed National

[19] Department of Work and Pensions, *Women and Pensions: The Evidence* (London, 2005), pp. v–vi and 23.

[20] *Social Insurance and Allied Services, Report by Sir William Beveridge*, Cmd 6404 (1942), pp. 121, 143–5.

[21] E. Philip Davis, 'Is There a Pensions Crisis?', *Geneva Papers on Risk and Insurance: Issues and Practice*, 29, 3 (July 2004), 343–70.

[22] A. Budd and N. Campbell 'The Roles of the Public and Private Sectors in the UK Pension System', in M. Feldstein, *Privatizing Social Security* (Chicago IL, 1998).

[23] National Association of Pension Funds, 'Key Facts', www.napf.co.uk/policy/keyfacts/index.cfm.

Pension Savings Scheme, its demise (in which the Treasury played a key role) merits particular attention. Eventually, as Pemberton shows, Labour introduced a compromise scheme in the mid-1970s—the ill-fated State Earnings-related Pension Scheme (SERPS), whose replacement (the State Second Pension) will revert to a flat-rate pension from 2007.

Thus, state earnings-related pensions in post-war Britain, like state pensions more generally, always played a residual role. Since the Second World War, governments of all political complexions have consistently expected the commercial, private sector to fill the gap. First, they encouraged employer-provided, occupational schemes, in both the public and private sectors, as alternatives to state earnings-related pensions. In the benign economic conditions, and tight labour markets, of the post-war 'golden age' the Treasury sought to minimize the future burden on the exchequer by encouraging employers to 'contract out' of the earliest state earnings-related pension introduced in 1959. As Howard Glennerster (Chapter 4) and Whiteside (Chapter 8) describe, employers (who already offered occupational pensions) and many trade unions (who saw an attractive pension deal as compensation for wage restraint policies) were happy to oblige. The problem with this approach, as Pemberton notes in Chapter 3, was that it excluded the low-paid, the self-employed, and those not in continuous paid employment. Thus, successive governments, together with their social partners, connived in a system that failed to help the majority of the population.

The most notable casualties of policies transferring responsibility for pensions away from government were women, as is made clear by Pat Thane (Chapter 5), Jay Ginn (Chapter 6), and Baroness Hollis (Chapter 7) in this volume. Occupational pensions never provided adequately for women, and do not do so now. Women are disproportionately employed in unskilled, service, or manual jobs which do not provide any occupational pension. Women are, however, more likely than men to work in the public sector, hence a slightly higher proportion of women than of men who are in full-time work are currently eligible for an occupational pension. But only a minority of women remain in full-time work throughout adult life, not least, as Ginn points out, because they are much more likely than men to care for children and elderly parents. For similar reasons, they also tend to have lower incomes. Even in the public sector, because they are heavily concentrated in the lower income levels in, for example, the National Health Service, their pensions tend to be lower than men's. In 2001/2, for example, the median income of women with a private pension even in the highest, professional/managerial, class was 55 per cent of that of men in the same class.[24]

Moreover, the rapid post-war expansion of occupational pensions was not sustained. As Pemberton, Hills, Whiteside, and Clark (Chapter 10) note in this volume, membership of occupational schemes peaked in 1967 at just over half the workforce and has been dropping ever since. This decline has recently accelerated with a shift from defined-benefit schemes (mainly based on final salary) to defined-contribution schemes in which the pension paid is dependent on the level of an individual's contributions and investment performance. Gordon Clark considers this change, its causes, and its possible consequences, more fully. It typically involves lower contributions (with employers reducing their level of contributions when the new schemes are established), higher costs, and a transfer of risk to contributors, who are generally poorly placed to determine risk levels and investment strategies.[25] Its causes are complex, involving increasing regulation (itself intended to correct market failure), the challenges of globalization (leading to restructuring and changed human resource management), the pricking of the 'dot com' equity bubble in 2000, and the introduction of accounting standard FRS17, which requires pension liabilities to be declared on a firm's balance sheet at current market prices. By 2004, two-thirds of traditional final-salary schemes had closed to new entrants and 24 per cent of the UK's largest companies were considering abandoning occupational pensions.[26] Clark is profoundly pessimistic about the future.

Thus, the hopes of successive post-war governments that occupational schemes would become pension providers for most people have never been fulfilled; they are increasingly unlikely so to develop in the future. From the early-1980s government policy shifted to encouraging individuals to purchase private pension plans.[27] This was a disastrous failure. Most notably the ensuing 'outrageous selling practices, aberrant salesmen [and] dubious transfer values', the Maxwell debacle, and, more

[24] Arber and Ginn 'Ageing and Gender'.

[25] ONS, *Pension Trends*, 1, 5.

[26] *Financial Times*, 2 July 2004, 'FT Money', 22.

[27] D. Blake, *Pension Schemes and Pension Funds in the United Kingdom* (Oxford, 2003), p. 19. This strategy continued after the election of a Labour government in 1997, with a projected reduction of the state's contribution to pensioners' retirement income from 60 per cent to 40 per cent over the ensuing forty years. See Department of Social Security, *A New Contract for Welfare: Partnership in Pensions* (London, 1998).

recently, the Equitable Life saga, contributed to a catastrophic decline in consumers' trust in pension companies.[28]

This led government to expand its regulation of private pension providers. But regulation is not just a recent phenomenon. Growing regulation of both private and occupational pensions has been a persistent feature of the post-war years. Since 1973, the state has steadily intervened to secure consumer protection and pensioner rights, eliminate discrimination, clarify marketing procedures, prevent misappropriation of company pension funds for other purposes, guarantee the solvency of funds, and block the use of pension funds for tax avoidance. The Minimum Funding Requirement (MFR), established in 1995, was designed to guarantee the security of private occupational pension schemes and, most recently, a Pension Protection Fund (PPF), financed by the industry, has been created to compensate members of funds which collapse with insufficient assets to cover their liabilities. As David Blake puts it, 'the cement never sets on British pensions legislation'.[29] Increasing regulation aimed to correct market failure but it also raised compliance costs, depressed investment returns over the long term, helped reduce market signals of 'best value' for potential customers, and made the system more complex. Not that this has guaranteed private pensions: on the contrary, despite the MFR, occupational schemes continue to be wound up and some have collapsed abruptly without warning yet the government has refused compensation.[30] Critics claim that the PPF will not be able to compensate future victims in full. Yet the taxpayer continues to underwrite some public-sector schemes, most notably those covering MPs and the central civil service. This not only creates a Disraelian 'two nations' of future pensioners; it exacerbates uncertainty and adds another dimension to the complexity preventing public comprehension of the British pension system.

As Pemberton's contribution demonstrates, regulation is not the only factor contributing to this growing complexity. Both occupational and personal pensions are private, so they are protected by private financial contracts that cannot be unilaterally restructured by government. In this respect, British occupational and earnings-related pensions differ from

[28] J. Black and R. Nobles, 'Personal Pensions Misselling: The Causes and Lessons of Regulatory Failure', *Modern Law Review*, 61, 6 (1998), 789.
[29] Blake, *Pension Schemes*, preface to 2nd edn.
[30] The government was censured in March 2006 for its failure to strengthen the MFR, to reflect changes in longevity and investment performance, and for failing to make clear to scheme members the risks they would face should their employer go out of business, but it rejected both the accusation and the idea of compensation. See Parliamentary and Health Service Ombudsman, *Trusting in the Pensions Promise*, HC 984 (London, 2006).

those found in continental Europe, as Whiteside's chapter shows. Breaking these contracts creates immediate political as well as financial costs. Coupled with the short time-horizons of most politicians, this has encouraged successive reforms to add to the system rather than abolishing or amending it in whole or part, thus fostering complexity. As Howard Glennerster points out, the history of post-war pensions is a history of the creation of 'a maze of such complexity that users cannot make sensible decisions about their own lives'.[31] Unsurprisingly, under circumstances of growing complexity and declining trust, sales of private pension plans have been disappointing, particularly to those on low incomes, and employers are increasingly reluctant to offer occupational schemes.[32]

These long- and medium-term problems for both occupational and privately purchased pensions have been compounded both by the Chancellor's decision to cut the tax exemption of pension fund returns in 1998 and the sharp falls in global financial markets since the millennium. This has resulted in very disappointing returns on financial products, including endowment mortgages and retirement annuities as well as pension funds. The funding crisis that has ensued has been worsened by the fact that optimistic employers (sometimes in compliance with Inland Revenue rules) took advantage of the prolonged boom in the 1990s to take 'contribution holidays' or raided their pension funds to finance corporate restructuring. In combination with new international accounting standards which require companies to publish the present value of future pension liabilities on their balance sheets, this fuelled the employers' flight from occupational pensions. It also further compounded consumer mistrust and confusion and exacerbated the poor take-up of private pension plans.[33]

In short, as John Hills points out in Chapter 12, the private sector has proved unable to fill the gap created by the initial inadequacy of UK state pensions, let alone the subsequent progressive reductions in state provision. Indeed, as the Pensions Commission has noted, far from expanding to fill the gap created by the inadequacies of the state schemes, 'Britain's

[31] See also A. Hedges, *Pensions and Retirement Planning*, Department of Social Security Research Report 83 (London, 1998); A. Smith and S. McKay, *Employers Pension Provision Survey 2000*, Department of Work and Pensions Research Report 163 (Leeds, 2000); S. Ward, *Resolving the Pensions Dilemma*, Work Foundation: Current Affairs Policy Brief 2 (London, 2002).

[32] Office of Fair Trading, *Report of the Director General's Inquiry into Pensions*, vol. 1 (London, 1997), p. 77; R. Sandler, *Sandler Review: Medium and Long-term Retail Savings in the UK* (London, 2002), p. 9; Blake, *Pension Schemes*, p. 240; Pensions Commission, *First Report*, p. 92.

[33] V. Mayhew, *Pensions 2000: Public Attitudes to Pensions and Planning for Retirement*, Department of Social Security Research Report 130 (Leeds, 2001).

funded pension system is in serious decline',[34] a conclusion Gordon Clark endorses in Chapter 10.

A New Pension Settlement for the Twenty-first Century?

The impending crisis in British pensions has given rise to a national debate unprecedented since the publication of the Beveridge Report. In its proposals for extensive reform, the Pensions Commission hopes to plug the holes in the current state system for those (mainly women) with interrupted careers and caring responsibilities.[35] It also aims to overcome barriers to private provision caused by cost, complexity, and misunderstanding. It seeks to keep employers involved in providing occupational pensions. It advocates a more sustainable system of state pensions to cope with rising longevity, prevent the spread of means-testing to a majority of pensioners (an estimated 70 per cent by 2050 if the present system were to remain unchanged), and maintain improvements in the relative standards of living of the poorest pensioners. Overall, it attempts to create a system that is less complex and more transparent. These are ambitious objectives. How does the Commission propose to achieve them?

Essentially, the proposed reform has three parts. First, the Commission recommends raising the state pension age to 67, or perhaps 69, by 2050.[36] A higher pension age creates the precondition for a second recommendation: a more generous basic state pension created by allowing the earnings-related second state pension to evolve into a flat-rate top-up to the present scheme. The basic state pension is to be re-indexed to average earnings. Pension rights will become universal by switching the basis of rights to a state pension from contributions to residency, thus helping those whose caring responsibilities and interrupted careers have prevented regular contributions in the past. The cost of state pensions will rise from 6.2 per cent to 8 per cent of GDP (7.5 per cent if retirement at 69 is adopted).[37]

[34] Pensions Commission, *First Report*, p. 80.

[35] Pensions Commission, *Second Report*, p. 4.

[36] The lower of these proposed ages ensures that the rise in the state pension age reflects the predicted future rises in longevity; the higher age acknowledges the rise in longevity since 1946.

[37] Pensions Commission, *Second Report*, p. 12; Department of Work and Pensions, *Simplicity*, p. 3; H. M. Treasury, *Long-term Public Finance Report: An Analysis of Fiscal Sustainability* (London, 2002), pp. 4 and 43. Whether this is really a 'rise' in state pension spending as a proportion of GDP is debatable since the Commission, along with many others, challenges the government's optimistic assumption that the current level can remain stable for the foreseeable future.

These changes underpin the Commission's third proposal, automatic enrolment of all workers into a National Pensions Savings Scheme (NPSS), funded by contributions equal to 4 per cent of salary, though with the right to opt out. The Commission thus seeks to avoid the government's fear that increased pension contributions will be viewed by the public as higher taxation by sustaining the convention of voluntarism—while assuming that inertia will work against opting-out unless the worker belongs to a contracted-out occupational scheme.[38] It envisages a 'modest' (one might say very modest) contribution of 3 per cent by the employer, and an additional 1 per cent state contribution in the form of tax relief/tax credit.[39] As noted earlier, the NPSS proposal recalls Labour's 1957 National Superannuation Scheme in that it will be funded, and the funds will be invested in the stock market. Recalling Beveridge's strictures on economies of scale, contributions would be collected via payroll deduction (almost certainly via pay-as-you-earn), thus allowing the Commission to envisage a low annual management charge of 0.3 per cent or less. Unlike the 1957 scheme, however, contributions would accumulate in individual accounts rather than being rolled together in a single fund with significant redistribution between contributors. Further, again unlike the earlier scheme, contributors will be encouraged to 'top up' their pension pot with voluntary supplementary contributions. In this way, the Commission's proposals pose a much bigger threat to the financial services industry than national superannuation ever did.

History and Policy

In making its proposals for radical change, however, the Pensions Commission may have failed sufficiently to acknowledge the historical roots of the crisis that it seeks to address and which may shape options for change. Its second report devoted only two pages to discussing the impact of the past. Yet, in its proposals for reform of the state pension system, it had to recognize that the legacy of the past required that its unified flat-rate pension be built on the existing basic state pension and state second pension. Equally, the Commission appears to have underestimated the historic aversion of the Treasury to raising pension spending

[38] Pensions Commission, *Second Report*, pp. 62–75 and 108–13. The Commission's assumptions about the desirability of auto-enrolment are derived from having examined 401,000 pension schemes in the USA, with and without auto-enrolment, and New Zealand's planned 'Kiwi-saver' scheme.
[39] Pensions Commission, *Second Report*, p. 133.

(discussed in several chapters in this volume). We are not surprised that the Commission's proposals were instantly attacked by the Treasury as 'unaffordable',[40] or that, as one Whitehall official put it, the Chancellor became immediately engaged in 'a deliberate attempt to undermine and discredit Lord Turner's calculations'.[41]

Despite the Pensions Commission's efforts, it is hard to see how its proposals can be said to solve the past and present problem concerning women and pensions. As Ginn notes (Chapter 6), redistribution is necessary for women to accumulate an adequate independent pension and the Commission's recommendations are not strong in this respect. One radical solution, advanced by Johnson in Chapter 11, would be for pension entitlement to be accumulated by virtue of parenthood. For Baroness Hollis (see Chapter 7), this does not go far enough. She notes that child-rearing is not the only unpaid service provided mainly by women; so is unpaid caring for ageing people. The Pensions Commission has acknowledged this in its proposals to improve the system of credits for the state second pension for those undertaking social care. Hollis, however, is extremely sceptical of the state's ability successfully to monitor the complex transitions in and out of, and the varying extent of, caring responsibilities.

Many commentators, including Hollis, note that the problem of female old-age poverty is mainly rooted in the current relationship between pension entitlement and paid employment; they advocate a 'citizen's pension', a tax-financed pension paid to all citizens who meet a residence qualification. Hollis and others argue that this is affordable. The net cost by 2030 of a pension at the 2005 threshold for means-testing (£105 per week or 22 per cent of national average earnings) is estimated at around £3 billion. This is less than one-third of the £10 billion savings which will result from the planned raising of women's state pension age from 60 to 65 between 2010 and 2020. Furthermore, the National Insurance (NI) Fund has a growing surplus, due to paying price-linked benefits while collecting earnings-linked contributions. By March 2006 the surplus is projected to be £34.6 billion, of which £25 billion can be treated as usable surplus, above the reserve which must be kept for prudential reasons. If current policies continue, the surplus will be about £60 billion by 2009. This is a

[40] BBC News, 'Brown Rejects Key Pensions Plan', 24 November 2005, http:news.bbc.co.uk/go/pr/fr/-/1/hi/uk_politics/4465652.stm; 'Turner Hits Back on Pensions', *Financial Times*, 24 November 2005; A. Rawnsley, 'How Appropriate—A Row about Retiring', *The Observer*, 27 November 2005.

[41] 'Brown Warns Turner that Real Value of Pension Credit could Fall after 2008', *Financial Times*, 24 November 2005.

convenient extra source of revenue for the Treasury, but it could fund better pensions. Income to the NI Fund could be further increased by raising or abolishing the Upper Earnings Limit on contributions to the State Second Pension. There would also be savings on the considerable cost of administering means-tested schemes. Also, as the Pensions Commission's second report suggests, a further source of finance in the longer term would result from gradually raising the state pension age.

Notably, the Pensions Commission shied away from such proposals in respect of past contributions, though it did propose future accruals of basic state pension rights on a citizenship basis. As Johnson notes in Chapter 11, the principal argument against moving immediately to a citizen's pension is that it would undermine the contributory principle that has long underpinned state pensions in Britain. Johnson asserts that such arguments are flawed because the contributory principal has long been a sham; national insurance pensions are actually funded on a 'pay-as-you-go' basis. As Harris and Pemberton point out in their chapters, this misconception dates back to Beveridge's negotiations with Keynes, and Ernest Bevin's shortening of the transition to full pension entitlement. Both authors describe the latter as a sleight of hand that wrapped a pay-as-you-go system in the mantle of national insurance, implying that accumulated contributions delivered a pension on retirement. A transition to a citizen's pension would expose this assumption as a deception and break what Pemberton notes is often perceived as a firm contract between individual contributors and the state. Thus, there is not just an economic cost–benefit equation to be determined here; a political judgement must be made about the electoral consequences of revealing the illusionary nature of post-war 'national insurance'.

The Commission may also have underestimated potential opposition from the pensions industry to its proposal for a National Pensions Savings Scheme, even though there is a clear historical precedent in the industry's reaction to Labour's National Superannuation proposals in 1957. Thus, while the NPSS proposal was welcomed by large employers, compulsory employer contributions produced the expected howl of protest from small businesses.[42] And, as fifty years ago, the reaction from the pensions industry was also hostile. The Association of British Insurers has decried this 'new, expensive and risky quango' while claiming, like its predecessors,

[42] Confederation of British Industry, 'Turner Report "Most Serious Proposal for Pension Reform Yet"', press release, 30 November 2005; Federation of Small Businesses, 'FSB Says Yes to Pensions Debate, No to Employer Compulsion', press release, 30 November 2005; British Chambers of Commerce, press release, 30 November 2005.

that the expertise and infrastructure of the existing private sector alone could 'put the vision into effect'.[43] As Clark notes, the NPSS embodies a break with market solutions to pensions and a return to a social democratic approach. This has enormous potential implications for UK investments in equity markets that have yet to be fully discussed, or perhaps even fully appreciated. It also cuts against the grain of Labour's acceptance of the market, which will surely have important political implications.

The resistance of the pensions industry to the NPSS proposals highlights a key problem. The 'perverse dynamics of UK pensions', noted by Glennerster, are strongly related to the system of UK governance, a system that history shows is poorly adapted to the construction of the sort of consensus that the government professes itself eager to achieve. An historical perspective demonstrates, not the existence of past consensus over pensions, but the extent of past political bickering over pensions systems, generating multiple policy trajectories that have provoked confusion, expense, and mistrust. The concentration of policy-making in the Treasury has allowed pension politics to degenerate into a technical debate on pension finance based on behavioural economics dominated by models of rational choice, whose conclusions are imposed by regulatory fiat. Consensus is not created by top-down imposition of new rules. Confidence and trust are best achieved not by financial incentives but by open deliberation and debate. In this respect, Britain has something to learn from its European neighbours, to whose pension debates we now turn.

The British Pensions Crisis in Comparative Perspective

Britain is not the only country struggling with problems of pension reform. Recent decades have witnessed global changes in pension provision, shifting responsibility away from states and towards more individualized systems that should, preferably, operate on a funded basis. Such revisions, promoted by the World Bank, have fostered the recalibration of pension provision between the three 'pillars': the first being state-funded pensions, the second private occupational schemes, the third voluntary personal saving.[44] The object of policy has generally been to promote the

[43] 'Insurers Likely to be Frozen Out Unless Products Delivered at Cheap Enough Prices', *Financial Times*, 1 December 2005.

[44] World Bank, *Averting the Old Age Crisis: Policies to Protect the Old and Promote Growth* (Oxford, 1994).

second and third while reducing the first: a strategy long pursued by British governments of all political complexions, as our contributors show. All European economies have reappraised their established pension systems; even in the USA recent reform debates focused on the extension of private pension provision (see Chapter 13 by Steven Sass). Demographic change, rising global competition, the retirement of the baby-boom generation, a shorter working life born of prolonged education—coupled in Europe with the collapse of state socialism and a surge in early retirement consequent on industrial restructuring—have presented common problems. Such factors are forcing departures from established pension schemes. The outcomes of some key debates, illustrating how other countries have tackled these problems, are addressed in the fourth section of this volume.

Although many countries have reformed their pension systems in recent years, they have done so on the basis of different historical legacies. Pension restructuring and reform has been most radical in the ex-Soviet block, where pension rights are now more firmly attached to contributory records, replacing the universal state-funded schemes classically associated with state socialism. Here, as Katharina Müller shows in Chapter 15, the shift has been both radical and swift: separating pensions from state budgets, establishing second-tier schemes, and promoting privatized provision—all in the context of rising unemployment following accelerated industrial restructuring. As Müller argues, such reforms have severely damaged future social equity and, thanks to the high unemployment currently characterizing many of these countries, are creating widening pension disparities between different groups and especially disadvantaging women. The prospect of a decent pension for many poor people currently unable to find work appears very small. While the situation is less severe in the new EU member states, the heavy burden imposed on future pensioner generations by the rising importance of funded systems introduced along lines promoted by the World Bank may undermine future stability. Müller points up the similarity between the reforms promoted in the ex-Soviet block states and those initiated a decade earlier in Latin American countries. Recent appraisals of the latter now indicate their weaknesses in terms of incomplete coverage and very low pensions, especially among poorer people least able to save for their old age.[45] This does not bode well for the future viability of some East European schemes that are over reliant on privatized provision. Equally it highlights how, in countries

[45] World Bank, *Keeping the Promise of Old Age Income Security: Latin America*, 2004, www.redsegsoc.org.uy/BM-Summary.pdf.

apart from Britain, the creation of pension policies reliant on funded private provision has not offered pension security to poorer workers.

Western European politicians have approached the pensions crisis in a more circumspect fashion. The foundations for reform also differ radically from the old socialist regimes—and from the widespread private arrangements that characterize British pensions. First, many basic state pension schemes in continental Europe were founded on the principles of Bismarckian social insurance. Unlike the British system of flat-rate contributions and flat-rate benefits, both contributions and benefits under Bismarckian social insurance schemes reflect previous earnings. Thus state schemes do not redistribute from rich to poor. They sustain established social hierarchies, and women's pensions, although more generous than in Britain, reflect the contributions made by their husbands, unless these women have worked themselves. Second, West European states, either directly or indirectly, have been more centrally involved in pension provision and in guaranteeing pension security than the British government. Whiteside's contribution (Chapter 8) shows how, in post-war West Europe and Scandinavia, state intervention universalized and rationalized occupational and professional earnings-related pensions. In Italy, Germany, and Sweden—analysed by Karl Hinrichs (Chapter 16) and Maurizio Ferrera (Chapter 14)—this translated into direct state provision of generous earnings-related pensions. In France and the Netherlands, legislation endowed the social partners with powers to operate state-ratified schemes guaranteeing similar levels of pension security, but independent of government.[46] The system favoured by Frank Field's Pensions Reform Group, and outlined in Chapter 9, is based on similar principles. When cuts became necessary in continental European systems, the pain was shared equitably, in contrast with the UK, where the pain has been disproportionately borne by unfortunate minorities whose companies have collapsed. Moreover, in Britain and the USA, pension debates have been overwhelmingly shaped by the impact of pension funds on future economic growth, reflecting the dominance of market-based frameworks of policy justification. In West Europe at least, more attention has been paid to questions of pension governance and public accountability as the means to guarantee social equity. In consequence, pensions have been more generous and more secure.

[46] N. Whiteside, 'Adapting Private Pensions to Public Purposes: Historical Perspectives on the Politics of Reform', *Journal of European Social Policy*, 16, 1 (2006), 43–54. Also see her contribution to this volume.

The focus for West European reform has therefore been to restructure long-established pension systems to contain present and future costs. This has stimulated considerable opposition. Reform agendas have been roughly similar: to individualize pension rights by tightening the relationship between contributions and pension benefits; to contain early retirement; to restructure pension formulae (for example, to institute longer periods of contribution or tighter wage-indexing); and to create contribution credits to compensate for periods of unemployment and unwaged social care. Such initiatives have been put in place in different contexts: each country has different political priorities. To compensate for lower pension benefits, governments are promoting prefunded complementary pension schemes (the second pillar) on a voluntary or obligatory basis; voluntary individual pension plans (the third pillar) are also growing. The social consequences of such reform are visible in terms of growing pension insecurity and rising income inequality in old age. As Müller demonstrates, this has been most pronounced in East European states, where state-based pensions have not merely been cut, but have virtually disappeared.

One of the current problems with Bismarckian schemes in West Europe, notably Germany, lies in their association with high levels of unemployment—a problem exacerbated by German reunification, leading to extensive restructuring of the old East German economy that created massive unemployment there. Raising contributions to fund a growing army of pensioners translates into higher labour on-costs, encouraging employers to relocate in cheaper regions (notably Eastern Europe), and thereby generating higher levels of unemployment in Germany (a problem also encountered in France). Hence, as Hinrichs shows, one of the main priorities for German governments has been to limit the burden of employers' insurance contributions. Pension funding has been subsidized by the state, an unstable strategy as Germany is currently failing to meet its obligations to keep public expenditure below 3 per cent of GDP, as demanded by the Eurozone's Stability and Growth Pact. As Ferrera shows, the Maastricht Treaty also shaped developments in Italian pensions, justifying lower state expenditure on pensions to enable Italy to be admitted into the 'euro club'; but the euro also delivered a substantial dividend in the shape of lower interest rates, and thus lower government debt servicing costs, which could be used to service the transition. Equally, as Müller's chapter demonstrates, economic issues have shaped the reconstruction of pensions in East Europe; the liberalization of state-run economies has required the development of capital markets for internal investment purposes, where none existed previously. Pension funds are extremely useful for this process. In each case, therefore, the pressures of globalization, translated by the requirements of the European Central Bank for Eurozone members, set the direction and pace of pension reforms that reduce the role of the state and expand that of the financial services sector in creating income security in old age.

Recent pressures have created novel initiatives in what are termed parametric reforms (the adaptation of existing schemes to new circumstances). The notional defined-contribution (NDC) system, perfected in Sweden and Italy (as Hinrichs and Ferrera indicate) and adapted by some East European states (as Müller describes), has aroused much interest. This scheme facilitates the transition from pay-as-you-go (PAYG) collective state pensions to more individualized schemes without imposing a double burden on the younger generation (who would otherwise have to save for their own pension while continuing to pay for that of their parents). Under NDC, state pension rights become formally attached to the individual contribution record but pension funding continues to operate on a PAYG basis. By sustaining standardization of pension benefits in accordance with cohort life expectancy and the individual contributory record, NDC bypasses some risks inherent in purely commercial schemes (that the pension provider might mismanage funds or go bankrupt; that unexpected market downturns might penalize some retirees, etc.). Necessarily, as demonstrated in Sweden and Italy, such a system requires recognition of (and compensation for) non-contributory periods due to unemployment, sickness, and caring for dependent relatives. It does, however, tie pension rights very closely to labour market participation, thereby exacerbating problems for women, which are examined below.

The other major issue has been the creation of supplementary funded pensions: while these are becoming increasingly common, the question remains, on the continent as in Britain, whether such pension saving should be obligatory or voluntary. British experience has demonstrated the problems with voluntary schemes. As noted by the Turner Commission and by contributors to this volume, lack of trust and the complexity of available choices have generated low levels of coverage. Further, voluntary schemes create huge problems with 'persistence': chasing contributors raises transaction costs and irregular contributions create a small pension pot.[47] The result is an income in old age that is lower than means-tested social assistance, necessitating complex 'tapering' of means-tested supplements to sustain incentives to save—itself a cause of extra

[47] Pensions Commission, *First Report*, pp. 256–7.

administrative expense. That poorer workers are reluctant to participate is no surprise: this problem has been with us for well over a century.[48]

In consequence, as Hinrichs shows, the voluntary German *Riester-Rente*, like its British counterpart, is not well subscribed. Similarly, Müller finds that, in the ex-communist states, future pension security is threatened by individual histories of partial (or no) contributions. On the other hand, the alternative of compulsory second-tier schemes has been put in place in both Italy and Sweden, as Hinrichs and Ferrera show. Both retain choice on questions of fund investment; in Italy, some of these are closed schemes negotiated by collective agreement on an occupational basis. Unlike in Britain, the issue of compulsion has proved acceptable, possibly because the more social democratic nature of pension governance elsewhere in Europe has enabled the creation of collective confidence in the viability of such systems.

So what lessons can Britain learn from overseas experiment and experience? Do other countries offer better protection to women—who, under the British system, so evidently lack real protection? The answer has to be a qualified 'yes'. On the one hand, as Hinrichs indicates, the extensive subsidies granted by the Swedish state in particular for both first- and second-tier pensions for periods spent on childcare, elder-care, or in unemployment do protect the pension rights of women on retirement. This is a country with high full-time female labour market participation rates; it also has redistribution embedded in the first tier at least: both help women to gain a decent pension. As in Britain and Italy, large-scale female participation in the public sector has proved beneficial to Swedish women's retirement prospects. But Sweden has a much larger public sector than most countries. On the other hand, evidence has emerged in Southern European states that individualized schemes with state contributions for unwaged work have fractured pension rights while failing to erase gender inequalities.[49] Any pension scheme that relies primarily on labour market status as a basis for determining pension benefits is liable to discriminate against women. Their career paths are liable to be more fractured and promotion prospects and levels of pay more limited than those of their male colleagues. In the ex-communist states, women's pension prospects have been all but obliterated by the withdrawal of state support. British women are more likely to work part-time and are overwhelmingly concentrated in low-paid employment; the gender gap in

[48] P. Thane, *Old Age in British History* (Oxford, 2000), p. 186.

[49] R. Trifiletti, 'Southern European Welfare Regimes and the Worsening Position of Women', *Journal of European Social Policy*, 9, 1 (1999), esp. 53.

earnings is one of the highest in Europe and translating this automatically into a gender gap in pension provision would not cure the current problem. We think that a tax-funded citizen's pension is essential in Britain to reduce risks of old-age penury among women, rather than a reversion to an NDC plus funded supplement along Swedish lines.

Perhaps the main lesson to be learned concerns less the content of policy than the process by which decisions have been reached and solutions introduced. In Britain, Italy, and Germany, the process of pension reform has been what Hinrichs terms 'a never ending story'. A stream of legislative proposals has reached the statute book in each of these countries; change has been piecemeal and erratic, all too often—as in Britain—driven by the short-term electoral calculations of politicians. Open methods of policy-making in other West European countries have required continuous negotiation with the social partners; concessions and amendments are used to win support. While this has generated a confused public, in Italy at least, such processes have led the trade unions to understand the limits of political possibility—creating a sounder foundation for collective policy development. In this regard, Swedish policy-making is exemplary. The pension problem was, by common consent, removed from the arena of party political debate in the early 1990s. The situation was subject to extensive collective deliberation and, once acceptable compromise was reached, the agreed solution was put in place as one single piece of legislation. Collective trust was sustained and—even though the principles of Swedish pension policy were completely revolutionized by the new scheme—public understanding and approval were guaranteed. The single solution avoids the problems of complexity currently bedevilling British pensions.

Looking at the confused morass of our current agencies and schemes, developed ad hoc over time by politicians of all political persuasions, with minimal public discussion, we conclude that agreement among our politicians on such an approach to an essential policy issue is devoutly to be wished. The proposal of the Pensions Reform Group, described by Frank Field in Chapter 9, for a form of pensions governance at arm's length from Westminster and Whitehall, comparable with the role of the Monetary Policy Committee at the Bank of England, offers one possible way forward. The Pensions Commission offers another. It would be excellent if real political consensus could be reached and a sound foundation established for the future. It takes forty years to save for a pension: in this policy area at least, history really matters. This volume shows us why this is so.

Bibliography

Official Publications

Department of Social Security, *A New Contract for Welfare: Partnership in Pensions* (London, 1998).

Department of Work and Pensions, *Simplicity, Security and Choice: Working and Saving for Retirement* (London, 2002).

——, *Women and Pensions: The Evidence* (London, 2005).

H. M. Treasury, *Pre-Budget Report, 2000: Building Long-term Prosperity for All* (London, 2000).

——, *Long-term Public Finance Report: An Analysis of Fiscal Sustainability* (London, 2002).

House of Lords, Select Committee on Economic Affairs, *Aspects of the Economics of an Ageing Population*, vol. 1 (November 2003).

Office for National Statistics (ONS), 'Focus on Older People', May 2004, www.statistics.gov.uk/CCI/nugget.asp?ID=878&Pos=1&ColRank=2&Rank=224.

——, *Pension Trends*, 1 (London, 2005).

——, *Population Trends*, 122 (London, 2005).

Office of Fair Trading, *Report of the Director-General's Inquiry into Pensions*, vol. 1 (London, 1997).

Parliamentary and Health Service Ombudsman, *Trusting in the Pensions Promise*, HC 984 (London, 2006).

Pensions Commission, *Pensions: Challenges and Choices. The First Report of the Pensions Commission* (London, 2004).

——, *A New Pensions Settlement for the Twenty-first Century. The Second Report of the Pensions Commission* (London, 2005).

Social Insurance and Allied Services, Report by Sir William Beveridge, Cmd 6404 (London, 1942).

World Bank, *Averting the Old Age Crisis: Policies to Protect the Old and Promote Growth* (Oxford, 1994).

——, *Keeping the Promise of Old Age Income Security: Latin America*, 2004, www. redsegsoc.org.uy/BM-Summary.pdf.

Other Publications

Arber, S. and J. Ginn, 'Ageing and Gender: Diversity and Change', *Social Trends*, 34 (London, 2004).

Banks, J., C. Emmerson, Z. Oldfield, and G. Tetlow, *Prepared for Retirement* (London, 2005).

Black, J. and R. Nobles 'Personal Pensions Misselling: The Causes and Lessons of Regulatory Failure', *Modern Law Review*, 61, 6 (1998), 789–820.

Blake, D., *Pension Schemes and Pension Funds in the United Kingdom* (Oxford, 2003).

Budd, A. and N. Campbell 'The Roles of the Public and Private Sectors in the UK Pension System', in M. Feldstein, *Privatizing Social Security* (Chicago IL, 1998).

Congdon, T., *Providing for Pensions: Savings in a Free Society* (London, 2005).

Hedges, A., *Pensions and Retirement Planning*, Department of Social Security Research Report 83 (London, 1998).

Mayhew, V., *Pensions 2000: Public Attitudes to Pensions and Planning for Retirement*, Department of Social Security Research Report 130 (Leeds, 2001).

Mullan, P., *The Imaginary Time Bomb: Why an Ageing Population Is Not a Social Problem* (London, 2000).

——, 'Ageing and the Pensions Crisis', *Spiked*, 8 December 2005, www.spiked-online.com/articles/0000000CA4E3.htm.

Philip Davis, E., 'Is There a Pensions Crisis?', *Geneva Papers on Risk and Insurance: Issues and Practice*, 29, 3 (July 2004), 343–70.

Sandler, R., *Sandler Review: Medium and Long-term Retail Savings in the UK* (London, 2002).

Smith, A. and S. McKay, *Employers Pension Provision Survey 2000*, Department of Work and Pensions Research Report 163 (Leeds, 2000).

Thane, P., *Old Age in British History* (Oxford, 2000).

Trifiletti, R., 'Southern European Welfare Regimes and the Worsening Position of Women', *Journal of European Social Policy*, 9, 1 (1999), 49–64.

Ward, S., *Resolving the Pensions Dilemma*, Work Foundation: Current Affairs Policy Brief 2 (London, 2002).

Whiteside, N., 'Adapting Private Pensions to Public Purposes: Historical Perspectives on the Politics of Reform', *Journal of European Social Policy*, 16, 1 (2006), 43–54.

Britain's System of Pensions

2.
The Roots of Public Pensions Provision: Social Insurance and the Beveridge Plan

JOSE HARRIS

The Pensions Problem

William Beveridge and his Report on *Social Insurance and Allied Services* of 1942 continue to occupy a pivotal position in the history of social security provision in Great Britain, Europe, and the wider world into the twenty-first century. Despite sixty years of subsequent pensions legislation—some of it very radical and innovative in its own right—the framework and principles of the Beveridge Plan are still cited as a fundamental clue to, and constraint upon, current social problems and policies. Indeed, an international commemoration of the sixtieth anniversary of the Beveridge Plan, organized by the Dominican Papal University in Rome in November 2002, bore witness to its continuing international resonance across a wide spectrum of political identities.[1]

In the context of pensions, this sense of an enduring Beveridge legacy is in many ways surprising, since Beveridge was not and did not pretend to be an expert on old age, in the way that he was an acknowledged authority on labour markets and unemployment insurance. His key ideas on the reform of old-age pensions, as initially set out during the early stages of the Beveridge Committee in 1941, were to be extensively and pragmatically pared down in the final version of his Plan of 1942, in order to meet what he foresaw as the fiscal and economic scarcities of the post-war era. And when it came to actual legislation in 1946, the Labour government of that period departed from Beveridge's recommendations in a

[1] Luigi Troiani (ed.), *Dopo Beveridge Reflessioni sul welfare con ristampa anastatica de Il Piano Beveridge* (Rome, 2005).

number of significant ways, most notably in evading Beveridge's long-term commitment to pensions based on the principle of 'subsistence'.[2]

So why is Beveridge still seen as a monumental figure in the evolution of pensions finance—identified in some quarters as the invisible hand behind the chronic underfunding of British old-age pensions provision, in others as the architect of the inadequately funded system and subsequent over-spending that has led to the currently perceived fiscal-cum-demographic pensions crisis? One rather trite answer might be that the Beveridge Plan for long had an iconic and morally imperative status in British post-war popular mythology, a status that made it difficult to break with its principles. But this, if true, simply begs the question of why Beveridge's ideas were so popular and seemingly so authoritative. I shall try to suggest some fuller answers to these questions, first by summarizing what Beveridge's ideas about pensions actually were; and then by identifying ways in which they appeared to him, and to many others at the time, to address both individual income needs and the wider structural realities of British post-war society.

German and British Models

Although Beveridge's long public career in social policy had been mainly concerned with the quite different sphere of unemployment insurance, his ideas about old-age pensions did not spring from nowhere in 1941, but dated back to the year 1907, when he had been a young investigative journalist for the radical conservative newspaper, the *Morning Post*. There, in a long series of articles, he had described and analysed the state-organized, insurance-financed, sickness, accident, and old-age-pension schemes introduced since the 1880s by the imperial government in Wilhelmine Germany. These schemes were compulsory for all grades of German manual workers (and were shortly to be extended to all white-collar employees as well): they were financed on a virtual pay-as-you-go basis by income-related insurance contributions from workers and employers, with a small subsidy from public funding. Such schemes were centrally managed by administrative and statistical experts, but at the same time incorporated representatives of working-class organizations into their day-to-day management and administrative machinery. German pensions were paid not at a fixed age, but to elderly contributors when they became individually no longer able to work, regardless of

[2] The National Insurance Act of 1946 introduced 'full' pensions immediately, without the build-up to subsistence over sixteen years envisaged in the Beveridge Plan, but at a much lower rate than the eventual subsistence-level pensions proposed by Beveridge.

financial means or personal moral character. In all of this the German system starkly contrasted with the means-tested public doles payable to destitute old people in England out of the local Poor Rate; and they contrasted even more strongly with the means-and-morality-tested pensions, financed out of general taxation, introduced for people over 70 by the Asquith Old Age Pensions Act of 1908. In Beveridge's view, the advantage in these contrasts lay almost entirely with the German system; and he was highly critical of the Asquith scheme for penalizing savings, fostering fraud and concealment, and stereotyping 'a vision of the State as Lady Bountiful' by vesting pensions management in the hands of amateur committees of the local great and good. Thus, many aspects of Beveridge's mature social philosophy were already clearly present in these early articles of 1907.[3] In particular, the young Beveridge's deep aversion to means tests as morally and functionally pernicious, his goal of making social security not just a crutch for destitution but a badge of modern citizenship, and his linking of pensions not to a fixed age of retirement but to declining ability to work—all gave expression in embryonic form to some of the key underlying principles of his Plan of 1942.

'All-in' Insurance

In 1908 Beveridge moved from journalism into a new career as a senior civil servant and personal adviser to Winston Churchill at the Board of Trade. There he was instrumental in inserting many of his ideas about social insurance into the unemployment provisions of the 1911 National Insurance Act. But not until the early 1920s, by which time he had become director of the London School of Economics, did he return to the question of old-age pensions. This was in the context of the so-called 'all-in' debate on the unification of social insurance, stimulated by the famous Geddes Axe on public expenditure of 1921. In this debate (very resonant of similar controversies at the present day) reformers of all complexions were engaged in the exercise of trying to *expand* social welfare provision while simultaneously *reducing* overall costs.

Beveridge's contribution to this debate found expression in his Liberal Party pamphlet on *Insurance for All and Everything* published in 1924. In this he argued for administrative harmonization of all existing state insurance schemes, together with the introduction for the first time of an insurance-based retirement pension for those no longer able to work—a

[3] Articles by W. H. Beveridge, *Morning Post*, 16 Feb. and 21 Nov. 1906, and Sept. 1907.

scheme that would be 'universal' in coverage for workers earning below the income-tax threshold.[4] Despite the coincidence of timing, this pamphlet appears to have had little or no direct influence on the legislation for contributory old-age pensions (tacked on to the system of national health insurance) that was introduced by Neville Chamberlain in 1925.[5] But Beveridge's pamphlet is nonetheless of some interest both for the further light it throws on his approach to pensions, and also for some of the points that it left out. It clearly defined 'loss of earning power' as the event that should trigger entitlement to an old-age pension (rather than lack of means or reaching a certain age); and it strongly defended the principle of contributory insurance as the most politically and psychologically desirable form of public relief. Insurance, Beveridge argued, gave the beneficiary what was already his own by contractual right, and it was attuned to the needs not of economic and social failures but of 'perfectly normal persons . . . facing disorders endemic in modern society' (in other words not just the 'very poor', but the great mass of the working population). An unexpected gap in his scheme was that the pamphlet paid little or no attention to pension funding; it blithely assumed that pensions could be paid for out of current surpluses in the unemployment fund (this in 1924, on the brink of what was to prove one of the longest and deepest recessions in British economic history!).[6] A year later, however, at a conference of the London Council of Social Service, Beveridge struck a more cautious note. On this occasion, he drew attention to the mounting *demographic* threat to pensions posed by falling birth and death rates, condemned Chamberlain for reducing the state pension age from 70 to 65, and argued that the decline in both fertility and mortality ought to be leading to a *prolongation* rather than *shortening* of the citizen's working life.[7]

The Beveridge Plan

All this meant that, although Beveridge had some long-standing views about the underlying principles of pensions provision, at the time of his appointment as chairman of the Social Insurance Committee in June 1941 he had almost no specialist knowledge of pensions administration or pensions finance. He viewed social security questions very much through the

[4] W. H. Beveridge, *Insurance for All and Everything* (London, 1924), pp. 4–8, 30–1.
[5] Pat Thane, *Old Age in English History: Past Experiences, Present Issues* (Oxford, 2000), p. 322.
[6] Jose Harris, *William Beveridge: A Biography*, 2nd edn (Oxford, 1997) pp. 338–41.
[7] *Social Service Bulletin*, London supplement, June 1925.

lens of unemployment insurance, with its focus (at least in aspiration) on trying to maintain mobility and industrial efficiency and on getting beneficiaries back into gainful employment as quickly as possible.[8] Nor was Beveridge in any way *required* to be a pensions expert by those who appointed him, since his brief was simply to report on the possibilities of administrative rationalization between the numerous patchy, overlapping, and contradictory welfare schemes that had sprung up largely piecemeal over the previous half-century. Beveridge himself in 1941 had no intention of sticking to such a prosaic and unadventurous brief, and he soon found himself giving much more concentrated attention to pensions questions than he had originally envisaged. But nevertheless it should be stressed that, throughout his work on the drafting of the Beveridge Plan, making provision for poverty in old age was never his number one priority. Although he aimed for a scheme that would be simple, integrated, uniform, and universal in coverage for all different kinds of need, when it came to giving precedence to some needy groups over others, then the problems of child poverty, support for families, and relief and prevention of unemployment loomed very much larger in his mind than pensions for the elderly.[9] This was not because Beveridge was dismissive of the needs of the aged poor: but 'old age' *per se* he simply refused to see as a problem. As he told the lobbyists of the National Federation of Old Age Pensions Associations, it was simply 'absurd, if I may say so, to call people of 60 upwards old'. This was a view not unconnected to the fact that at the time of writing his report he was himself a hyperactive swimming, tennis-playing, mountain-climbing, ambitious, and argumentative 63-year-old, who felt he had an unending future of academic research, public service, and possibly even political office stretching before him!

Pensions Finance

Nevertheless, pensions came to loom disproportionally large both in Beveridge's thoughts and calculations and in discussions with his committee, because the sheer volume of projected pensions finance threatened to overwhelm and shipwreck what were perceived as other more important priorities. Beveridge's initial draft plan, as sketched out towards the

[8] In addition to his earlier work in designing the 1911 state unemployment insurance scheme, Beveridge from 1934 had acted as chairman of the Unemployment Insurance Statutory Committee, set up to disentangle contributory insurance from unconditional benefits (Harris, *William Beveridge*, pp. 345–9).
[9] Harris, *William Beveridge*, ch. 16.

end of 1941, envisaged a unified system of flat-rate subsistence-level National Insurance benefits, payable in the event of sickness, disability, unemployment, retirement, industrial injury, and various lesser contingencies.[10] Among the latter was a range of special entitlements for women, including a benefit for what would nowadays be called 'home carers'. He envisaged that such benefits would henceforth be available to all classes in the community, and would be financed by three-way contributions from insured persons, employers, and the national exchequer. In addition, subsistence-level family allowances for all children and a comprehensive free national health service were to be financed largely by direct taxation. Rather surprisingly, Beveridge did not at this stage link his pension proposals to retirement or inability to work, proposing instead a simple age qualification of 60 for women and 65 for men (a suggestion that was rather out of line with his usual approach to pensions, and may have been influenced by the fact that the principle of insurance pensions at a fixed age had been conceded by the Chamberlain Act of 1925). This early draft was composed by Beveridge as a kind of Platonic template (what I believe is now known as 'blue-sky thinking') rather than as a detailed programme for action; but it nevertheless generated a flurry of alarm, almost amounting to panic, in official and Treasury circles. Beveridge himself had made a rough estimate that the non-contributory elements in his draft plan would raise exchequer spending on social services by about 30 per cent, and he was horrified when the government actuary (who served as one of the 'official' members of the committee) calculated the increase as more like 300 per cent. J. M. Keynes, who was a strong supporter of Beveridge's overall objectives, warned him that his figures needed also to be revised upwards to take account of wartime inflation, and that the whole package would cost the taxpayer £535 million in its first year of operation. (This was equivalent to nearly 60 per cent of total central government expenditure for 1937, i.e. the last 'normal' peacetime year before public spending had been seriously inflated by rearmament.) Lionel Robbins and others in the Economic Section of the War Cabinet predicted that such a level of expenditure would seriously hamper post-war industrial reconstruction: and Treasury alarm was not assuaged when Robbins's colleague James Meade cheerfully remarked that it could all be met by 'socialization of property' and a 'capital levy'. The result was that Keynes, Robbins, Government Actuary Sir George Epps, and several members of his committee were all briefed to persuade

[10] The National Archives: PRO, CAB 87/76, 'Basic Problems of Social Security with Heads of a Scheme', 11 Dec. 1941.

Beveridge to 'see sense' and to adjust his proposals to what was 'economically reasonable'.[11]

These pressures led to severe pruning of the scope and level of Beveridge's proposals on family allowances and on special benefits for women; but since by far the largest financial slot in his social security budget was occupied by provision for old age, it was inevitably pensions that bore the brunt of these pressures for economy. Even so, Beveridge did not climb down easily, strongly resisting pressures to abandon the principle of subsistence, to limit his scheme to the non-tax-paying classes, or to put his whole enquiry on hold until after the end of the war. He also rejected proposals from various bodies giving evidence before his committee, who suggested that it would be simpler and more economical to fund benefits, including pensions, from income tax, or that more money might be raised from graduated rather than flat-rate contributions.[12] Instead he reverted to his long-standing view that 'old age' in itself was not a problem, and that people could be persuaded by the prospect of slightly higher pensions to defer retirement until they were no longer able to work. During the summer of 1942, however, he reluctantly came to the conclusion that even a deferred retirement arrangement would not in itself be adequate to meet the financial shortfall and that insurance-based pensions at full subsistence level could not therefore be paid from the start of the new scheme. Instead, he accepted a suggestion from Keynes that subsistence pensions (for all but the minority already covered by the Chamberlain scheme of 1925) would have to be phased in gradually over a period of sixteen years.[13] In the interim, those who retired without adequate private savings would continue to rely on the supplementation of their insurance pensions by means-tested public assistance. By 1965, Beveridge estimated, pensioners reliant on assistance would have dwindled to a tiny fraction of the elderly population, composed largely of those who through sickness or disability had never been able to work. Aside from this tiny minority, poverty in old age would by that date have been effectively abolished by universal social insurance.[14]

[11] Harris, *William Beveridge*, pp. 398–402.

[12] *Social Insurance and Allied Services, Memoranda from Organisations* (Cmd 6405, 1942), Paper 7, 'Summary of Memorandum of Evidence from PEP'; British Library of Political and Economic Science (hereafter 'BLPES'), Beveridge Papers, VIII, 27, James Meade to Norman Chester, 28 Aug. 1941.

[13] Harris, *William Beveridge*, p. 401.

[14] *Social Insurance and Allied Services* (Cmd 6404, 1942), pp. 90–101, 126–8, 131, 141, 175.

The Legacy of Beveridge

The practical aftermath of all this is well known, and doesn't need recounting in detail. In the final version of the Beveridge Plan, the projected increase in real costs to the exchequer at the start of the new social security scheme was to be confined to about 33 per cent. The post-war Labour government, constrained by the desperate shortages that Beveridge himself had predicted, understandably held back from committing itself to full 'subsistence' benefits in 1946, particularly for the most numerous and expensive class of beneficiaries, namely pensioners. Over subsequent decades, inflation, demographic change, consumerism, changes in family life, the restructuring of labour markets, and growing popular resistance to the high tax levels of wartime and post-war taxation all conspired to erode both the socio-economic structures and the normative assumptions on which Beveridge's proposals and predictions of 1942 had been based. Such changes have occurred far beyond the boundaries of Britain, and in 2006 there is probably no 'advanced' country without its recurrent 'pensions crisis' in one form or another. The question remains to be addressed, however, of how far the present-day pensions problem in Britain can be traced back to the structural and intellectual legacy of Beveridge. On this point I should like to conclude with a few tentative suggestions.

First, the *demographic issue*. Beveridge had spent much of his adult life pondering what he saw as the dangerous conjunction of declining fertility and mortality; and the birth-rate question was addressed in great detail throughout the Beveridge Report. The same was not true, however, of declining mortality. No one could have been more conscious than Beveridge of changing patterns of life expectancy; but, advised by Sir George Epps, he explicitly excluded any attempt to anticipate such patterns in the Beveridge Report. If life expectancy substantially increased, the government actuary conceded, then the future pensionable population 'may be materially in excess of my estimates', but the extent of such changes could be nothing more than guesswork in the prevailing context of prolonged economic crisis and global war.[15] Beveridge did, however, constantly stress the notion of old age as a moving frontier, and the financial and practical advantages of a flexible age of retirement. 'It would be reprehensible and unjustifiable', he argued, 'to give a full subsistence-

[15] *Social Insurance and Allied Services*, Appendix A, 'Finance of the Proposals of the Report relating to Social Insurance and Security Benefits', *Memorandum by the Government Actuary*, pp. 180, 210.

level income to every citizen, as a birthday present on his reaching a particular age.'[16]

Second, one might explore Beveridge's *costing of pensions*. As we have seen, Beveridge pared down his pension plans to a fraction of their original cost, and very powerful Treasury and actuarial searchlights were trained on every last detail of his pension proposals. Nevertheless, there was an element of sleight of hand in Beveridge's public presentation of the long-term costs of old-age pensions. Although this was never spelt out in so many words, the tables and calculations set out in the government actuary's memorandum on the financing of Beveridge's Social Security Budget seem to indicate that a very much larger exchequer subsidy (or much higher insurance contributions) would in the long run be needed if subsistence-level pensions were to be adopted and indefinitely maintained (and this without factoring in any provision for increase of life expectancy).[17] That this was an arithmetical error on Beveridge's part, or Sir George Epps's, seems inconceivable. What seems much more likely is that it stemmed from the influence of Keynes, who constantly pressed him to concentrate on immediate post-war problems, and not to bother too much about the distant actuarial future. 'The future can well be left to look after itself', Keynes had commented on Beveridge's original draft. 'It will have far more resources for doing so than the immediate present.'[18]

Third, there is the question of Beveridge's *provisions for women*, on which there has been much heated debate. As we have seen, Beveridge's original proposals had included a range of special benefits for women (grants for setting up home, domestic help during sickness, payments for care of aged relatives, and insurance benefits for divorcees, deserted wives, and what were known as 'domestic spinsters'), but these largely fell by the wayside in the course of paring down costs. In the final report, employed *single* women were to be insured on virtually the same basis as men, though with a minimum retirement age of 60 rather than 65. *Non-employed married women* (i.e. housewives) were to be insured largely as domestic appendages of their husbands; while *employed married women* were to have the choice either of contributing on the same basis as employed single women, or of opting out and being subsumed like housewives under the provision for their husbands. There were several aspects of these complex arrangements that appear somewhat surprising.

[16] BLPES, Beveridge Papers, VIII, 33, 'The Problem of Pensions', 19 Aug. 1942; IXa 37(1), Beveridge to Keynes, 20 Aug. 1942.

[17] *Social Insurance and Allied Services*, Appendix A, p. 209.

[18] BLPES, Beveridge Papers, IXa, 37(1), Keynes to Beveridge, 17 Mar. 1942.

One is the fact that, despite his anxiety about pensions costs and his concern for administrative symmetry, Beveridge proposed an earlier retiring age for independent women, even though their life expectancy was longer than men's (thus significantly privileging a small minority of women over all other contributors). The reasoning behind this anomaly is unclear, but was probably linked to the fact that an earlier retiring age for women had been built into the Chamberlain legislation of 1925. More controversial, however, were Beveridge's proposals for the large majority of women, both married and unmarried, who spent the bulk of their adult lives outside the labour market. Beveridge in other contexts was an active sponsor of equal rights for women: he regarded running a home as a skilled and honourable 'occupation', and he was well aware that more than three-quarters of poverty in old age was female. (Indeed in 1908 he had suggested that the Asquith non-contributory pension scheme should be solely confined to women—who, unlike men, very rarely had lifetime earnings that were adequate for long-term saving.) Nevertheless, in 1942 his proposal for women with primarily domestic functions fitted rather uncomfortably into a scheme so closely linked to the labour market, and where the most appropriate qualification for benefits, even for old-age pensioners, was defined as loss of capacity to work or 'interruption of earnings'. Beveridge defended these proposals by arguing that social security schemes had to reflect social reality, and that at the previous census 'seven out of eight of all housewives . . . made marriage their sole occupation'[19] (an assumption that may have fitted the 1930s, and even the immediate post-war era, but was to sit very awkwardly with longer-term future trends). What was perhaps surprising here, in view of Beveridge's very high evaluation of homemaking and motherhood as economic as well as social roles ('occupations' that were at least as valuable to the community as paid employment) was that no attempt was made in his report to treat these activities as insurable work. Historians should be cautious about upbraiding actors in past epochs for what they didn't think of doing: but Beveridge would almost certainly have approved the notion of 'crediting' mothers, housewives, and home-carers with insurance contributions during their years outside the labour market—if only someone had suggested it to him, or if he had thought of it for himself!

Fourth and last, I should like to comment on an aspect of Beveridge's scheme that was in no sense his intention, but was nevertheless to be of major significance for the long-term evolution and character of British old-age pensions. This was the quite unexpected (and at the time wholly

[19] *Social Insurance and Allied Services*, p. 49.

undetected) lease of life that Beveridge's scheme was to give to the structural and functional legacy of the supposedly discredited *Poor Law*. This may seem a very odd comment, given the triumphalist celebration of the 'abolition of the Poor law' with which 'universal' insurance-based pensions were launched in the late 1940s, and their reinforcement by various kinds of 'graduated' and 'occupational' insurance schemes from the late 1950s.[20] Despite its negative reputation, however, the Poor Law and its related institutions had played for many centuries a very much more central, functional, and indispensable role in many aspects of social life in Britain than most classic accounts of its history would have us believe.[21] Unpleasant as the Poor Law may have been in many aspects, it had supplied even in its harshest periods the basic means of livelihood to large numbers of destitute people; and during the early twentieth century the more liberal welfare institutions that had evolved out of the Poor Law (such as public assistance, hospital care, and many forms of provision for specially disadvantaged groups) had continued to play an essential role in many people's lives. Even Beveridge's 'Platonic' blueprint of a universalist social security plan in 1941 had contained many residual functions for the successor institutions of the Poor Law; and the cuts imposed during 1942 on many of the 'insurance' aspects of that blueprint meant that those residual functions loomed even larger in the final text of the Beveridge Plan. Nowhere was this more evident than in the transitional arrangements for pensions, which were to be explicitly dependent in their early years on the legal and structural inheritance of poor relief (though now to be administered with 'decency and humanity'). Such a compromise was of course meant to be purely temporary. But, from the start of the new arrangements, 'national assistance' pension rates were always substantially higher than contributory-insurance pension rates, even at the full level payable from the start to those who had been insurance contributors since 1926. In the decades that followed, British governments, faced with the twin problems of inflation and increased longevity, were constantly tempted by, and fell into, the cheaper option of raising the basic pension level for the 'means-tested' few (or relatively few) rather than for the universalist many. This was in marked contrast to the opposite trend in much of Western Europe over the same period, where insurance benefits increasingly outstripped payments to those on residual

[20] Hansard, HC Debs, 5th ser. (1947–8), vol. 443, cols 31–2.

[21] Jose Harris, 'From Poor Law to Welfare State? A European Perspective', in Donald Winch and Patrick K. O'Brien (eds), *The Political Economy of British Economic Experience, 1688–1914* (Oxford, 2002), pp. 409–38.

public relief.[22] Thus, by a strange paradox, what was widely seen at the time as the progressive implementation of the Beveridge Plan, eventually shifted the pattern of British old-age pensions provision in a direction quite different from, and opposite to, the one that Beveridge himself had originally envisaged.

Bibliography

Beveridge, W. H., *Insurance for All and Everything* (London, 1924).

Flora, P., *State, Economy, and Society in Western Europe 1815–1975* (Frankfurt, 1983).

——, *Growth to Limits: The Western European Welfare States since World War II* (Berlin, 1986–7).

Harris, J., *William Beveridge: A Biography*, 2nd edn (Oxford, 1997).

——, 'From Poor Law to Welfare State? A European Perspective', in Donald Winch and Patrick K. O'Brien (eds), *The Political Economy of British Economic Experience, 1688–1914* (Oxford, 2002).

Social Insurance and Allied Services, Report by Sir William Beveridge, Cmd 6404, and *Memoranda from Organisations*, Cmd 6405 (London, 1942).

Thane, P., *Old Age in English History: Past Experiences, Present Problems* (Oxford, 2000).

Troiani, L. (ed.), *Dopo Beveridge Reflessioni sul welfare con ristampa anastatica de Il Piano Beveridge* (Rome, 2005).

[22] Peter Flora, *State, Economy, and Society in Western Europe 1815–1975* (Frankfurt, 1983), vol. 1, pp. 546–7; and Peter Flora (ed.), *Growth to Limits: The Western European Welfare States since World War II* (Berlin, 1987), vol. 4, pp. 111, 327, 395, 400–1, 517.

3. Politics and Pensions in Post-war Britain

HUGH PEMBERTON

Understanding the politics of post-war British pensions in its broadest sense is imperative if we are to understand the nature of the pensions crisis that Britain faces, and essential too if we are to devise effective solutions to address that crisis. This chapter surveys the development of Britain's overall system of pensions since the Beveridge Report, focusing in particular on the reasons why the system became steadily more complex as time went by, and on the lessons of history for those seeking to address that complexity. We will begin by first discussing the current crisis of complexity in British pensions. We will then briefly survey recent work on path dependence in pensions before going on to examine developments in British pensions after the publication of the Beveridge Report in 1942, focusing in particular on the two succeeding decades.

The Pensions Commission, appointed by the government to review British pensions, and to make recommendations on future policy, rightly decided that it must necessarily examine Britain's overall system of pensions provision, not just the crisis in voluntary pensions provision. In its first report, the Commission bluntly concluded: 'The UK has the most complex pension system in the world.'[1] This complexity is clearly a major contributor to Britain's present pensions 'crisis'. In the arena of state pensions, for example, while the basic pension is relatively easy for employees to understand, the earnings-related state pension is not. Not least because there are actually three of them. All opaque to the average citizen. All costly to administer

Complexity is also a problem in occupational pensions. For example, it is a fundamental reason why most employers provide no occupational

[1] Pensions Commission, *Pensions: Challenges and Choices. The First Report of the Pensions Commission* (London, 2004), p. 210.

pension scheme for their staff.[2] Moreover, lack of employee understanding arising from complexity has almost certainly aided employers in their recent flight from defined-benefit schemes in favour of defined-contribution schemes in which the confused employee is expected to take the investment decisions (and all the risks), and into which employers typically make much lower contributions.[3]

If anything, problems with privately purchased pensions are even greater than those of occupational schemes. Almost half those of working age have no more than a 'patchy' knowledge of pensions.[4] The complexity of the pension choices facing individuals is a major factor in the relatively low rate of take-up (even though over half those of working age fear they will receive little or nothing by way of state pension), and in poor persistence when plans are purchased. These effects have been exacerbated by the erosion of trust in the system produced by the mis-selling scandal that followed Conservative reform of the system in 1986—to which an important contributor was consumers' lack of awareness due to complexity. In addition, of course, complexity raises administration costs, and consequently reduces returns on investment. This is a further disincentive to saving.[5]

So, there is complexity in all three areas of the system—state, occupational, and private—not least because in addition to the basic state pension Britain actually has at least nine pension systems—more if one counts the innumerable variations in these schemes over time, or counts the various pensions-related welfare benefits that exist in parallel with, and to support the weaknesses of, Britain's increasingly inadequate system of pensions provision. But why is Britain's overall system of pensions, both public and private, so complex? And why does that complexity seem to be increasing? One clue lies in the foreword to the Pensions Commission's first report, which notes:

> The problems of the British pension system today reflect the cumulative impact of decisions and commitments made, and of policies rejected, often with unintended consequences, by governments over several decades.[6]

[2] A. Pickering, *A Simpler Way to Better Pensions* (London, 2002), p. 2.
[3] A. Hedges, *Pensions and Retirement Planning*, Department of Social Security Research Report 83 (London, 1998).
[4] V. Mayhew, *Pensions 2000: Public Attitudes to Pensions and Planning for Retirement*, Department of Social Security Research Report 130 (Leeds, 2001).
[5] Pickering, *Simpler Way*.
[6] Pensions Commission, *First Report*, p. vi.

In other words, if we are to understand the present crisis in British pensions, and if we are to solve it effectively, we have to understand the history of the development of the UK pension system over the long term.

Surprisingly, however, discussion of the history of that development and of the implications of that history for solving the present pensions crisis is conspicuous mostly by its absence. It is notable, for example, that the recent second report of the Pensions Commission devoted only two of its 460 pages to any consideration of how the present systems developed, and none to the implications of that development for present and future policy.[7] The nearest we get in the literature to a discussion of how the historical development of pensions in Britain might have shaped present policy options is the argument that a key problem in meeting demands for radical change is the impossibility of starting with a blank sheet of paper in pensions. Those who emphasize such problems either implicitly or explicitly cite the path-dependent nature of pensions, and thus emphasize the problem of history for any radical reform of British pensions.[8] In doing so, they appeal to a developing scholarly literature on the constraints on policy posed by path dependence in pensions.[9]

I do not propose to examine path dependency theory in detail here. It derives from the argument of economists and economic historians such as Paul David, Brian Arthur, and Kenneth Arrow that technologies can embody increasing returns arising from scale economies and coordination effects, and that this can result in early entrants cornering a market even though better technologies come along later.[10] The idea that increasing

[7] Pensions Commission, *A New Pensions Settlement for the Twenty-first Century. The Second Report of the Pensions Commission* (London, 2005).
[8] Such as R. Brooks *et al.*, *A New Contract for Retirement* (London, 2002); or the third report of the House of Lords Work and Pensions Committee, *The Future of Pensions*, 2 April 2003, http://www.publications.parliament.uk/pa/cm200203/cmselect/cmworpen/92/9202.htm.
[9] For example, P. Pierson, *Increasing Returns, Path Dependence and the Study of Politics* (Florence, 1997); P. Pierson, 'Increasing Returns, Path Dependence and the Study of Politics', *American Political Science Review*, 94, 2 (2000), 251–67; G. Bonoli, *The Politics of Pension Reform: Institutions and Policy Change in Western Europe* (Cambridge, 2000); J. Myles and P. Pierson, 'The Comparative Political Economy of Pension Reform', in P. Pierson, *The New Politics of the Welfare State* (Oxford, 2001); M. Haverland, 'Another Dutch Miracle? Explaining Dutch and German Pension Trajectories', *Journal of European Social Policy*, 11, 4 (2001), 308–23.
[10] P. David, 'Clio and the Economics of QWERTY', *The American Economic Review*, 75, 2 (1985), 332–7; B. W. Arthur, 'Self-reinforcing Mechanisms in Economics', in Philip W. Anderson, Kenneth J. Arrow, and David Pines (eds), *The Economy as an Evolving Complex System* (Reading MA, 1989); B. W. Arthur, *Increasing Returns and Path Dependence in the Economy* (Ann Arbor MI, 1994); B. W. Arthur, 'Competing Technologies, Increasing Returns, and Lock-in by Historical Events', *Economic Journal*, 99, 394 (Mar. 1989), 116–31; and K. J. Arrow, 'Increasing Returns: Historiographical Issues and Path Dependence', *European Journal of the History of Economic Thought*, 7, 2 (2000), 171–80.

returns might lead to path dependence was pounced on by those for whom political and economic institutions could be seen as the underlying determinant of economic performance. Thus, for example, Douglas North argued that institutions might also become 'locked-in' by increasing returns derived from high fixed costs, by learning effects over time, by coordination effects, and by adaptive expectations.[11] Building on the work of North and others, Paul Pierson argues that path dependence is an important feature of political life in general, and the political life of welfare states in particular, as a consequence of institutional inertia, the non-market nature of public policy, and short political time horizons.[12] Indeed, in the context of welfare states, there seems to be general agreement among historical institutionalists in political science that 'pensions policy is a locus classicus for the study of "path-dependent" change' as a consequence of its very long time-horizons.[13]

Yet, if one looks at the development of British pensions over the past half-century or so what immediately strikes one is the fact that the system has been subject to major reform at least once a decade—which does not really suggest a locked-in system. This is important because whether or not the system is 'locked-in' has major implications both for understanding why the complexity of the overall system seems to inexorably increase and for any attempts to reform the system. The question of whether or not British pensions are 'locked-in' lies at the heart of this chapter which will now go on to examine developments in British pensions in the two decades after the publication of the Beveridge Report in 1942, and then briefly consider the course of subsequent developments. In doing so, four points will be emphasized. First, the dynamics of continual change over more than half a century suggest that Britain's overall pensions system is far from 'locked-in'. Second, an important feature of the way that the system developed was the discrepancy between the long-term nature of pensions and short-term political horizons. Third, it is clear that individual elements within the overall system *did* become 'locked-in'. Finally, a combination of short-term political horizons and long-term lock-in at sub-system level acted together to encourage the accumulation of elements within the system; British pensions therefore demonstrated a systemic tendency for the complexity of the system as a whole to increase.

[11] D. North, *Institutions, Institutional Change, and Economic Performance* (Cambridge, 1990).
[12] Pierson, *Increasing Returns*; Pierson, 'Increasing Returns'; P. Pierson (ed.) *The New Politics of the Welfare State* (Oxford, 2001).
[13] Myles and Pierson, 'Comparative Political Economy', p. 306.

The Beveridge Settlement

Britain's system of pensions when the Beveridge Committee was appointed in 1941 already exhibited signs of sub-system accumulation. First, there was the 1908 non-contributory and means-tested scheme, administered by Customs and Excise and paid through post offices. Second, there was the 1925 contributory scheme, part of the National Health Insurance system, which by 1938 covered around 21 million contributors but which paid pensions for only five years from age 65, after which the pensioner proceeded to the 1908 scheme but without means-testing.[14] In addition, backing up this system was a system of supplementary pensions paid to approximately 250,000 of the poorest pensioners by the Assistance Board.[15]

In 1946, however, Britain shifted to a state-run universal contributory pension paid at a flat rate until death; a structure backed by a parallel system of National Assistance payments which Beveridge, erroneously as it turned out, expected would largely wither away after a transitional period during which employee contributions would build up to yield a full pension.[16]

Beveridge's achievement in creating a unified universal state pension was, nonetheless, remarkable. That this was the case was due to the exceptional conditions of the Second World War, which therefore represented a critical juncture at which Britain had the chance to address the shortcomings of pre-war pensions and create, for the first time, a system of adequate pension provision for all. The war had two effects which allowed both contractual lock-in and increasing returns in pensions to be transcended (or at least minimized). First, the war contributed to a solidaristic environment and to a faith in the capabilities of the state that reduced the political costs of moving to the new national insurance pension.[17] Second, wartime inflation reduced the real financial costs of compensating members of the existing schemes.

Nevertheless, the new national insurance pension did reflect path dependencies set up by the preceding arrangements. At root, Beveridge's proposals largely retained the structure of the contributory and actuarially

[14] *Social Insurance and Allied Services*, Cmd 6404, 'The Beveridge Report' (London, 1942), p. 213; J. Macnicol, *The Politics of Retirement in Britain, 1878–1948* (Cambridge, 1998), p. 214.
[15] Macnicol, *Politics of Retirement*, p. 351.
[16] Beveridge, *Social Insurance*, p. 141.
[17] Paul Addison, *The Road to 1945*, 2nd edn (London, 1994), pp. 211–28, 279–92; J. Harris, *William Beveridge* (Oxford, 1997), p. 369.

funded 1925 scheme, made use of the existing 1925 scheme machinery in which contributions were collected through a stamped card, and involved flat-rate contributions and benefits.[18]

Moreover, despite the achievement that the 1946 scheme represented, it did not entirely meet its objectives. First, Beveridge's main task was to bring the 1908 and 1925 schemes together under a single administrative umbrella.[19] This was successful in that the new system involved a combination of the principles lying behind the two schemes, but the 1908 scheme continued for those who had retired without ever contributing to the 1925 scheme. Beveridge's second task was to move to a universal contributory pension—a task that was successfully achieved. Third, Beveridge had to bring pensions paid up to 'subsistence' (in other words devise a system that would pay a pension that would be enough to live on)[20] in order to eliminate the need for supplementation by the Assistance Board. This objective was not achieved, a failure that was of profound significance because it meant that the new pension was from the start inadequate.[21] Finally, the system as implemented was not fully funded, as Beveridge had intended.

Beveridge's concept of 'national insurance' implied a funded scheme in which an employee's contributions would purchase specific future benefits. In fact, even under Beveridge's proposals this was not entirely the case. The decision to pay full pensions sooner than Beveridge had envisaged (by dropping his twenty-year transition period, or 'golden staircase', to full pension rights) then made it even less so. Instead, full pensions were to be paid immediately to those insured since 1925. For those who had joined after 1925 a full pension would be paid after only ten years of contributions. For Bevin, and for other members of the Cabinet Committee on Reconstruction Priorities overseeing the translation of the Beveridge plan into legislation, the long delay envisaged by Beveridge to allow contributions to build up was simply not practical politics. A more

[18] B. Ellis, *Pensions in Britain, 1955–1975* (London, 1989), pp. 1–2; H. Glennerster and M. Evans, 'Beveridge and His Assumptive Worlds: The Incompatibilities of a Flawed Design', in J. Hills *et al.*, *Beveridge and Social Security* (Oxford, 1994), p. 60.

[19] Macnicol, *Politics of Retirement*, p. 352.

[20] Although the concept of 'subsistence' raised several issues, being very difficult to define. Beveridge's definition, for example, was notably lower than the measure employed by Rowntree (J. Veit-Wilson, 'Muddle or Mendacity? The Beveridge Committee and the Poverty Line', *Journal of Social Policy*, 21 (1992), 269–301) and its level tended to vary between regions and between individuals depending on personal circumstances (R. Lowe, 'A Prophet Dishonoured in His Own Country? The Rejection of Beveridge in Britain, 1945–1970', in J. Hills *et al.*, *Beveridge and Social Security*, pp. 120–2).

[21] Macnicol, *Politics of Retirement*, p. 325.

generous settlement seemed essential given the sacrifices made by those of working age during the 1930s Depression and in the Second World War.[22] This made short-term political sense for Labour. It mollified an electorate eager to put the poverty of the 1930s and the suffering of war behind it and build a universalist new welfare state as soon as possible. However, Labour's decision severely weakened the finances of the new state pension by making it essentially an 'unfunded scheme' that was not based on actuarial principles—in that an employee's contributions did not build up a fund out of which a pension would be paid to them in retirement.[23] Instead the system was pay-as-you-go (PAYG) with current pensions paid out of current contributions which (on the Treasury's own admission) were no more than 'a regressive poll tax', the level of which was determined by an 'arbitrary guess by the Actuary as to what is affordable'.[24] The concept of national insurance was therefore essentially a 'fiction'.[25] In effect, a political sleight of hand had been employed to allow the immediate payment of benefits, the cost of which would not have to be redeemed for many years.

This shift to a pay-as-you-go funding basis was, however, concealed from contributors, who continued to view national insurance in effect as a financial contract between them and the state in which their contributions purchased rights to a fully funded future pension. Not only was the new state system immediately 'locked-in' by this implicit contract, Labour's relaxing of the transitional arrangements envisaged by Beveridge meant that the pension it would deliver was bound to be inadequate. With the golden staircase demolished, the Treasury viewed the plan to increase the level of the pension up to 'subsistence' as ruinous to the long-term financing of the National Insurance Fund.[26] In order to obtain Treasury support, the level of the pension had to be set lower than subsistence (with National Assistance used to target benefits on the really needy) and the level of the pension was not indexed to rise in line with inflation.[27] As we shall see, this too was to have important repercussions in the 1950s.

Moreover, the implicit financial contract between contributors and the state reflected the decision to adopt a universal flat-rate pension. This was

[22] Macnicol, *Politics of Retirement*, pp. 390–4; N. Timmins, *The Five Giants* (London, 2001), p. 136.
[23] D. Gladstone (ed.), *British Social Welfare* (London, 1995), p. 83.
[24] The National Archive (hereafter TNA): Public Record Office (hereafter PRO) T 227/415, note by Miss Whalley, 'NHS and National Insurance contributions', 1 May 1956.
[25] Lowe, 'Prophet Dishonoured', p. 123.
[26] Macnicol, *Politics of Retirement*, pp. 353–4; Timmins, *Five Giants*, pp. 136–7.
[27] D. Fraser, *The Evolution of the British Welfare State* (Basingstoke, 1984), pp. 230–1.

a function of the political conditions of the time. Wartime deprivation had been both widespread and relatively equally felt. Beveridge was thus 'interpreting and responding to, rather than creating the spirit of the times'.[28] The problem was that it assumed a world of fair shares in deprivation. While this made sense in the context of the war years and of the 1930s, the inflexibility of the flat-rate approach was to prove a major constraint in the very different conditions of the post-war years. A system of flat-rate contributions tied the level of that contribution to what the lowest-paid worker could afford. This made it very difficult to raise the level of the pension—what Helen Fawcett has termed the 'Beveridge straitjacket'.[29] This straitjacket, reinforced as it was by the existence of a firm financial contract in the mind of individual contributors, was to prove a major constraint which shaped the development of pensions policy during the decade and a half after 1945.

The Growth of Occupational Pensions in the 1950s

The contractual nature of the flat-rate 'Beveridge straitjacket' left the new system poorly placed to deal with the changed conditions of the 1950s for two reasons. First, the rising prices experienced in the post-war economy eroded the real value of the new pension. An increase in 1951 restored its real value and thereafter it was again raised several times in response to rising prices. Nevertheless, it fell below the rate of National Assistance—a poverty benchmark. Moreover, each rise was conceded with great reluctance by the Treasury which was all too aware of the looming deficit in the National Insurance Fund as a consequence of the decision to abandon Beveridge's golden staircase to full pension rights. The prospect of the 'growing army' of employees who were about to retire having paid only ten years contributions filled the Treasury with considerable alarm. It was further concerned that each rise in the pension would require payments to be financed by current contributions that it had hoped to use to bolster the finances of the National Insurance Fund.[30]

If the Treasury was reluctant to maintain the real value of the state pension for fear of the cost to the exchequer—in a situation in which the level of the contribution must necessarily be tied to what the poorest

[28] Addison, *Road to 1945*, p. 17; Harris, *Beveridge*, pp. 406–7.
[29] H. Fawcett, 'The Beveridge Strait-jacket: Policy Formulation and the Problem of Poverty in Old Age', *Contemporary British History*, 10, 1 (1996), 20–42.
[30] Ellis, *Pensions*, p. 3; M. Hill, *The Welfare State in Britain: A Political History since 1945* (Aldershot, 1993), p. 57; Timmins, *Five Giants*, p. 193.

could afford to pay—it was even more reluctant to accede to demands that the pension should reflect not just the increase in prices but the greater increase in average earnings that was such a notable characteristic of the post-war 'golden age'. With the state pension locked-in to a minimalist solution, and with employees in a strong bargaining position in the labour market as a consequence of full employment, there was an increasing gap between workers' expectations of the pension they should receive and the reality of what they would actually receive. This led to considerable pressure for their future pensions to reflect the increase in their earnings.[31] This demand was increasingly met by a rapid rise in the number of occupational pension schemes offered by employers as an addition to the state pension.

Occupational pension schemes were not new. Hitherto, however, they had been largely confined to public servants and higher-paid private-sector employees. Firm data on numbers are lacking, but in 1936 a large-scale statistical survey by the Ministry of Labour found that about 8 per cent of workers were in private-sector occupational pension schemes, with a further 5 per cent in public-sector schemes.[32] Before the war, therefore, occupational pensions were the preserve of a minority. By 1954, however, the Phillips Committee was noting that occupational pension schemes were becoming major providers of pensions.[33] By 1956 the proportion of workers in occupational schemes had leapt to 33 per cent, most of this growth having occurred since the end of the war, and the figure was rising by 2.3 per cent a year. At this rate more than half of all workers would be covered by 1964.[34]

Some of the enormous growth in the membership of occupation pension schemes was a consequence of the rise in the number of government employees that accompanied the expansion of the state after 1939. To some extent, it was deliberately cultivated by the Conservative government—both for ideological reasons and for reasons of short-term

[31] Although Hill, *Welfare State*, p. 57 implies that there was no such pressure there is ample evidence to the contrary: not least the minutes of the Cabinet's National Insurance Committee (TNA: PRO CAB 134/2246, National Insurance Committee, meetings and memoranda, 1957 *passim*), and the Labour Party's proposals for 'national superannuation' which are outlined in the next section, see Labour Party, *National Superannuation: Labour's Policy for Security in Old Age* (London, 1957).

[32] L. Hannah, *Inventing Retirement: The Development of Occupational Pensions in Britain* (Cambridge, 1986), p. 40.

[33] *Report of the Committee on the Economic and Financial Problems of the Provision for Old Age*, Cmd 9333 (London, 1954).

[34] Government Actuary, *Occupational Pension Schemes: A Survey by the Government Actuary* (London, 1958).

expediency, since an expansion of occupational pensions might reduce pressure to increase the level of the state pension.[35] Much of the growth, however, was organic: the result of a desire on the part of employees for earnings-related pensions—which in turn was the product of the inadequate level of state pension produced by the financial consequences of the 1946 settlement and the barrier to its reform posed by its contractual nature. This demand for earnings-related pensions was increasingly met by employers eager to offer employment packages that would help to improve staff retention in a tight labour market. By 1967, membership of such schemes had reached 53 per cent of the working population.[36] Occupational pensions had moved from a 'niche' position to a central role in Britain's system of pension provision.

Like the 1946 'national insurance' pension, this new element in mass pension provision was also locked-in. Partly this might be seen as the product of 'increasing returns' in that the value of such pension funds, and the number of contributors, grew rapidly, thus giving the funds considerable market and political power. But pension benefits under an occupational scheme were also accrued as a matter of contractual right under the rules of the scheme.[37] This immediately locked-in such schemes. An employee in an occupational scheme would contribute a proportion of their income to the scheme with, in many cases, an additional contribution on the employee's behalf by the employer or, in some cases, the employer might pay the whole value of the contributions for that employee. As long as the employee remained in the scheme until retirement (and as long as the fund remained solvent) they were effectively guaranteed a pension (generally calculated as a percentage of their final salary). For those who stayed, therefore, the contractual commitment by the scheme was both firm and potentially very long-term.

Thus, because the 1946 settlement had resulted in a minimalist state pension immediately locked-in by contractual obligations, it had created the conditions for the development of a parallel and extensive system of private occupational pensions provision on a vastly greater scale than had been expected at the time of the Beveridge Report.[38] As a consequence, by the mid-1950s Britain effectively had two systems of mass pension provi-

[35] L. Dennett, *A Sense of Security: 150 years of the Prudential* (Cambridge, 1998), p. 349.
[36] Government Actuary, *Occupational Pensions Schemes: Third Survey by the Government Actuary* (London, 1968).
[37] D. Blake, *Pension Schemes and Pension Funds in the United Kingdom* (Oxford, 2003), pp. 94–5.
[38] Hannah, *Inventing Retirement*, p. 44.

sion to provide workers with an adequate pension, rather than the one envisaged by Beveridge; with each of these sub-systems locked-in by contractual obligations.

The Adoption of a State Graduated Pension

Although the rapid growth of occupational schemes filled a gap in the market for many employees, the Phillips Report noted in 1954 that two-thirds of workers still remained wholly dependent on a flat-rate state pension which was not keeping pace with rising earnings. The desire to bring these excluded workers within the orbit of earnings-related pensions was an important driver of moves to reform the state pension during the mid-1950s.[39]

In 1957, the opposition Labour Party produced a set of proposals for an all-embracing system of 'national superannuation' which was intended to extend the benefit of earnings-related pension benefits to all. The proposed scheme would pay a pension equal to approximately 50 per cent of income at retirement.[40] To finance this, higher contributions would be required. These would be invested by the state in stocks and shares in order to build up a large fund out of which the considerably improved pension would be paid. (There is a striking resemblance between this proposal and the National Pensions Saving Scheme (NPSS) proposed by the Pensions Commission in its second report, although Labour's 1957 scheme did not involve individual accounts.)[41] Labour's proposal for 'half-pay on retirement' was unusually well thought-out and envisaged a scheme 'as advanced as any under discussion in the social democratic parties of Europe'.[42] It could be expected to play well electorally and it therefore encouraged the Conservative government to bring forward its own proposals for reform of the 1946 state pension.[43]

In theory, one way of satisfying the desire for earnings-relation in pensions was simply to encourage the private sector to expand its operations and provide occupational pensions to all. This was the solution favoured by the Minister for Pensions in early discussions in the Cabinet's National

[39] Hannah, *Inventing Retirement*, p. 55.
[40] Labour Party, *National Superannuation*, pp. 17–19.
[41] For details of the NPSS, see Pensions Commission, *Second Report*, ch. 10.
[42] Fawcett, 'Beveridge Strait-jacket', 25.
[43] Ministry of Pensions, *Provision for Old Age*, Cmnd 538 (London, 1958).

Insurance Committee and pushed aggressively by him thereafter.[44] Such an approach was a reflection of a powerful commitment to private-sector solutions among many Conservatives (and among many officials). It was also the product of a high degree of institutional inertia in the Ministry of Pensions as it sought to defend its implementation and administration of the 1946 institutional settlement on pensions. Yet, as the life assurance companies themselves acknowledged, it was never going to be possible for the private sector to provide occupational pensions for all workers because it would be unprofitable to deal with the very large number of small firms in the British economy.[45]

This inability of the private sector to deliver earnings-related pensions for all employees implied an extension of the existing state pension. The question was how extensive should this be and how feasible was reform of the existing national insurance pension? Ian Macleod, then Minister of Labour, with the support of Prime Minister Harold Macmillan, produced initial proposals to compel employers to set up and contribute to a private occupational pension scheme or to enter a new state scheme of equivalent generosity—which Macleod intended would encompass both the flat and supplementary pension.[46]

After considerable debate within government during 1957 and 1958, however, the intention to instigate a radical reorganization of the 1946 state scheme was dropped. This was a critical moment in the development of Britain's system of state pensions and, by extension, in the development of the private sector. Instead of a relatively ambitious recasting of the Beveridge system, as envisaged by Macleod's proposals, the flat-rate pension was retained and a separate, and not particularly generous, earnings-related (or 'graduated') state pension was introduced.

Paul Bridgen has argued that the limited nature of the new graduated state pension was a product of a strong anti-state culture in the

[44] See, for example, TNA: PRO CAB 134/2246, 8 March 1957, NI(57)8 'A supplementary pensions scheme: the Treasury view', memorandum by the Financial Secretary to the Treasury; CAB 129/88, 16 September 1957, C(57)205, 'Supplementary Pension Schemes', memorandum by the Minister of Pensions and National Insurance ('The September Plan'); CAB 129/88, 11 October 1957, C(57)211, 'Old age pensions: note by the Secretary to the Cabinet'; and PRO CAB 129/93, 9 July 1958, C(58)145, 'Pensions', memorandum by the Secretary of State for the Home Department and Lord Privy Seal.

[45] The Archive of the Life Offices' Association (hereafter LOA): Ms 28376/101, 3 Dec. 1958, minutes of a meeting between the Minister of Pensions and representatives of the Joint Committee of the LOA and Associated Scottish Life Offices.

[46] TNA: PRO CAB 134/2246, 6 May 1957, NI(57)12, 'National pension scheme: note by the Minister of Labour' ('The Life Offices' Plan', also known as 'The May Plan').

Conservative Party.[47] There is truth in this. Those who opposed Macleod's scheme, such as the Minister of Pensions (John Boyd-Carpenter) and the Chancellor and his Treasury ministers (Peter Thorneycroft, Enoch Powell, and Nigel Birch), reflected antipathies on the right of the party to a greater role for the state in providing pensions (and to the greater state control of the assets that would accrue in the sort of comprehensive and generous contributory scheme envisaged by Labour). By creating deadlock in the Cabinet at a time of pressing need to produce a new scheme to defuse the threat posed by Labour's proposals, they were able to secure a decision to adopt a less ambitious scheme, even if this was clearly going to be inadequate in the long term. As Macmillan noted to ministers, 'In the long run we shall all be dead and before some of these calculations mature we may well be a Communist society or destroyed by a bomb. So do not let us bother too much as long as we do not spend too much for the next two or three years.'[48] Short-term expediency was of greater concern than long-term effectiveness.

Bridgen underestimates, however, the part played in the government's adoption of a limited scheme of earnings-relation by sub-system lock-in. First, the pressing need to solve the finances of the National Insurance Fund, coupled with the flat-rate design of the 1946 pension, fed Treasury opposition to a generous state earnings-related pension. The National Insurance Fund, despite much lower unemployment than had been anticipated in 1946, was due to move into deficit in 1958 and this deficit was expected to rise to £250 million by 1966.[49] At this level, the deficit would amount to about 7 per cent of the total value of current annual public expenditure. In the opinion of the Treasury, any reform of the state pension should be directed at solving this financial crisis. In fact, it is notable that the debate in Whitehall about the future of the state scheme swiftly moved away from a debate about how to improve the level of the 1946 national insurance pension. Instead, it rapidly centred on the question how to devise a scheme that would appear to offer improved benefits, while in reality using the higher contributions that would result from earnings-relation to bail out the National Insurance Fund.[50]

[47] P. Bridgen, 'The One Nation Idea and State Welfare: The Conservatives and Pensions in the 1950s', *Contemporary British History*, 14, 3 (2000), 86.
[48] TNA: PRO CAB 129/88, 22 July 1957, C(57)176, 'Pensions', memorandum by the Prime Minister.
[49] TNA: PRO CAB 134/2246, 8 March 1957, NI(57)8, 'A supplementary pensions scheme: the Treasury view', memorandum by the Financial Secretary to the Treasury.
[50] See TNA: PRO CAB 129/88, 27 July 1957, C(57)181, 'National Insurance changes', memorandum by the Chancellor of the Exchequer ('The August Plan') for the most definitive statement of this aim.

Second, as we have noted, the 1946 settlement had created the erroneous impression that national insurance contributions purchased specific pension benefits. This had created an apparent contract between each contributor and the state which at once fed the desire for 'reform', by undermining the finances of the National Insurance Fund, and made the abolition of the flat-rate pension all but impossible. The enduring nature of the flat-rate 'contract' meant that Macleod's initial plan, all the subsequent competing plans considered by the government, and the Cabinet's final compromise plan were forced, either explicitly or implicitly, to assume its continuation.[51] Likewise, Labour's proposals also envisaged a continuation of the flat-rate scheme. Rodney Lowe has suggested that the adoption of a state graduated pension in 1961 represented a decisive break with at least two of the four key principles of Beveridge's (1942) proposals; involving as it did the abandonment of flat-rate contributions and benefits.[52] The truth, however, is that policy-makers were forced to accept that the contract represented by the 1946 settlement could not be broken. Consequently earnings-relation had to be implemented as a new element in the state scheme. The flat-rate pension continued, as did flat-rate contributions. The break in respect of the flat-rate principle was confined to the raiding of the new earnings-related scheme (the 'graduated pension') to subsidize the deficit in the funding of the flat-rate pension (thus solving the emerging deficit over the short term but creating a significantly larger problem in the medium to long term).

Finally, the growth of occupational schemes was by now a *fait accompli*. As we have already noted, this immediately introduced problems of contract path dependence as well as path dependency effects arising over time from increasing returns. By 1956 there were over 8 million employees in such schemes and around 300,000 pensions in payment. This was therefore now a business of considerable size, able to spend large sums on policy research, on lobbying opinion formers, briefing the press, advertis-

[51] TNA: PRO CAB 134/2246, 6 May 1957, NI(57)12, 'National pension scheme: note by the Minister of Labour' ('The Life Offices' Plan', also known as 'The May Plan'); TNA: PRO CAB 134/2246, 24 June 1957, NI(57)23 / NI(O)(57)28 (Revise), 'Second report by officials' ('The June Plan'); TNA: PRO CAB 129/88, 27 July 1957, C(57)181, 'National Insurance changes', memorandum by the Chancellor of the Exchequer ('The August Plan'); TNA: PRO CAB 129/88, 16 September 1957, C(57)205, 'Supplementary Pension Schemes', memorandum by the Minister of Pensions and National Insurance ('The September Plan'); TNA: PRO CAB 129/93, 9 July 1958, C(58)145, 'Pensions', memorandum by the Secretary of State for the Home Department and Lord Privy Seal; a useful summary of the competing plans can be found in TNA: PRO CAB 129/88, 11 October 1957, C(57)211, 'Old age pensions: note by the Secretary to the Cabinet'.

[52] Lowe, 'Prophet Dishonoured', pp. 122–3.

ing and publicity, and on mobilizing trade union opposition (the importance of which is emphasized by Noel Whiteside in her chapter in this volume).[53] Its interests, as both parties realized, must be taken into account and the industry could no longer be ignored as it had been in 1946.[54] The fact that the proposals of the Life Offices' Association formed the basis of the government's initial plan for earnings-relation in the state system is therefore highly significant.[55] Its influence is also evident in the final proposals of the Labour Party. Under both plans provisions were made to allow occupational schemes to 'contract-out' of the new earnings-related state pension, effectively encouraging the continued growth of such schemes, despite the fact that allowing them to do so significantly weakened the finances of the state scheme.[56]

The construction of a state earning-related pension was therefore highly constrained by sub-system lock-in generated initially by contractual obligations and then by increasing returns. The result was a 'graduated state pension' that was limited in its scope, used to bail out the National Insurance Fund over the short term, and which had to be installed on top of the existing state scheme in order to respect the national insurance contract. Rather than 'reform', therefore, we see a further element added to the pensions system, one which embodied its own path dependencies that would then ensure its long-term survival.

Subsequent Developments

By 1961, therefore, a system of mass pensions that had been characterized basically by a single element in 1946 now had three elements (four if one includes the system of additional voluntary contributions (AVCs) associated with occupational pensions).[57] Each element was locked-in by

[53] See, for example, LOA: Ms 28376/89, 'Retirement Pensions: the State Scheme, Occupational Schemes and the Future', *passim*; and LOA: Ms 28376/90–28376/96, minutes of the Publicity Joint Committee of the LOA and Associated Scottish Life Offices, April 1957–June 1958, *passim*.

[54] See, for example, the terms of reference set by the Prime Minister for the Cabinet's National Insurance Committee in its devising of a new scheme at TNA: PRO CAB 134/2246, 14 May 1957, NI(57)13, 'Reconstitution of the committee', note by the Secretary to the Cabinet.

[55] TNA: PRO CAB 134/2246, 6 May 1957, NI(57)12, 'National pension scheme: note by the Minister of Labour' ('The Life Offices' Plan', also known as 'The May Plan').

[56] Labour Party, *National Superannuation*; Ministry of Pensions, Cmnd 538. The ability of the Life Offices to resist Labour's proposals does not bode well for the success of the Pensions Commission's proposed National Pensions Savings Scheme.

[57] More again if one were to include supplementary welfare benefits.

contractual obligations and by gradually increasing returns. In the case of occupational pensions and the state graduated pension the contract was explicit. In the case of the state basic pension it was implicit, but nonetheless it would be a brave government that would choose to revoke 'rights' acquired under a contract which most workers saw as explicit. Increasing returns further contributed to lock-in, but the existence of a contract ensured that lock-in was a fact as soon as contributions to a new element began.

It might be argued that the development of three parallel sub-systems was simply a product of filling in what has come to be seen as the standard three tiers of pension provision—a basic pension provided by the state, an additional earnings-related element, and finally an additional voluntary component (via AVCs to occupational schemes)—rather than the product of path dependency. Yet, a brief survey of subsequent developments shows that this process of sub-system accumulation has continued. Each of the elements in place by 1961 endures today, despite a number of subsequent major 'reforms' (see Figure 3.1).

At best, reform has involved the 'cold storage' of rights under a given pension when a new element has been introduced. In 1978, for example, the state graduated pension was apparently superseded by Labour's state earnings-related pension, but in fact this 'reform' was unable to integrate

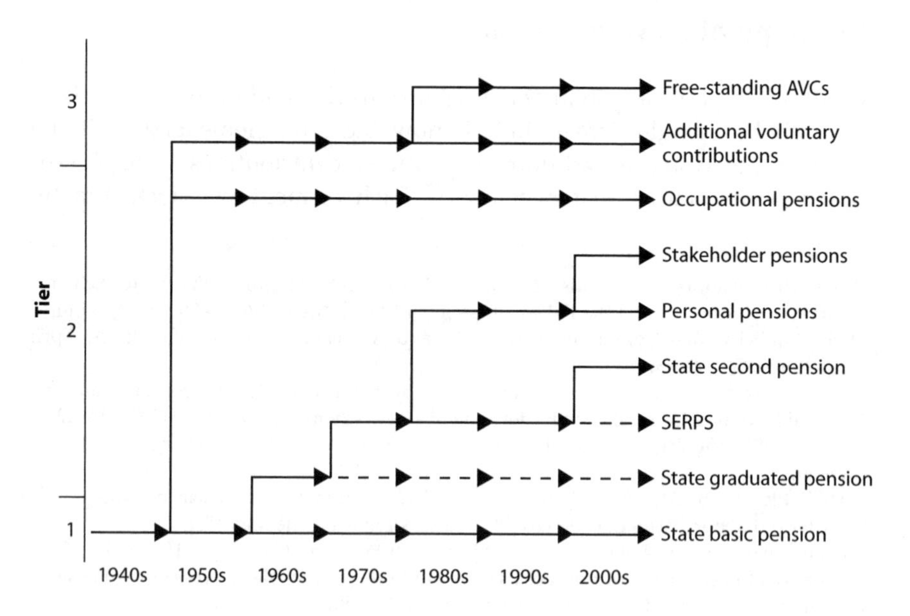

Figure 3.1. Contract path dependence in UK pensions.

into the new scheme the Conservatives' graduated pension. Contributors to the graduated pension retain an entitlement to its benefits to this day and the scheme will continue until the death of the last contributor, which may well not be until the 2060s. Similarly, while Labour's recent introduction of the state second pension sees an end to contributions under the state earnings-related pension scheme (SERPS), it does not end pension rights under SERPS which will therefore likely also live on until the death of its last contributor, perhaps until the 2080s.

More commonly, 'reform' has involved the installation of a new system of pensions in parallel with the old. In the 1980s, for example, the Conservatives' wish to abolish SERPS was thwarted by the fact that contributors to SERPS felt themselves to be directly purchasing rights to an earnings-related pension in retirement and were reluctant to see the scheme ended. Such was the opposition that the Thatcher administration found it much easier simply to introduce a new system of mass personal pensions in addition to rather than as a replacement for SERPS. As Sir John Hoskyns remarked, this was 'a major admission of defeat' by the Conservatives.[58] Similarly, Labour's recent introduction of stakeholder pensions was an addition to personal pension plans, not a replacement.

The consequence of sub-system contractual lock-in has been that if one traces the development of mass pensions in Britain since 1946 one finds a steadily rising number of elements in the overall system (see Figure 3.1). This sub-system accumulation has led to rising complexity and decreasing efficiency (in other words, 'decreasing returns') in the system as a whole. Indeed, complexity has become a significant problem in all areas of the UK's overall system of pensions.

In the arena of state pensions, for example, there are actually three state earnings-related pensions: the state graduated pension, the succeeding state earnings-related pension (SERPS), and the new state second pension. They are costly to administer because they are extremely complicated and there is only a tenuous link between contributions paid and benefits received.[59] None of the individual elements of state earnings-related provision as a whole is well understood by the public.

In occupational pensions, complexity was identified by the Pickering Report as a fundamental reason for 71 per cent of employers providing no

[58] Blake, *Pension Schemes*, p. 89.

[59] A. Budd and N. Campbell, 'The Roles of the Public and Private Sectors in the UK Pension System', in M. Feldstein, *Privatizing Social Security* (Chicago IL, 1998); P. Johnson, R. Disney, and G. Stears, *Pensions: 2000 and Beyond: IFS Retirement Income Inquiry*, vol. 2 (London, 1996); Office of Fair Trading, *Report of the Director General's Inquiry into Pensions* (London, 1997), p. 88.

occupational pension scheme for their staff.[60] Moreover, the complexity of both the pensions system as a whole, and of the occupational pensions system in particular, has played a part in the recent transition by many employers to defined-contribution schemes—which are typically run in parallel with the old defined-benefit scheme, with new recruits being admitted to the defined-contribution scheme. Occasionally, and increasingly since the introduction of the new Financial Reporting Standard (FRS) 17 in 2001, employers have closed the existing defined-benefit scheme and forcibly moved workers onto a defined-contribution basis. However, where this has occurred, as with reform in state earnings-related pensions, those benefits have effectively been put into cold storage, thus leaving the employee with two benefit entitlements from the same employer. These are radical changes in which employers have been aided by the fact that the complexity of Britain's pensions system means workers generally have a very low level of understanding of their occupational scheme.[61] The potential costs of transfer have therefore typically been quite low. Nevertheless, most employers have plainly judged that the political and commercial costs of interfering with workers' *existing* benefits are so high as to preclude this approach. Thus, change in occupational pensions acknowledges a degree of sub-system lock-in and is typically achieved only by the introduction of further complexity into the system.

If anything, the impact of complexity on privately purchased pensions is even greater. Although more than half those of working age fear that they will receive little or nothing by way of a state pension, take-up of private pension plans is worryingly low. A major factor in the relatively low rate of take-up, and in poor persistence when plans are purchased, is the complexity of Britain's pensions system. Almost half those of working age have no more than a 'patchy' knowledge of pensions.[62] As the chief executive of the Pensions Advisory Service noted, complexity is a 'major barrier to the ordinary citizen's understanding of their pension position'.[63] As Ruth Kelly, then economic secretary to the Treasury, acknowledged in 2003, such is the level of confusion among consumers that 'It is almost impossible for anyone to make rational choices [about their pensions]'.[64] Complexity, by reducing consumer understanding, inhibits effective pension planning and decision-making and it discourages pension accumu-

[60] Pickering, *Simpler Way*, p. 2.
[61] Hedges, *Pensions*.
[62] Mayhew, *Pensions 2000*.
[63] Quoted in *The Guardian*, 8 July 2002.
[64] Quoted in the *Sunday Telegraph*, 5 October 2003.

lation.[65] Although these effects have been exacerbated by the erosion of trust in the system produced by the mis-selling scandal, complexity was itself an important contributor to this because of consumers' lack of understanding of pensions. Finally, the fact that complexity raises administration costs, and consequently reduces returns on investment, is a further disincentive to saving.[66]

Conclusions

Britain's system of pensions, both public and private, has been subject to major reforms at least once a decade since 1946. The system, therefore, appears to be anything but locked-in. Nevertheless, while lock-in does not seem to apply at the macro-level, this survey has demonstrated that lock-in does appear to apply at the sub-system level.

Sub-system lock-in has been fed by 'increasing returns' in terms of high set-up costs, institutional inertia, the rising numbers of contributors and pensioners in the sub-system, learning effects, and the costs and coordination problems of abolishing the sub-system and transferring its contributors, pensioners, and liabilities into a superseding scheme. However, sub-system lock-in has primarily been caused by the contractual nature of British pensions—explicit financial contracts in the case of privately purchased pensions, explicit financial contracts between employers and employees in the case of occupational pensions, and implicit financial contracts between workers and the state in the case of the various state pensions.

This phenomenon of sub-system contractual lock-in lay behind the initial post-war shift to, and the subsequent rapid development of, occupational pensions. Reform of the flat-rate state pension was then highly constrained by contractual lock-in in both occupational pensions and the 1946 flat-rate state pension. The government simply found that it was easier to add a new element to the existing flat-rate state pension than to reform it. This pattern of sub-system accumulation has continued so that Britain now has nine parallel systems of mass pension provision (excluding supplementary systems of welfare benefits and tax credits).

[65] Hedges, *Pensions*, p. 117; *Sandler Review: Medium and Long-term Retail Savings in the UK* (London, 2002); A. Smith and S. McKay, *Employers' Pension Provision Survey 2000*, Department of Work and Pensions Research Report 163 (Leeds, 2000); S. Ward, *Resolving the Pensions Dilemma* (London, 2002).

[66] Pickering, *Simpler Way*.

Reform has therefore always been possible, in that there was nothing to stop the development of a brand new pensions system. Any change, however, has always had to be grafted on to the existing system due to sub-system lock-in, and the shape of any new element has often been affected by the existence of, and the political difficulty and financial cost of abolishing, these other elements. This has created not a single locked-in trajectory of institutional development but the widening array of locked-in sub-systems shown in Figure 3.1. This in turn has led to mounting problems of complexity, to increasing system inefficiency, and thus to what one might term 'decreasing returns' in the system as a whole.

This systemic tendency to increasing complexity and decreasing systems efficiency as a consequence of contractual lock-in at the sub-system level is insufficiently recognized. There is a widespread acknowledgement that Britain's system of pensions has become unnecessarily complex but too little recognition of the important role played by contractual lock-in both in creating this complexity and in limiting the possibility of ameliorating it.[67]

We need to be more aware, or perhaps more honest in acknowledging, both that sub-system contractual lock-in exists, and that the effects it gives rise to represent a substantial constraint on present policy options. It is noticeable that the Pensions Commission, for example, in crafting its proposals for reform of the state pension system to promote private saving, found itself having to acknowledge a 'trade-off between the benefits of a radically simplified system and the implementation complexities of radical change'.[68] In the event, it felt unable to recommend a move to a single unified state pension owing in large part to the 'major transitional complexities' involved.[69]

Nevertheless, because contractual lock-in operates at the system level in Britain rather than at the level of the system as a whole, it also presents us with an opportunity to effect reform—because at the macro-level the system is not locked-in. Change is therefore possible, albeit at the price of a probable further increase in the level of system complexity.

The opportunity to change the system, however, presents us with a major challenge—to avoid 'reform' that serves merely to make the situa-

[67] For example, Hedges, *Pensions*; Mayhew, *Pensions 2000*; Office of Fair Trading, *Report into Pensions*; Department of Work and Pensions, *Simplicity, Security and Choice: Working and Saving for Retirement* (London, 2002); Inland Revenue, *Simplifying the Taxation of Pensions: Increasing Choice and Flexibility for All* (London, 2002); Pickering, *Simpler Way*; *Sandler Review*, 2002; Ward, *Resolving the Pension Dilemma*; Pensions Commission, *First Report*.

[68] Pensions Commission, *Second Report*, p. 8.

[69] Pensions Commission, *Second Report*, p. 9.

tion worse over the long term. A consistent theme in the developments in post-war pensions discussed in this chapter has been the contradiction between the long-term nature of the pension contract and the short-time scale of politics. Short-term political horizons encourage quick fixes that, while they may address short-term political needs and/or the ideological predilections of the party currently in power, may have deleterious consequences by creating new sub-systems that are both locked-in and poorly constructed. In the longer term this creates pressure for political reform, thus setting up a cycle of sub-system accumulation, rising complexity, and decreasing efficiency in the system as a whole.

In 1997, the minister responsible for pensions in the incoming Labour government acknowledged the cumulative failure of British pensions, the mounting complexity and decreasing efficiency of the system, the malign tendency to 'reform' the system every ten years or so, and the tendency for such reform to be dominated by short-term political horizons rather than long-term needs.[70] The implication was that Labour would do things differently. Plainly, given developments in the succeeding five years, it did not.

Yet the government's decision in December 2002 to set up the Pensions Commission and to encourage a national debate about how best to address the pensions crisis was encouraging. David Blunkett's professed intention to 'reach out to the other major political parties because we need a lasting solution for the decades ahead—not a quick fix' was also welcome.[71] Mr Blunkett has gone, of course, but the principal lesson of history is that his instincts were right. Unfortunately, despite his successor's claim that the Pensions Commission's proposals are the framework for achieving a national consensus on the way forward, the whispering campaign mounted against those proposals in the immediate aftermath of its second report rather suggest that this lesson has not been learnt.[72]

Note: I am grateful to Paul Bridgen, Paul Johnson, Rodney Lowe, John Macnicol, Fiona Ross, and Mark Wickham-Jones for a number of fruitful discussions on path dependency and pensions policy; and to the comments of those who attended

[70] J. Denham, unreported speech by the Parliamentary Under-Secretary of State for Social Security, 12 July 1997, http://www.dss.gov.uk/mediacentre/pressreleases/1997/jul/sp_120797.htm.

[71] D. Blunkett, Secretary of State for Work and Pensions, speech to the National Association of Pension Funds Conference, Manchester, 12 May 2005, http://www.dwp.gov.uk/aboutus/2005/13_05_05.asp.

[72] J. Hutton, Secretary of State for Work and Pensions, 'National pensions day to focus on Turner', 18 January 2006, http://www.dwp.gov.uk/mediacentre/pressreleases/2006/jan/pens43–180106.asp.

presentations by me of papers relating to this topic at the American Political Science Association annual conference, Boston, 2002; annual conference of the Political Science Association, Lincoln, 2003; Department of Economic History, London School of Economics, 2003; the annual conference of the European Social Policy Analysis Network (ESPAnet) in November 2003; and the British Academy's conference 'Where has it all gone wrong: the past, present, and future of British pensions', 15 June 2005.

Bibliography

Items that provide a useful introduction to the issues discussed in this chapter are marked with an asterisk.

Primary Sources

Archive of the Life Offices' Association (LOA), Guildhall Library, London

LOA: Ms 28376/89, 'Retirement Pensions: the State Scheme, Occupational Schemes and the Future'.

LOA: Ms 28376/90–28376/96, minutes of the Publicity Joint Committee of the LOA and Associated Scottish Life Offices, April 1957–June 1958.

LOA: Ms 28376/101, 3 Dec. 1958, minutes of a meeting between the Minister of Pensions and representatives of the Joint Committee of the LOA and Associated Scottish Life Offices.

The National Archive (TNA), Public Record Office (PRO), Kew

TNA: PRO T 227/415, Miss Whalley, 'NHS and National Insurance contributions', 1 May 1956.

TNA: PRO CAB 134/2246, National Insurance Committee, meetings and memoranda, 1957 *passim*.

TNA: PRO CAB 134/2246, 8 March 1957, NI(57)8, 'A supplementary pensions scheme: the Treasury view', memorandum by the Financial Secretary to the Treasury.

TNA: PRO CAB 129/88, 22 July 1957, C(57)176, 'Pensions', memorandum by the Prime Minister.

TNA: PRO CAB 134/2246, 6 May 1957, NI(57)12, 'National pension scheme: note by the Minister of Labour' ('The Life Offices' Plan', also known as 'The May Plan').

TNA: PRO CAB 134/2246, 24 June 1957, NI(57)23 / NI(O)(57)28 (Revise), 'Second report by officials' ('The June Plan').

TNA: PRO CAB 129/88, 27 July 1957, C(57)181, 'National Insurance changes', memorandum by the Chancellor of the Exchequer ('The August Plan').

TNA: PRO CAB 129/88, 16 September 1957, C(57)205, 'Supplementary Pension Schemes', memorandum by the Minister of Pensions and National Insurance ('The September Plan').

TNA: PRO CAB 129/88, 11 October 1957, C(57)211, 'Old age pensions: note by the Secretary to the Cabinet'.
TNA: PRO CAB 134/2246, 14 May 1957, NI(57)13, 'Reconstitution of the committee', note by the Secretary to the Cabinet.
TNA: PRO CAB 129/93, 9 July 1958, C(58)145, 'Pensions', memorandum by the Secretary of State for the Home Department and Lord Privy Seal.

Official Publications

Blunkett, D. Secretary of State for Work and Pensions, speech to the National Association of Pension Funds Conference, Manchester, 12 May 2005, http://www.dwp.gov.uk/aboutus/2005/13_05_05.asp.
Denham, J., speech by the Parliamentary Under-Secretary of State for Social Security, 12 July 1997, http://www.dss.gov.uk/mediacentre/pressreleases/1997/jul/sp_120797.htm.
Department of Work and Pensions, *Simplicity, Security and Choice: Working and Saving for Retirement* (London, 2002).
Government Actuary, *Occupational Pension Schemes: A Survey by the Government Actuary* (London, 1958).
——, *Occupational Pensions Schemes: Third Survey by the Government Actuary* (London, 1968).
House of Lords, *The Future of Pensions.* The third report of the House of Lords Work and Pensions Committee, 2 April 2003, http://www.publications.parliament.uk/pa/cm200203/cmselect/cmworpen/92/9202.htm.
Hutton, J., Secretary of State for Work and Pensions, 'National pensions day to focus on Turner', 18 January 2006, http://www.dwp.gov.uk/mediacentre/pressreleases/2006/jan/pens43–180106.asp.
Inland Revenue, *Simplifying the Taxation of Pensions: Increasing Choice and Flexibility for All* (London, 2002).
Ministry of Pensions, *Provision for Old Age*, Cmnd 538 (London, 1958).
Office of Fair Trading, *Report of the Director General's Inquiry into Pensions* (London, 1997).
Report of the Committee on the Economic and Financial Problems of the Provision for Old Age, Cmd 9333, 'The Phillips Committee' (London, 1954).
Sandler Review: Medium and Long-term Retail Savings in the UK (London, 2002).
**Social Insurance and Allied Services*, Cmd 6404, 'The Beveridge Report' (London, 1942).

Other Publications

Addison, P., *The Road to 1945*, 2nd edn (London, 1994).
Arrow, K. J., 'Increasing Returns: Historiographical Issues and Path Dependence', *European Journal of the History of Economic Thought*, 7, 2 (2000), 171–80.
Arthur, B. W., 'Self-reinforcing Mechanisms in Economics', in Philip W. Anderson, Kenneth J. Arrow, and David Pines (eds), *The Economy as an Evolving Complex System* (Reading MA, 1989).

——, 'Competing Technologies, Increasing Returns, and Lock-in by Historical Events', *Economic Journal*, 99, 394 (March 1989), 116–31.
——, *Increasing Returns and Path Dependence in the Economy* (Ann Arbor MI, 1994).
Blake, D., *Pension Schemes and Pension Funds in the United Kingdom* (Oxford, 2003).
Bonoli, G., *The Politics of Pension Reform: Institutions and Policy Change in Western Europe* (Cambridge, 2000).
Bridgen, P., 'The One Nation Idea and State Welfare: The Conservatives and Pensions in the 1950s', *Contemporary British History*, 14, 3 (2000), 83–104.
Brooks, R. *et al.*, *A New Contract for Retirement* (London, 2002).
Budd, A. and N. Campbell, 'The Roles of the Public and Private Sectors in the UK Pension System', in M. Feldstein, *Privatizing Social Security* (Chicago IL, 1998).
David, P., 'Clio and the Economics of QWERTY', *American Economic Review*, 75, 2 (1985), 332–7.
Dennett, L., *A Sense of Security: 150 years of the Prudential* (Cambridge, 1998).
Ellis, B., *Pensions in Britain, 1955–1975* (London, 1989).
*Fawcett, H., 'The Beveridge Strait-jacket: Policy Formulation and the Problem of Poverty in Old Age', *Contemporary British History*, 10, 1 (1996), 20–42.
Fraser, D., *The Evolution of the British Welfare State* (Basingstoke, 1984).
Gladstone, D. (ed.), *British Social Welfare* (London, 1995).
Glennerster, H. and M. Evans, 'Beveridge and His Assumptive Worlds: The Incompatibilities of a Flawed Design', in J. Hills *et al.*, *Beveridge and Social Security* (Oxford, 1994).
*Hannah, L., *Inventing Retirement: The Development of Occupational Pensions in Britain* (Cambridge, 1986).
*Harris, J., *William Beveridge* (Oxford, 1997).
Haverland, M., 'Another Dutch Miracle? Explaining Dutch and German Pension Trajectories', *Journal of European Social Policy*, 11, 4 (2001), 308–23.
Hedges, A., *Pensions and Retirement Planning*, Department of Social Security Research Report 83 (London, 1998).
Hill, M., *The Welfare State in Britain: A Political History since 1945* (Aldershot, 1993).
*Hills, J. *et al.* (eds), *Beveridge and Social Security* (Oxford, 1994).
Johnson, P., R. Disney, and G. Stears, *Pensions: 2000 and Beyond: IFS Retirement Income Inquiry*, vol. 2 (London, 1996).
*Labour Party, *National Superannuation: Labour's Policy for Security in Old Age* (London, 1957).
Lowe, R., 'A Prophet Dishonoured in His Own Country? The Rejection of Beveridge in Britain, 1945–1970', in J. Hills *et al.*, *Beveridge and Social Security* (Oxford, 1994).
*Macnicol, J., *The Politics of Retirement in Britain, 1878–1948* (Cambridge, 1998).
Mayhew, V., *Pensions 2000: Public Attitudes to Pensions and Planning for Retirement*, Department of Social Security Research Report 130 (Leeds, 2001).
Myles, J. and P. Pierson, 'The Comparative Political Economy of Pension Reform', in P. Pierson, *The New Politics of the Welfare State* (Oxford, 2001).
North, D., *Institutions, Institutional Change, and Economic Performance* (Cambridge, 1990).
Pensions Commission, *Pensions: Challenges and Choices. The First Report of the Pensions Commission* (London, 2004).

——, *A New Pensions Settlement for the Twenty-first Century. The Second Report of the Pensions Commission* (London, 2005).
Pickering, A., *A Simpler Way to Better Pensions* (London, 2002).
*Pierson, P., *Increasing Returns, Path Dependence and the Study of Politics* (Florence, 1997).
——, 'Increasing Returns, Path Dependence and the Study of Politics', *American Political Science Review*, 94, 2 (2000), 251–67.
—— (ed.), *The New Politics of the Welfare State* (Oxford, 2001).
Smith, A. and S. McKay, *Employers' Pension Provision Survey 2000*, Department of Work and Pensions Research Report 163 (Leeds, 2000).
Timmins, N., *The Five Giants* (London, 2001).
Veit-Wilson, J., 'Muddle or Mendacity? The Beveridge Committee and the Poverty Line', *Journal of Social Policy*, 21 (1992), 269–301.
Ward, S., *Resolving the Pensions Dilemma* (London, 2002).

4. Why So Different? Why So Bad a Future?

HOWARD GLENNERSTER

There is still a major comparative question to be answered about the United Kingdom's pension history and its present dilemmas. Harris, Pemberton, and Johnson in this volume go some way to answering it but not, I think, the whole way.

While virtually all European countries with advanced welfare states are worrying about how to cut back their state pension generosity, and sometimes partially succeeding, the UK faces the opposite problem. It is offering its citizens both inadequate and very varied pensions for the future. We must find ways to make them more generous and less varied.

Yet the UK is no novice in the pension field. It began providing state pensions at the beginning of the twentieth century. It was not *the* leader but *a* leader. It was certainly not a laggard. The UK has been unusual in Europe in developing a large private occupational pensions sector built on and fostering sophisticated financial markets in the City of London. It is not alone in the first respect. The Netherlands and Switzerland have large occupational and private coverage. But it is highly differentiated. The coverage of these schemes there is more extensive and even. The apparently reasonable average private pension income in the UK hides a wide variety of coverage—from none at all to relatively generous.[1]

The UK relies more on means-testing than any other European country. No one thinking of the UK as conforming to the 'Beveridge model' would have expected that. Beveridge was so adamant that this was not what the British people desired.

[1] Pensions Commission, *Pensions: Challenges and Choices. The First Report of the Pensions Commission* (London, 2004), pp. 62–9; comparative modelling by colleagues at LSE/ SAGE shows the extent of this variation.

Poor Theories

So why has all this happened? General 'welfare regime' explanations that put the UK and the USA together as 'Anglo Saxon' nations with powerful individualist value systems simply do not fit the case.[2] How did the UK come to pioneer a National Health Service available free at the point of use to all its citizens funded out of general taxation? If a residual means-tested ethic is so pervasive in the UK why did that happen? Why was Beveridge's contention that the opposite was true, that the British people loathed means-testing, so warmly welcomed at the time? How did the USA come to develop a much more generous, universal, and redistributive social security (i.e. pension) scheme?

I would argue that different policy spheres in any one country are shaped by different patterns of established interests. Both employers and trade unions in the UK had an interest in developing occupational pensions at key times in British pension history given the way the Beveridge Report was framed and implemented. But the pattern of trade union power was not the same in, for example, the Netherlands and the Scandinavian countries and that gave rise to another pattern of pension provision, as Whiteside shows in her chapter in this volume.

Trade union and medical professional interests were more favourably aligned to universal provision in the case of the National Health Service. Trade unions and the Labour movement more generally felt the pre-Second World War National Health Insurance system was unfair to occupations that carried high health risks. They wanted national risk-pooling. The foot soldiers who provided the service—the GPs who were 'panel' doctors in the state insurance scheme—wanted to continue with their secure state incomes even if their rich consultant colleagues felt differently.[3] In short, the politics of health and pensions were different. The role of the trade union movement was key in that difference, as we shall see. So, too, was the role of the trade union movement in the other European countries that developed strong occupational pensions, notably the Netherlands. Here almost universal inclusion in such schemes was achieved through powerful centralized tripartite bargaining between the unions, employers, and the government. No such mechanisms have ever existed in the UK. When they were tried in the late 1940s and late 1970s they were used to try to check wage inflation and fell apart very quickly.[4]

[2] G. Esping-Andersen, *The Three Worlds of Welfare Capitalism* (Cambridge, 1990).

[3] C. Webster, *The Health Services since the War*, vol. 1 (London 1988), p. 61.

[4] See N. Whiteside in this volume for more on this theme.

The Australian pattern of compulsory contributions to private occupational schemes also relied on powerful national collective bargaining to create it. Switzerland has compulsory membership of occupational schemes set at a more modest level than in the Netherlands. This scheme was a response to growing support for a more generous German-style pension scheme that came from the left in politics. Hence there was a need for a counter-scheme that had to be inclusive though private. This does not fit well into the 'welfare regime model'.

Pemberton is surely right to question whether traditional 'path dependency' theory fits the bill either. The whole notion of path dependency is that a country may find a good or a 'good enough' policy framework at one point in its history and then sticks with it even though a better framework might become available. It does so because the established interests oppose change and there are other efficiency costs of change in a well developed system.

But what if the initial path is not a good one? What if the path is not a path but a maze of such complexity that users cannot make sensible decisions about their own lives? Moreover, what if, at each stage when policy is discussed, governments decide to add a baffling extension to the maze? Why do not the respective consumer and producer interests in a democracy not rebel and force through a more sensible path in the undergrowth? Path dependency theory has no ready answer.

The issue here is not just complexity: many European pension systems are complex in the sense that they have multiple administrative structures for different occupational groups. The UK's complex structures interact in *destructive* ways. How did that happen?

The key reason seems to be that for a long period a range of interests was quite happy with the way things were going. On average, present pensioners are not devastatingly poor in comparison with other countries, though they suffer a larger fall in income than in most other European countries. Indeed the present generation of pensioners is better off than others who preceded them. The accumulation of State Earnings-related Pension Scheme (SERPS) rights and membership of occupational schemes has done well for many. The wide variation in their incomes and poor futures that are on offer are one key problem. But it is the general collapse of occupational schemes and the winding-down of SERPS that pose the main problem.

There were powerful private and governmental interests that opposed a coherent state solution or a comprehensively regulated private one. The Treasury had fought Beveridge hard to reduce the expense of his flat-rate scheme whose logic depended on the flat rate being 'adequate'. Beveridge was acutely aware that he had to leave room open for the friendly societies and the private pension industry to continue. But it will not do simply to blame the Treasury and private interests. The trade union movement played its part, as I shall argue.

Nor will poor information do as a theory. For a time the underlying weakness was obscured by the demographic gains of the post-war period. There was a growing labour force and new members were contributing to new schemes long before benefits had to be paid out. Later on, stock market gains and poor actuarial advice produced 'a fool's paradise of irrational exuberance' as the Pensions Commission called it.[5] We need a fuller account of this period in the 1980s and 1990s. It suited the short-term interests of government and large firms to go along with this fiction, but why was the labour movement so slow to unmask it? As Johnson points out in this volume the economic analytics were well understood long before this, even if they were not by Beveridge. The trade unions were highly critical of the actions of employers like Maxwell who defrauded their members. They asked for, and to some extent got, tighter regulation of pension schemes.

But, of course, to have drawn attention to the long-term deficits in occupational pension schemes would have required pressing employers to raise employees' contributions as well as asking more from employers. That would put a single union at a competitive disadvantage. What might be negotiated as a national bargain between all employers and all unions was not possible on a plant-by-plant or union-by-union basis.

In short, we need a different theoretical starting point to explain the present dilemmas. It has to take account of the labour market and the particular structure of the trade union movement in the UK and its relationship to the Labour Party.

The Perverse Political Dynamics of UK Pensions

There are some key points in UK post-war pension history. The first is, of course, the drafting of the Beveridge Report itself and the immediate post-war response to it which Harris and others discuss in this volume, as have others.[6] This set British pensions down a maze rather than a path. It was not the scheme's early effectiveness but the set of perverse political incentives

[5] Pensions Commission, *First Report*, p. 125.

[6] See, for example, the contributions of J. Harris, J. Macnicol, R. Lowe, H. Glennerster, and M. Evans in J. Hills, J. Ditch, and H. Glennerster (eds), *Beveridge and Social Security: An International Retrospective* (Oxford, 1994).

it set in train that are the key. Pensions were set low in comparison to the wage of the average industrial worker. It was in the interests of both large employers and individual trade unions to develop a parallel system of occupational pensions. The 1950s and 1960s was a period of considerable labour shortage. Large firms wanted to retain their skilled labour in which they had invested a good deal of training. Occupational pension schemes that penalized members for leaving their employer fitted their needs exactly. Trade unions were in fierce competition for members, and one way to attract and keep them was to negotiate a good pension deal for their members with an employer. But the structure of the UK trade union movement meant that these deals were part of their competitive strategy for winning members, not part of some nationwide collective agreement covering wages and pensions as in the Netherlands. The very weakness of the state scheme was lifeblood to trade union power and recruiting potential.

The low state pension and the rising occupational pension membership on offer to over half the population meant that the state pension became increasingly marginal to the median or marginal voter. In contrast, in the USA in 1935 the Federal Government had begun to create a national compulsory and wage-related scheme that used some of the revenue from richer contributors to pay reasonable pensions to poorer workers. It was expanded to cover most members of the population and was relied on as a key component of the average worker's income in retirement. Collective bargaining agreements were built *on top* of it. Thus, the politics of US pensions have been very different from those of the UK. Every time a Republican president has sought to weaken the system it has led to outrage from the average, middle-of-the-road American voter. That was true in Reagan's time and proved similarly with President George W. Bush. In the UK the basic pension was eroded with little outcry after 1980.

The second key decision taken by the Churchill government in 1951 was to challenge the Beveridge Plan and to appoint a committee headed by a wartime critic of the Plan to review it. In a passage that might have been written by today's World Bank economists that committee's report saw the state scheme running into deficit, having to raise taxes, and hence deterring the savings on which the economy depended. It emphasized the importance of private occupational and funded schemes as a source of savings in the economy[7] but, in a line the Treasury has held to ever since, it rejected compulsion. The state scheme had, by implication, to be

[7] *Report of the Committee on the Economic and Financial Problems of the Provision for Old Age*, Cmd 9333, 'The Phillips Committee' (London, 1954), p. 34.

sufficiently ungenerous to foster such schemes which were rapidly expanding at that point.

The Labour Party did begin to challenge this situation in the 1950s. Knowing Brian Abel Smith, a young lecturer at the LSE, from Cambridge days, Peter Shore, in the Labour Party Research Department, persuaded Richard Crossman, the pension spokesman for the National Executive Committee of the Labour Party, to use the expertise of Titmuss, Abel Smith, Peter Townsend, and Tony Lynes at the LSE to come up with a post-Beveridge answer. The result was *National Superannuation*.[8] That policy document essentially adopted the US model—as the Swedes and the Germans did at about the same time. Indeed, papers describing their new schemes were one of the first set put to the committee.

If the UK had at that point, or in the mid-1960s, gone for such a change we might today have a national pension scheme not unlike that of Sweden, or Germany, or the USA. We did not and we failed to do so not just because of the powerful private pension lobby but because the unions themselves were worried by the impact a universal wage-related scheme would have on their hard-won and prized private occupational schemes that they had secured for their members. A truly universal compulsory scheme would have destroyed such schemes or heavily curtailed them. Workers could not afford to pay into both a reasonably generous state scheme and a generous private scheme on top. So the unions negotiated in the Labour Party the arrangement that has been the hallmark of the UK pattern ever since. Workers and firms could opt out of the second wage-related state scheme if their own scheme met certain basic conditions. But that limited the scope for redistribution within the new state scheme. The better organized and better-off workers were not in the state scheme. Their contributions could not be used to subsidize poorer contributors on anything like the scale needed or to the extent that happened in the USA.

By this time, 1959, I was working in the Labour Party Research Department, attracted in no small way to the job by reading the challenging academic analysis at the back of *National Superannuation*. I was not put to work on pensions. The team that had worked on it was still there refining it and looking at sickness and unemployment benefits. However, I did share a room with the secretary to the working group. Regularly he would come back fuming from one of the working party meetings, complaining about the stiff opposition that was still being shown by the TUC representative on the committee. In general the unions wanted a more generous flat-rate pension not a wage-related one. They wanted to minimize

[8] Labour Party, *National Superannuation: Labour's Policy for Security in Old Age* (London, 1958).

the impact the scheme would have on the private schemes that covered their members. The Titmuss/LSE group wanted to make the scheme more generous, to link it to prices and rising average earnings, to cover women more generously, and to enable benefits of it and the private pension schemes to be transferable between jobs. They knew that this would pose more and more difficult conditions for the private schemes to meet and they hoped in the long run this would mean that the scheme did indeed become all but universal. The occupational schemes would be marginalized or become small additions to the basic superannuation scheme. Such, at least, Abel Smith explained to me as a member and later chair of the Young Fabians. (It was a group to which, as an elder member of the Fabians, Abel Smith acted as an 'uncle'.) But that, of course, was precisely what the TUC representative feared, I suspect.

In a little noticed passage, *National Superannuation* had said: 'Before final conclusions are reached about actual figures further research would be necessary, as well as further negotiations with interested parties—for example the Trade Union Congress.'[9] To that, the TUC was holding the Labour Party.

I think this little bit of personal history helps to explain the otherwise very odd sequence of events after the Labour Party won the 1964 general election. National superannuation had been a central plank of the elections of 1959 and 1964. Yet nothing happened to implement it until Crossman returned to the case after his appointment as Secretary of State for Health and Social Security in 1968. The Bill to implement the 1958 policy fell when the Labour Party lost the 1970 election. The other measures to introduce wage-related sickness and unemployment benefits, which the unions favoured, were implemented by the 1964–70 government.

A version of the national superannuation policy was legislated as the State Earnings-related Pension Scheme (SERPS) in 1975 and came into force in 1978. Only a year later Mrs Thatcher came to power. SERPS was hardly born before it was to be cut back and powerful incentives given to join private personal pensions. It never had the chance to gather average-voter, middle-Britain support as the US, Swedish, and German schemes had. The period 1958–68 turns out, in retrospect, to be as crucial as the period 1942–8.

As we have already seen, the apparent golden years of occupational pensions that followed were nothing of the sort in reality. It was not in the short-term interests of either firms or unions to face up to what was happening. But what about government? It was relying on the private

[9] Labour Party, *National Superannuation*, p. 31.

sector to deliver its strategy. But its regulatory and strategic oversight was minimal.

When things began to go wrong, the occupational structure changed and corporations took pension holidays; the machinery of government was not capable of getting to grips with the diversified system that the 1950s legacy of weakly regulated schemes had bequeathed. The trade unions were never fully represented in, much less partners in, the running of pension schemes as they were on the continent. Nor was the government machine set up to worry very much about the private sector. The Ministry of Pensions and National Insurance saw its job as running state pensions.

This struck me in the early 1990s when a team of very able young Treasury officials from Sweden visited me at the LSE. They had been taken out of normal duties to think about the future of the whole of the Swedish pension system and its long-term viability. Their work led to an all-party commission that worked for four years and in the end an agreed Swedish approach emerged. Nothing equivalent happened here. The old Pension and National Insurance Ministry in the UK was primarily concerned with state pensions and opting-out conditions, not with old-age security and equity in occupational pensions more generally. There was no interest group powerful enough to bring pressure to bear on government until the scale of the private pension scandals grew.

Will the Future be Different?

So the question for today is: has this coalition of negative and complacent forces, collective myopia, and weak governance changed or is it likely to change? Several points can be made.

- Outside the public sector, trade unions matter less than they did. Though here they are showing themselves unwilling to face the realities of demographic change. However, their members are now worried about their pension futures.
- Firms no longer see occupational pensions as a great bonus to labour recruitment and retention but as a large risk.
- The private pensions industry badly wants a coherent state framework and a basic state floor on which it can build. Regulatory requirements are now seen as the government's responsibility.

So there may just be political space for a positive programme from government which could build a lasting framework around which interests could converge.

The Pensions Commission is at last providing a coherent framework for debate. I think its report is one of the very best state papers on the subject since the Second World War.[10] For the reasons set out above it could be sown in a favourable climate. Demography is on the side of politicians taking an interest. There are growing numbers of grey voters. Some parts of the private sector may see the proposals boosting business rather than taking it away. Others may not.

On the more negative side:

- The first point to come strongly from Jose Harris's contribution in this volume is that you cannot see pension policy in isolation from the other claims on the public purse and political priorities more generally. The post-war world had many such claims—post-war economic reconstruction, housing reconstruction, and a sharp rise in the birth rate that left governments struggling to prevent class sizes rising to forty and to build new schools in time to house the growing numbers of children.
- Current political pressures have led the present government to devote about 3 per cent more of the GDP to health and education. That is 3 per cent that could have gone on pensions and did not. The scope for more public spending as a solution to the pension problem is strictly limited now. The days of steadily rising public spending as a percentage of GDP may be over. It is a common failing of specialists in one part of social policy to talk as if they had a monopoly of virtue or at least a prime claim to resources.
- Another important point Harris makes is to draw attention to the critical interaction between pension policy and public assistance. No full history of pensions is possible without it. The very humanization and nationalization of public assistance for the elderly in the Second World War and afterwards made a means-tested, poverty-targeting approach more politically feasible. Getting current pensioners cash has always been given preference over long-term reconstruction. What was true in 1946 was true again in 1964. When the majority the Wilson government obtained was so small—only four—current poor pensioners and voters dominated policy to the exclusion of the long term. Exactly the same was true in 1997 when Labour was elected with a much larger majority. Moreover, the very improvements that

[10] Pensions Commission, *A New Pension Settlement for the Twenty-first Century. The Second Report of the Pensions Commission* (London, 2005).

have been made to means-tested pensioners' incomes since 1997 make any universal solution, public or private, more expensive. We have been here before—several times.

On the other hand, and most important for today, there is the scope of what Beveridge attempted. Here we must admire and try to emulate him. Whatever the weaknesses of the Beveridge Plan its great virtue was to attempt a comprehensive strategy. It was one that did not just deal with the state's role. Beveridge saw the state providing a platform for voluntary saving and voluntary action. He saw the interaction between public, individual, and private action. The pensions system needs to be seen whole.

Surely this is the lesson we should draw from the mistakes we have made since the Second World War in pensions policy. The Pensions Commission has given us a chance to do just that.

Bibliography

Esping-Andersen, G., *The Three Worlds of Welfare Capitalism* (Cambridge, 1990).

Hills, J., J. Ditch, and H. Glennerster (eds), *Beveridge and Social Security: An International Retrospective* (Oxford, 1994).

Labour Party, *National Superannuation: Labour's Policy for Security in Old Age* (London, 1958).

Pensions Commission, *Pensions: Challenges and Choices. The First Report of the Pensions Commission* (London, 2004).

Pensions Commission, *A New Pension Settlement for the Twenty-first Century. The Second Report of the Pensions Commission* (London, 2005).

Report of the Committee on the Economic and Financial Problems of the Provision for Old Age, Cmd 9333, 'The Phillips Committee' (London, 1954).

Webster, C., *The Health Services since the War*, vol. 1 (London 1988).

Women and Pensions in Britain

5. The 'Scandal' of Women's Pensions in Britain: How Did It Come About?

PAT THANE

Introduction

Alan Johnson, secretary of state for work and pensions until the 2005 election, commented, during his all-too-brief tenure of the office, on the need for 'radical reform to tackle the scandal of women's pensions'.[1] He was referring to the fact that, in 2005, just 19 per cent of women pensioners were entitled to the full basic state pension (itself insufficient to live on without a supplement) compared with 92 per cent of men.[2] The first report of the Pensions Commission, chaired by Adair Turner, pointed out that, in addition:

> Current female pensioners receive much lower levels of occupational pension because during working life they had much lower levels of employment, a greater tendency to be in part-time work, lower average earnings, and a greater tendency to work in service sectors where pension provision was less prevalent.[3]

The two main 'pillars' of the British pension system throughout the past century were state and occupational pensions. Both have failed most older women.

Younger women now spend longer periods in paid work than earlier age cohorts and average female earnings have risen, but a gender gap in work opportunities and pay, and in capacity to save, remains. Hence, a large disparity in pension entitlement between men and women is likely

[1] *The Guardian*, 8 March 2005.

[2] Press release, Fawcett Society and Age Concern Joint Response to the Government's Principles for Pension Reform, 24 February 2005.

[3] *Pensions: Challenges and Choices. The First Report of the Pensions Commission* (London, 2004), p. 262.

to continue for the foreseeable future if present pension arrangements continue.

None of this should be news. The obstacles to women building an adequate pension have been known ever since state pensions were first proposed in Britain over a century ago. The challenges were the same then as now: women did, and do, outlive men; women were/are likely to be poorer than men in old age because they had/have lesser opportunities to save due to more restricted job opportunities, lower pay, and interrupted careers arising from caring responsibilities. They were/are more likely than men to experience poverty due to the ending of a partnership. One hundred years ago this was caused mainly by widowhood, now the chief cause is separation or divorce, but the proportion affected[4] and the material effects were/are similar. The current financial problems of older women are not simply a product of unprecedented recent demographic and social change such as the increased divorce rate. They have been evident for a very long time, but have never been tackled by policy-makers as enthusiastically as the pension needs of men. As Baroness Hollis has rightly pointed out: 'Pensioners are women and pensions are for women, but, for far too long, pensions policy has been designed for men.'[5]

The First British Pensions

The relative poverty of older women was the major reason why the first British state pensions, introduced in 1908, took a different form from the pioneering German scheme introduced in the 1880s. The German pensions were contributory and income related, components of the first ever national insurance scheme. The German model was subsequently adopted by a number of European countries. A similar scheme was strongly advocated for Britain at the time, but was rejected because the two schemes had very different objectives.[6]

The main motive for the introduction of pensions by the German state was Bismarck's desire to win the loyalty of key groups of German workers, to create a counter-attraction to the growing lure of socialism by demonstrating that the liberal state could provide income security in old

[4] Michael Anderson, 'The Social Implications of Demographic Change', in F. M. L. Thompson (ed.), *The Cambridge Social History of Britain, 1750–1950*, vol. 2 (Cambridge, 1990), p. 29.
[5] House of Lords Debates, 25 May 2005, col. 502.
[6] Pat Thane, *Old Age in English History: Past Experiences, Present Issues*, (Oxford, 2000), pp. 196–222.

age, sickness, or disability. The German pension scheme, like all social insurance schemes, required regular weekly contributions. Hence it excluded male workers who were paid too little or too irregularly to make the required contributions. Most women were excluded for the same reason.

The motivation behind British pensions was quite different. The long campaign for pensions from the 1870s was fuelled at least as much by concern about the high levels of poverty among older people as by issues around working-class politics. Old age was badly provided for by the long-established system of publicly provided poor relief, the Poor Law, because it gave too little support unless old people were prepared to give up their homes and enter the stigmatizing workhouse, which most would not until their situation was desperate, and sometimes not even then. Attempts to use the law to force children to support their ageing parents failed because it became apparent that most who could afford it already did so; the children of very poor old people tended also to be very poor.[7]

The first pension proposal to be taken seriously by the British state, in the 1870s, advocated compulsory saving into a state-guaranteed pension fund by all young people between entry to paid work and marriage. Thereafter, it was recognized, saving became difficult for most working-class men and impossible for most women. After investigation, it became obvious that most young people, especially women, did not earn enough to save for a worthwhile pension and, in any case, many of them helped support their families with their earnings and had no surplus for saving.[8]

After a succession of official enquiries the British government concluded that the clinching argument against a German-style social insurance pension was that the majority of the neediest older people were women, and very few women could afford to pay regular, adequate insurance contributions. No way could be found to include them in such a scheme. The government drew on the experience of the friendly societies. These developed during the nineteenth century as non-profit mutual institutions through which working people saved primarily in order to receive a weekly payment when unable to work due to sickness. Increasingly by the later nineteenth century they also provided a small weekly payment to those unable to work due to old age, though this sum was rarely sufficient to live on. The friendly societies provided invaluable support for better-off working men in regular employment. However, they covered no more than 6 million people at the beginning of the

[7] Thane, *Old Age in English History*, pp. 171–93.
[8] *Ibid.*, pp. 196–204.

twentieth century.[9] According to the 1901 census, 10 million males or more were employed in manual or other low-paid occupations.[10] Also, friendly societies had very few female members, and male contributions did not cover benefits for their families. The friendly society experience demonstrated clearly the limitations of contributory insurance as a solution to the challenge of providing pensions for the large poor, and predominantly female, sector of early-twentieth-century society.

Consequently, the first British state pensions were non-contributory. They were fixed at less than the estimated weekly cost of subsistence, to encourage saving and family support to supplement the pension, and were subject to stringent means and character tests, to exclude those who squandered their resources. The principles of the ancient Poor Law lived on in the new pension system. The pensions were paid from the late age of 70. It was well recognized at the time that many, probably most, older people became unfit for regular work by the time they reached their early sixties, earlier if they had worked for decades in heavy industry. The age of 70 was chosen on the insistence of the Treasury in order to cut costs: by that age many people were dead. Two-thirds of the first state pensioners were female. Throughout the history of the non-contributory pension, which lasted until 1948, remaining at a very low level of payment, three-quarters of pensioners were female.[11]

Pensions between the Wars

In 1925 the pension was supplemented by the extension of the National Health Insurance scheme (established 1911) to provide pensions between ages 65 and 70 for contributors, mainly male manual workers (higher paid, white-collar workers were excluded). Employed single women could contribute, but they paid lower contributions and received lower benefits on the, often incorrect, assumption that they had fewer family responsibilities than most adult men. Many such women supported siblings or older relatives. The insurance pension was a flat rate and fixed at the same, low level as the non-contributory pension which continued to be paid from age 70.

Also in 1925 the problem of poverty due to the ending of partnerships and single motherhood was acknowledged with the introduction of

[9] Paul Johnson, *Saving and Spending: The Working-class Economy in Britain, 1870–1939* (Oxford, 1985), p. 57.
[10] B. R. Mitchell and P. Deane, *Abstract of British Historical Statistics* (Cambridge, 1962), p. 60.
[11] Thane, *Old Age in English History*, pp. 194–235.

pensions for widows. The widow's pension was paid to all widows of insured men with children under the age of 14 at the time of the husband's death. It was set at the same low level as the old-age pension and was payable for life. Protest followed that this was unfair to women widowed at an older age who might have been out of the labour market for many years caring for husband and children and would find it difficult to support themselves, especially amid the high unemployment of the 1920s. In 1929 entitlement was extended to all widows of insured men from the age of 55. This assisted a substantial group of poor older women.

Occupational pensions expanded in Britain between the wars, but they disproportionately benefited men. On marriage, women were compelled to give up most forms of employment in which pensions were available—i.e. white collar jobs in the public sector, banks, etc.—and were obliged to exchange their pension entitlements for lump-sum marriage gratuities. Even after marriage, most women could not rely upon lifetime support from a male breadwinner. Even the minority married to men with occupational pensions (many of which were small) could not expect to inherit that pension. Some might receive their husband's (but not the employer's) contributions only, in a lump sum on his death. A fortunate few might receive their husband's pension for five years after his death. Since women could expect to live, on average, three to four years longer than men, and also married men, on average, five years older than themselves, these arrangements did not guarantee security for women for the entire period between widowhood and their own deaths.[12]

Women who did not marry did not fare better. Marriage rates at any time up to the Second World War were lower than later in the century: according to the 1931 census, in England and Wales, fewer than two-thirds of women aged 25–34 were married and about three-quarters of those aged 35–44. These were higher proportions than in the previous twentieth-century censuses.[13] Unmarried women generally had more restricted job opportunities, lower pay, and fewer opportunities for saving than men, even when they had equivalent qualifications. They were less likely to be in pensionable employment. Many were carers for ageing relatives.

To highlight these problems, in 1935 the National Spinsters' Pensions Association (NPSA) was formed to demand state pensions for unmarried women at age 55. It argued that, in addition to their other disadvantages,

[12] Leslie Hannah, *Inventing Retirement: The Development of Occupational Pensions in Britain* (1986), pp. 27, 95–6, 118.

[13] Mitchell and Deane, *Historical Statistics*, p. 16.

women were often forced into involuntary retirement at earlier ages than men, for various reasons: women's poorer health; discrimination by employers against post-menopausal women; and the fact that many unmarried women gave up work in middle life to care for ageing parents and could not, thereafter, find employment. The NPSA was founded in Bradford by Florence White who ran a small confectionery business. Its members were mainly working- or lower-middle-class women, including many textile workers, many of whom would have started work at ages 12 or 13.

A government enquiry found substance in these arguments: rates of unemployment among 'spinsters' over 45 were higher than among men of the same age, and they found it harder to regain employment; and women tended to show a marked deterioration in health from age 55 despite their longer life expectancy. The committee expressed concern about the numbers of women left in poverty after caring for elderly relatives.[14] In 1940 the state pensionable age for all women was reduced to 60. This was probably partly due to the NPSA's campaign , though the official explanation was that, since wives were, on average, five years younger than their husbands, the change was designed to ensure that married couples received their pensions at similar times.

But the level of pension remained very low. Government surveys during the Second World War found appalling levels of poverty among pensioners, most of them female, even after the introduction, also in 1940, of Supplementary Assistance, a means-tested boost to the already means-tested pension. One-third of all pensioners immediately qualified for this, again most of them female.[15] The poverty that was revealed, which horrified researchers, had often been kept private, secret even from close neighbours, as often it still is.

Beveridge and Women's Pensions

This was the situation Beveridge surveyed when he produced his influential Report in 1942. He recommended that state pensions should become universal and national insurance based, but remain flat-rate and minimal, 'guaranteeing the minimum income needed for subsistence'[16] but little more. To enjoy higher incomes and 'comfort' in retirement people should save, ideally through non-profit, mutual institutions such

[14] *Report of the Committee on Pensions for Unmarried Women*, Cmd 5991 (London, 1939).
[15] Thane, *Old Age in English History*, p. 355.
[16] *Social Insurance and Allied Services*, Cmd 6404 (London, 1942), p. 14.

as friendly societies. The long legacy of the Poor Law lived on: state assistance was to remain minimal.

Beveridge had long been aware of the difficulties of fitting women into an insurance system and about the specific problems facing women, including that not all of them experienced life-long, stable marriages. He clearly identified the main issues faced by women in seeking to provide for old age. Early in the deliberations over his Report, he proposed that the needs of women should be provided for in six different ways:

1. Employed single women would contribute as men did for comprehensive social insurance.
2. Married women would be entitled to a 'housewife's policy', based on their husbands' contributions. This would entitle them to a furnishing grant for setting up home (a 'marriage grant' in the final report); maternity grants and benefits; dependants' benefits when their husbands were sick, disabled, or unemployed; funeral benefit; widowhood and separation allowances; domestic help during sickness; and pensions in old age.
3. Employed married women could choose to rely on the housewife's policy or contribute separately as employed persons, but in the latter case with lower benefits than men, on the assumption that their housing was provided by their husbands.[17]
4. Widows would continue to draw pensions while they had dependent children, but thereafter 'every widow of working age and capacity' would be entitled to apply for 'training benefit' after which she would be expected to work and to contribute to the fund. As the final report put it: 'There is no reason why a childless widow should get a pension for life; if she is able to work she should work. On the other hand provision much better than at present should be made for those who, because they have the care of children cannot work for gain or cannot work regularly.'[18]
5. 'Unmarried wives'—i.e. cohabitees—would be entitled to the housewife's policy, with the exception of the furnishing grant and the widow's pension.
6. 'Domestic spinsters'—unmarried carers for elderly relatives who were not in paid work, and other categories of women—would be

[17] The majority of employed women took the housewife's option since it reduced their NI contributions though it lowered their pension entitlement. This opt-out was abolished with the introduction of SERPS in 1978 but still affects the later life income of many women.
[18] *Social Insurance and Allied Services*, p. 64, para. 153.

> classed as unoccupied persons and would contribute only to receive an old-age pension, i.e. they would not be eligible for sickness or unemployment benefits. The many who could not afford contributions (which would require an income of at least £75pa) would have no recourse but means-tested public assistance.[19]

Had they been implemented, these proposals would have established a framework with a greater capacity for flexible adaptation to social change later in the century than that established by the post-war Attlee government. In particular it could have adapted better to the increase in divorce and unmarried partnership, though it left untouched other problems such as that of the poorer single carer.

The proposals faced criticism, especially from women's organizations for not giving all women equal benefits with men. Beveridge, despite his real sympathy with women's needs, was devoted to the principle of National Insurance and could find no way to fit into it women who did not have work histories equivalent to those of men. He justified his recommendations for married women on the grounds that the work of the housewife in the home was as important socially and economically as waged work and merited equal recognition in the social security system. As he put it: 'The great majority of married women must be regarded as occupied on work which is vital though unpaid, without which their husbands could not do their paid work and without which the nation could not continue.'[20] 'The position of housewives is recognized in form and in substance . . . by treating them not as dependants of their husbands, but as partners sharing benefit and pension when there are no earnings to share.'[21] Hence it was reasonable that the male worker's contribution should cover benefits for his partner.

Behind this approach lay not only Beveridge's concern about the relative poverty of older women, which had been clear in his writings since the beginning of the century, but also the desire to reverse the pre-war decline in the birth rate and the consequent, projected growth in the proportion of older people in the population.[22] Beveridge believed that one important reason why housewives should be supported by the social security system was: 'In the next thirty years housewives as mothers have

[19] Jose Harris, *William Beveridge: A Biography*, 2nd edn (Oxford, 1997), pp. 392–3.

[20] *Social Insurance and Allied Services*, p. 49, para. 107.

[21] *Ibid.*, p. 52, para. 117.

[22] Pat Thane, 'The Debate on the Declining Birth-rate in Britain: The "Menace" of an Ageing Population, 1920s–1950s', *Continuity and Change*, 5, 2 (1990), 283–4.

vital work to do in ensuring the adequate continuance of the British race and of British ideals in the world.'[23] The Report stated:

> On marriage a woman gains a legal right to maintenance by her husband as a first line of defence against risks which fall directly on the solitary woman; she undertakes at the same time to undertake vital unpaid services and becomes exposed to new risks, including the risk that her married life may be ended prematurely by widowhood or separation . . . Moreover even if a married woman, while living with her husband, undertakes gainful occupation . . . her earning is liable to interruption by child-birth. In the national interests it is important that the interruption by childbirth should be as complete as possible; the expectant mother should be under no economic pressure to continue at work as long as she can and to return to it as soon as she can.[24]

Beveridge's assumptions appeared to be justified by the most recent census, of 1931, which showed that 'more than 7 out of 8 of all housewives, that is to say married women of working age, made marriage their sole occupation; less than one in 8 of all housewives was also gainfully employed'.[25] Reasonably enough, he expected this situation to continue after the war.[26]

Beveridge's proposals for benefits for deserted wives and 'unmarried wives' foundered partly on moral objections from those who feared that such provision would undermine the family, and partly on perceived practical problems concerning the treatment of 'guilty' wives who initiated the break-up of a marriage. These were dropped by the Attlee government.[27] Thereafter 'unmarried wives' were to be treated exactly as all unmarried women, and separated and divorced women were left, as before, to try to extract support from their partners in the courts or to manage on public assistance.

Pensions and Social Change after the Second World War

The greatest problem created by the pension system introduced by the Labour government in 1948 was not the treatment of unmarried, separated, and divorced women, or the presumed dependence of most women on a male 'breadwinner', problematic though these were, but the very

[23] *Social Insurance and Allied Services*, p. 53, para. 117.
[24] *Ibid.*, p. 49, para. 108.
[25] *Ibid.*, p. 49, para. 108
[26] *Ibid.*, p. 50, para. 111.
[27] *Ibid.*, pp. 391–8.

low level of pension payments, lower even than Beveridge had envisaged. Consequently, even when the pension was introduced in 1948, 638,000 (mainly female) people over age 60 had to supplement it with the means-tested National Assistance, also introduced in 1948. The number rose to almost 1 million in 1951. Surveys in the 1950s showed the continuing extent of poverty among older women. Townsend and Wedderburn found from a survey in 1959:

> Single and widowed women emerge as the largest problem group among the aged. Although twice the proportion of women as of men and couples receive national assistance, the women still have lower incomes. True, the women are more likely to be sharing a home with other people; but often they share only with another woman, perhaps a widowed sister, or a single daughter—that is, people who like themselves often have low incomes.[28]

Substantial numbers (again, mostly female) have continued ever since to depend on the means-tested supplement, which has gone through a number of changes of name and detail since 1948. Still, in late 2005, 1.3 million out of 1.9 million recipients of the means-tested Pension Credit were female.[29] Equally consistently since 1948, and of still greater cause of concern, has been the large number of people who have qualified for the supplement but failed to apply: still 20 per cent of eligible pensioners in 2005 do not take up the Pension Credit, under the most humane form of administration so far devised for this supplement. It is reasonable to assume that most of these, also, are female.

Beveridge's expectations about the post-war roles of women appeared to be borne out. Marriage rates rose and marriage became almost universal. The numbers of never-married woman fell sharply. The mean age at first marriage also fell to historically low levels, from 25.3 for women earlier in the century (and the norm for long before), to 22.6 in 1971.[30] This reduced the time available to most women to establish themselves in careers and accumulate pension savings between completing education and entering marriage and childbirth, the more so because the compulsory school-leaving age rose from 14 to 15 in 1947 and to 16 in 1972, and increasing numbers of young women stayed in education past the minimum leaving age. The declining marriage age was shared by female graduates. The birth rate also rose and births tended to be concentrated early

[28] Peter Townsend and Dorothy Wedderburn, *The Aged in the Welfare State* (London, 1965), p. 77.

[29] Department of Work and Pensions press release, 3 November 2005, 'Pensions Report Shows "Historical Divide" Faced by Women'.

[30] Jane Lewis, *The End of Marriage?* (Cheltenham, 2001), p. 30.

in marriage. Social disapproval, poor availability of childcare, full employment for men, and generally rising living standards ensured that mothers of young children were rarely in the paid labour market and almost never in full-time work.

The young women who married and had their children in the 1950s and 1960s and did not build up pensions in their own right, and who all too often experienced divorce in the 1970s and after, are now in or approaching pension age. They account for a great deal of current poverty among older women and will do so for some time since they can expect to live into their eighties, at least.

In what is now seen as a 'golden age' of full employment between the end of the Second World War and the early 1970s, marriage also experienced an historically quite unusual golden age: life expectancy rose and the number of relatively young widows fell, while divorce was difficult to obtain and relatively rare by more recent standards. It was the only period in history when the long-lasting marriage really was the norm.

In other respects Beveridge's expectations about post-war Britain were not quite fulfilled. Though mothers of young children were likely to stay at home, older women were increasingly in the workforce; indeed they were encouraged out of the home and into the workplace by the Attlee government, which was concerned about the labour shortage. The 'marriage bar' disappeared, though more slowly in some occupations than others. For the first time it became socially acceptable and possible for middle-class wives to work for pay once their children were grown, as it had not been previously. However, it remained difficult, even for the best qualified of them, to re-enter full-time or pensionable employment and all had discontinuous work records. Since the 1950s increasing numbers of married women have been in paid work for increasing lengths of time, though an exceptionally high proportion of the British female workforce continues to be in part-time work which is not, or is inadequately, pensioned.

Occupational Pensions and Women

Not until the 1980s did significant numbers of women enter employment which could potentially provide an adequate occupational pension or sufficient income to save for an adequate private pension. Yet still women's chances of building a pension sufficient even for moderate comfort in old age are less than those of men due to the persistently lower pay and promotion prospects and discontinuous work records of all but a minority of them.

In the immediate post-war period some occupational pension schemes still did not admit women on the grounds that they were likely to leave on marriage. Those which did so still often repaid the contributions as a 'dowry' on marriage. Some admitted women only at later ages than men, presumably once they were thought too old to marry. Viola Klein reported in 1965 that the minimum age of admission to pension schemes varied between 21 and 40 for women, whereas for men it was normally 21.[31] Even in 1966 an official enquiry by industrialists and trade unionists decided that the preservation of women's occupational pensions on marriage was unnecessary.[32]

Very slowly, pension annuities for widows were introduced into occupational schemes, typically providing one-third to one-half of the husband's (often low) pension. By 1971 only one-third of private-sector scheme members were eligible for this on death in service. For members who died after retirement, employers, under pressure from members, from the 1950s offered the opportunity for a male employee to take a lower pension in return for an enhanced pension for his widow: usually one-third to one-half of that paid while he was alive. Few eligible members took up this option because most initial pensions were low and the trade-off offered unfavourable.[33]

Provision for widows improved due to the requirements for occupational schemes wishing to contract out of the state earnings-related scheme (SERPS), introduced in 1978:

> In 1971 only 39% of male employees in private sector schemes had provision for widows' annuities on death in service; by 1979 the proportion was 89%. Many widows of deceased employees also benefited from a tax-free lump sum of around two years salary. Similar improvements, from 34% to 89% between 1971 and 1979 were also made in the coverage of widows following their husbands' deaths in retirement . . . It became the norm for good employers to offer widows' pensions at about half the level of the men's pension.[34]

Half of a not necessarily high pension was not a lot and only a minority of wives benefited, but it was better than before.

The two pillars of state and occupational pensions could do even less to provide for the growing numbers of divorced and separated women. The other change which Beveridge could not have foreseen was the rapid

[31] Viola Klein, *Britain's Married Women Workers* (London, 1965), p. 126.
[32] Hannah, *Inventing Retirement*, p. 18.
[33] *Ibid.*, pp. 119–20.
[34] Hannah, *Inventing Retirement*, pp. 120–1.

rise in divorce, separation, and unmarried parenting and partnership which followed the 1969 Divorce Act and accelerated during the 1980s. This ended the brief heyday of the long, stable marriage which guaranteed many women a very basic, if temporary, material security in old age. Not until 2000 did women (and men where appropriate) gain the right on divorce to receive a proportion of their former spouse's pension fund and to receive benefits independently (though few such 'sharing orders' had been taken out by 2005 and the advantages to women are limited).[35]

Conclusion

The current problems of poverty among older women are not new. The difficulties for women of providing for their old age have been known for over a century and have never gone away, but they have been evaded by successive governments, not least because they are hard to solve without considerable public expense. But what is the alternative? Of course, women, like men, should save all that they can, but there is no evidence that large numbers of the old women at present in poverty are suffering the just reward of improvidence in early life. Our pension system has been characterized by a state pension too low to live on and dependence on occupational and private pensions which cannot provide a comfortable old age to the low-paid and irregularly employed, most of whom are female. It is hard to believe that this miserable situation could have lasted for so long if the majority of victims had been men.

Bibliography

All items listed below provide a useful introduction to the issues discussed in this chapter.

Hannah, L., *Inventing Retirement: The Development of Occupational Pensions in Britain* (Cambridge, 1986).

Harris, J., *William Beveridge: A Biography*, 2nd edn (Oxford, 1997).

Johnson, P., *Saving and Spending: The Working-class Economy in Britain, 1870–1939* (Oxford, 1985).

Klein, V., *Britain's Married Women Workers* (London, 1965).

Lewis, J., *The End of Marriage?* (Cheltenham, 2001).

Mitchell, B. R. and P. Deane, *Abstract of British Historical Statistics* (Cambridge, 1962).

[35] See Jay Ginn's chapter in this volume.

Pensions Commission, *Pensions: Challenges and Choices. The First Report of the Pensions Commission* (London, 2004).
——, *A New Pension Settlement for the Twenty-first Century. The Second Report of the Pensions Commission* (London, 2005).
Report of the Committee on Pensions for Unmarried Women, Cmd 5991 (London, 1939).
Social Insurance and Allied Services. Report by Sir William Beveridge, Cmd 6404 (London, 1942).
Thane, P., 'The Debate on the Declining Birth-rate in Britain: The "Menace" of an Ageing Population, 1920s–1950s', *Continuity and Change*, 5, 2 (1990).
——, *Old Age in English History: Past Experiences, Present Issues* (Oxford, 2000).
Thompson, F. M. L. (ed.), *The Cambridge Social History of Britain, 1750–1950*, vol. 2 (Cambridge, 1990).
Townsend, P. and D. Wedderburn, *The Aged in the Welfare State* (London, 1965).

6. Gender Inequalities: Sidelined in British Pension Policy

JAY GINN

Introduction

'The UK state pension system is among the least generous in the developed world' admitted the Pensions Commission in its first report.[1] This reflects the explicit aim of both Conservative and New Labour governments since 1980 to reduce the share of pensions provided by the state and increase that provided by the private sector. Because women's lower pay and chequered worklife place them at a disadvantage in the private pension sector, the policy has reinforced the gender gap in pensions. Despite recent acknowledgement by the government's pensions minister that women's pensions are 'a national scandal', there is no sign of the radical shift in policy needed to remedy that situation.

This chapter first outlines the gender gap in later life income, showing how private pensions shape gender inequality in different ways according to women's marital status. Next it examines gender differences in working-age individuals' employment, earnings, and private (occupational or personal) pension scheme membership, focusing on the impact of motherhood on women's position. The following section considers alternative ways of protecting the pension income of carers. Finally, the Pensions Commission's 2005 proposals are evaluated in terms of women's pension needs.

[1] Pensions Commission, *Pensions: Challenges and Choices. The First Report of the Pensions Commission* (London, 2004).

The Gender Gap in Pension Income

Poverty

In most EU countries, older women bear a disproportionate share of poverty. However, the proportion of pensioners at risk of poverty is relatively high in Britain and it is also higher than for the British population as a whole.[2] Among British women aged over 65, 28 per cent had income below 60 per cent of national median household income in 2001, compared with 19 per cent of similarly aged men.[3]

In terms of personal income, older women in Britain are much poorer than older men, due mainly to smaller private pensions.[4] Three-quarters of pensioners receiving means-tested income support are women, almost all of them not married. In 2001, one-fifth of single and widowed women were poor enough to receive income support, as were two-fifths of divorced and separated women (Table 6.1a). Income declines with age group (Table 6.1b), so that one-fifth of women aged over 75 received income support. Because of low take-up of income support (at between two-thirds and three-quarters of eligible older people) the proportion in receipt underestimates the prevalence of poverty.

Means-testing has been justified as targeting resources on the poorest pensioners. However, the persistently low take-up of income support undermines the effectiveness of this strategy and is evidence of its unpopularity. The process of claiming is seen as complex, intrusive, and demeaning. 'The main barriers to claiming related to fears of appearing in need, losing independence and a feeling that people could manage on their own resources.'[5] Means-tested benefits are tainted for many with the image of poor relief, a handout associated with shame. Yet, as long as the basic state pension remains below poverty level, many British pensioners, especially women, will need some form of income support.

[2] Office for National Statistics (ONS), *Social Trends 2002* (London, 2003).
[3] European Commission (2003), *Joint Inclusion Report*, Statistical Annex, http://europa.eu.int/employment_social/soc-prot/soc-incl/sec_2003_1425_final_en.pdf.
[4] S. Arber and J. Ginn, 'Ageing and Gender: Diversity and Change', in *Social Trends* 34 (London, 2004), pp. 1–14.
[5] M. McConaghy, C. Hill, C. Kane, D. Lader, P. Costigan, and M. Thornby, *Entitled but not Claiming? Pensioners, the Minimum Income Guarantee and Pension Credit*, Research Report 197 (summary) (London, 2003), www.dwp.gov.uk/asd/asd5/rrs2003.asp.

Table 6.1. Percentage receiving income support* (was Minimum Income Guarantee) by (a) marital status, (b) age group. Men and women aged 65+.

	All	Men	Women
(a) Marital status			
Married/cohabiting	3	4	1
Single	17	13	20
Widowed	18	11	20
Divorced/separated	34	23	40
(b) Age group			
65–69	6	6	5
70–74	8	6	11
75–79	14	8	18
80–84	15	8	19
85+	18	11	22
ALL	11	7	13
*N***	3,356	1,474	1,882

* Respondents were asked if they were 'receiving [IS] in your own right: that is, were you the named recipient'. Those married to a named recipient would therefore respond negatively, even though the benefit is intended for the couple.
** Number of men and women in the General Household Survey aged 65 and over.

Source: Arber and Ginn (2004), using General Household Survey 2001/2.

Total Income

Table 6.2 shows how individual pensioner incomes vary with gender, marital status, class, and age, including state and private pensions, earnings, interest on savings, and any other income. Among men, those who were married had the highest income but, among women, those who were single (never married) and those who were widowed had the highest income (Table 6.2). The ratio of women's median income to men's, within each marital status, was highest for single women at 85 per cent and lowest for married women at only 33 per cent. The precarious financial position of older divorced women is evident; although their income was higher than that of married women, they had no prospect of inheriting a widow's pension.

Within each occupational class group, women's income was a fraction of men's and the gender gap was greatest in the highest class group, where women's income was only 52 per cent of men's. Older men's income declined with age group but women's did not, reflecting inheritance of widows' pensions and the influence of a means-tested floor. Overall, older women's individual income was only 57 per cent of men's.

Table 6.2. Median gross individual income in pounds per week by (a) marital status, (b) occupational class,* and (c) age group. Men and women aged 65+.

	Men £/wk	Women £/wk	Women's/men's %
(a) Marital status			
Married/cohabiting	171	56	33
Single	130	109	85
Widowed	144	112	78
Divorced/separated	125	92	74
(b) Occupational class			
Professional/managerial	287	148	52
Intermediate	142	99	70
Routine and manual	136	89	65
(c) Age group			
65–69	177	90	51
70–74	168	9	55
75–79	148	92	62
80–84	143	93	65
85+	123	92	75
ALL	161	92	57
N**	1,474	1,882	

* Based on own previous occupation and classified according to the National Statistics Socioeconomic Classification (NS-SEC).
** Number of men and women in the General Household Survey aged 65 and over.

Source: Arber and Ginn (2004), using General Household Survey 2001/2.

Private Pension Income

Differences in older people's incomes reflect mainly inequalities in the ability to save and build private (occupational or personal) pension entitlements during the working life.[6] For the minority of women receiving any private pension, their lower average amount reflects their previous domestic roles. The latter have much less effect on state pension income, due to redistributive features such as the flat-rate structure of the basic pension and widow's benefits at 100 per cent of the husband's entitlement.

Table 6.3 shows the proportions receiving private pensions among men and women aged 65 and over (a) and the median amounts for those with this source of income (b). Only two-fifths of older women had any

[6] J. Ginn and S. Arber, 'Gender, Class and Income Inequalities in Later Life', *British Journal of Sociology*, 42, 3 (1991), 369–96; J. Ginn, *Gender, Pensions and the Lifecourse: How Pensions Need to Adapt to Changing Family Forms* (Bristol, 2003a).

private pension income, including a widow's pension based on their deceased husband's private pensions, compared with over 70 per cent of men (Table 6.3a). A relatively high proportion, 61 per cent, of single (never-married) women had some private pension income and their median amount was higher at £70 per week than that of ever-married women and single men. Among divorced women, only one-third had any private pension income. Men's receipt and amount of private pensions were higher than women's within each occupational class group. Among those with a private pension, women's amount was just over half of men's (Table 6.3, last column).

Incomes of individuals from minority ethnic groups are lower than those of whites, and reliance on means-tested income support is greater.[7]

Table 6.3. Private* pensions by (a) marital status and (b) occupational class.** Men and women aged 65+.

	(a) % receiving		(b) Median amount for those with private pension		
	Men %	Women %	Men £/wk	Women £/wk	Women's/men's %
(a) Marital status					
Married/cohabiting	74	28	92	34	37
Single	52	61	65	70	108
Widowed	70	56	61	46	75
Divorced/separated	57	36	78	4862	
(b) Occupational class					
Professional/managerial	90	64	172	95	55
Intermediate	60	51	84	43	51
Routine and manual	62	34	50	28	56
ALL	71	43	83	44	53
*N****	1,474	1,882	891	694	

* Occupational or personal pensions, including survivor pensions.
** Based on own previous occupation and classified according to the National Statistics Socioeconomic Classification (NS-SEC).
*** Number of men and women in the General Household Survey aged 65 and over receiving some private pension.

Source: Arber and Ginn (2004), using General Household Survey 2001/2.

[7] R. Berthoud, *The Incomes of Ethnic Minorities* (Colchester, 1998).

Within most minority ethnic groups, older women have lower income than men, reflecting smaller income from private pensions.[8]

Working-age Women's Pension Accumulation: The Effect of Motherhood

I now turn to the question of working-age women's prospects in retirement. At any one time, about one-third of women are employed full-time, one-third part-time, and the remaining one-third are not employed. Consequently, women's private pension scheme membership lags far behind men's. Among full-time employees, just under 60 per cent of both men and women contribute to a private pension, but only 30 per cent of women part-timers do so.[9] Thus, approximately 30 per cent of women contribute to a private pension scheme at any time.

The gender gap in hourly pay is 18 per cent for full-timers and 40 per cent for part-timers, while weekly full-time pay is 25 per cent less for women than for men.[10] The gender gap in hourly pay is narrowing only very slowly.

For those with caring responsibilities, the effect of the gender gap in pay is magnified. Family responsibilities, especially motherhood, make full-time employment difficult. The 'family gap in pay'—or the wage loss due to the presence of dependent children—for women aged 24–44, after taking account of age, education, and other relevant variables, is relatively large in Britain; 8 per cent for one child and 24 per cent for two children.[11] Without children, a mid-skilled British woman could expect to earn £241,000 less over her working life than a similar man in the late 1990s. Having two children led to a further loss of £140,000.[12] Davies *et al.* estimated that a British, married, mid-skilled mother of two would receive only half the lifetime earnings of a similar childless woman.[13] For lone mothers (divorced, never married, or widows) the reduction in employment and earnings is even greater than for married mothers, due

[8] J. Ginn and S. Arber, 'Ethnic Inequality in Later Life: Variation in Financial Circumstances by Gender and Ethnic Group', *Education and Ageing*, 15, 1 (2000), 65–83.

[9] Women and Equality Unit (WEU), *Key Indicators of Women's Position in Britain* (London, 2002), fig. 6.5.

[10] ONS, *Social Trends 2003* (London, 2004).

[11] S. Harkness and J. Waldfogel, *The Family Gap in Pay: Evidence from Seven Industrialized Countries*, CASEpaper 29 (London, 1999).

[12] WEU, *Women's Income over a Lifetime* (London, 2000).

[13] H. Davies, H. Joshi, and R. Peronaci, 'Forgone Income and Motherhood: What Do Recent British Data Tell Us?', *Population Studies*, 54 (2000), 293–305.

to the difficulty of paying for childcare on a single income. Mothers' earnings loss relative to childless women extends throughout the working life, since gaps in employment and periods of part-time work tend to reduce occupational status[14] with part-timers frequently working below their potential.[15] Although tax credits subsidize childcare, market forces are pushing up costs and women with more than one child often cannot afford childcare. The rise in full-time employment among working-age British women has been glacially slow, rising only from 38 to 39 per cent between 1990 and 2000.[16]

Women's lower earnings mean that among those belonging to a private pension scheme, their contributions are smaller than men's. They often pay in only the minimum required to contract out of the State Second Pension, especially while they are raising children, whereas men can more easily contribute extra amounts above the minimum.[17] The cumulative effect over the working life of no/low contributions to a private pension leaves women with much lower pension income.

The impact of motherhood on British women's employment, earnings, and ability to contribute to private pension schemes is found at all levels of education. The research of Ginn and Arber[18] distinguishes six lifecourse categories for women:

1. Aged under 35 and childless
2. Youngest child aged under 5
3. Youngest child aged 5–9
4. Youngest child aged 10–15
5. No child under 16 still at home
6. Aged over 35 and childless.

Figure 6.1 shows the percentage of women employed full-time in these six categories. There was a dramatic reduction in full-time employment among mothers in each educational group. Even for graduate women, under half were employed full-time during the four stages of motherhood, and among those with children aged under 5 less than one-third were in full-time employment.

[14] S. Dex, *Women's Occupational Mobility: A Lifetime Perspective* (Basingstoke, 1987).

[15] D. Darton and K. Hurrell, *People Working Below Their Potential* (Manchester, 2005).

[16] OECD, *Employment Outlook* (Paris, 2001).

[17] D. Price, 'Marital Status, Money and Pensions: A Sociological Perspective on Women's Pension Scheme Participation', paper presented at the Work, Pensions and Labour Economics Study Group Conference, 18–20 July 2005.

[18] J. Ginn and S. Arber (2002), 'Degrees of Freedom: Can Graduate Women Avoid the Motherhood Gap in Pensions?' *Sociological Research On-line*, www.socresonline.org.uk/7/2/.

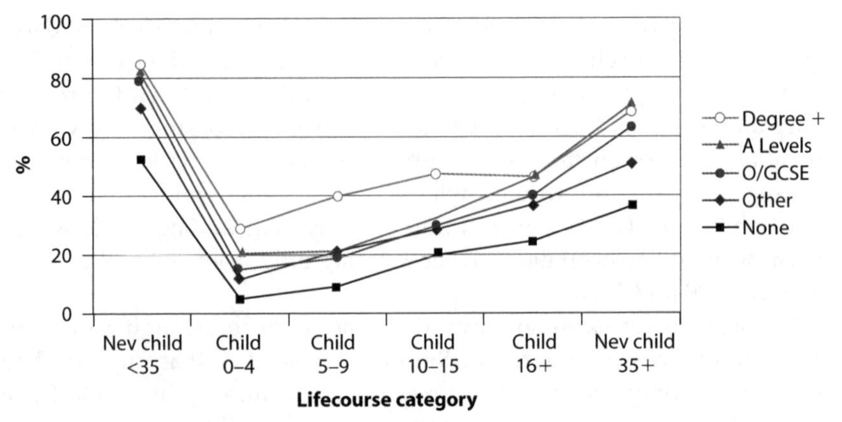

Figure 6.1. Percentage employed full-time by lifecourse category and education. British women aged 20–59.

Source: Ginn and Arber (2002).

Measuring the average earnings of all working-age women, including those not employed, provides an indication of the effect of motherhood on the eventual amount of a woman's private pension (Figure 6.2). British mothers had substantially lower median earnings compared with childless women. For women at all educational levels combined, median weekly earnings were zero for those whose youngest child was aged under 5. For mothers of children aged 5–9, median earnings were only 21 per cent of those of childless women aged under 35, while the proportion rose to 41 per cent for mothers of older dependent children. Mothers of children aged 5–9 earned on average only 17 per cent of the median earnings of men aged 20–59. Graduates maintained higher earnings across all lifestage categories, as would be expected, yet even graduate mothers experienced an initial fall in earnings to less than half that of childless graduates, on average.

Figure 6.3 shows private pension coverage according to age group and maternal status for all women aged 20–59, including those not currently employed. Among women with a child aged under 16 at home, pension coverage was under 40 per cent at all ages, whereas childless women had much higher pension coverage. Thus motherhood severely reduces women's opportunities for private pension accumulation.

The amount of private pension at retirement depends on a number of factors, including employment participation, hours of work, pay, and whether a generous and sustainable occupational pension scheme is available. Recently, many defined-benefit occupational pension schemes have closed or switched to a money-purchase basis, transferring the

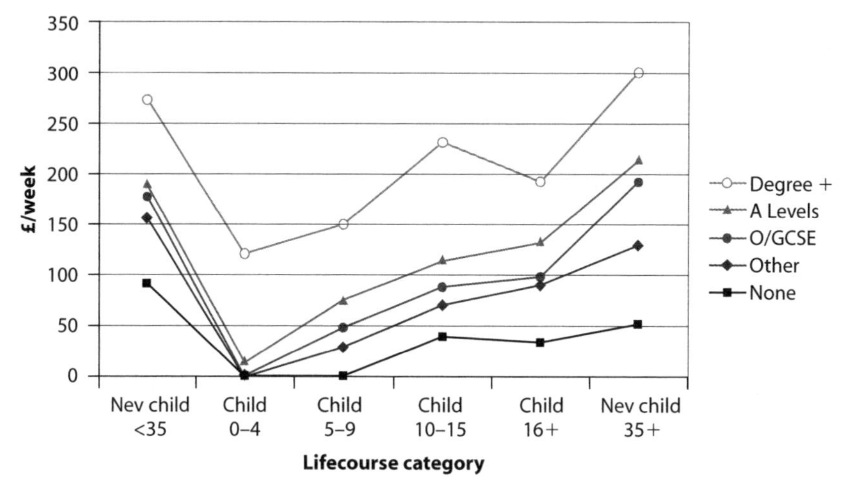

Figure 6.2. Median earnings by lifecourse category and education. British women aged 20–59.

Source: Ginn and Arber (2002).

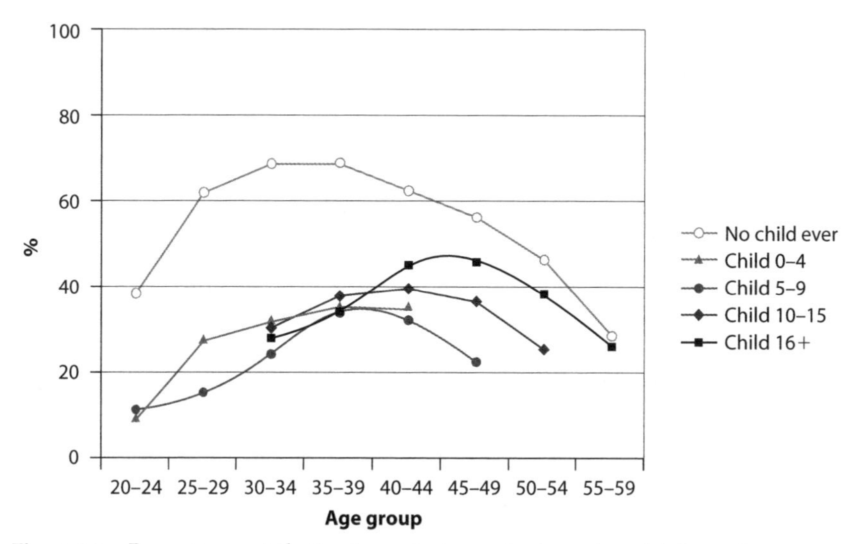

Figure 6.3. Percentage contributing to a private pension by maternal status and age group. British women aged 20–59.

Source: Ginn and Arber (2002).

market risk to employees and reducing the benefits they can expect (see Chapter 10 by Clarke in this volume). Because of this and the decline in the basic state pension, contributing to a private pension is less likely than in the past to provide sufficient pension income to avoid means-testing, especially for low earners and those with interrupted employment, most of whom are female.[19]

For the majority of women, pension disadvantage and risk of personal poverty in later life are unlikely to diminish in the foreseeable future, as acknowledged by the government[20] and the Pensions Commission's first report.[21] Furthermore, new patterns of pension disadvantage are emerging, influenced by partnership status, motherhood, class, and ethnicity. Thus the pension advantage enjoyed by single (never-married) older women is greatly reduced among midlife women and almost disappears in the youngest generation, due to the much higher marriage and motherhood rates since the Second World War compared with the pre-war period. Lone motherhood is more common among younger women due to social change since the 1970s.[22] Divorced mothers face particular problems. On average, children are 4–5 years old at the time of divorce. Hence, caring responsibilities are likely to restrict their mothers' earnings for a number of years after the divorce. They begin to 'catch up' on lost employment, earnings, and pension-building when their children are independent, but they nevertheless remain at high risk of poverty in later life because of the gap in their work and earnings histories due to child-rearing.[23] For this and other reasons, legislation allowing pension-sharing at divorce is unlikely to end divorced women's severe pension disadvantage.

Pension System Design and the Gender Gap in Pensions

European Community law on sex equality in pensions has brought benefits to women, notably by abolishing discrimination against those who are married.[24] Equal treatment has also extended some benefits to men. However, the effects apply only to paid workers. To improve gender

[19] J. Ginn, 'Pensions and Poverty Traps: Is Saving Worthwhile for Women?' *Journal of Financial Services Marketing*, 7, 4 (2003b), 319–29.

[20] Department of Work and Pensions (DWP) *Simplicity, Security and Choice*, Green Paper (London, 2002); DWP, *Women and Pensions: The Evidence* (London, 2005).

[21] Pensions Commission, *First Report*, ch. 8.

[22] J. Ginn, 'Parenthood, Partnership and Pensions: Cohort Differences Among Women', *Sociology*, 37, 3 (2003c), 493–510.

[23] J. Ginn and D. Price, 'Can Divorced Women Catch Up in Pension Building?' *Child and Family Law Quarterly*, 14, 2 (2002), 157–73.

[24] J. Sohrab, 'An Overview of the Equality Directive on Social Security and Its Implementation in Four Social Security Systems', *Journal of European Social Security*, 4, 4 (1994), 163–27.

equality in pensions, compensatory provisions in state pensions are needed to help those with caring responsibilities to obtain entitlements.

Three types of compensatory rules are distinguished by Luckhaus:[25]

- 'survivor' or 'derived' benefits, originally available only to widows in recognition of their past years of financial dependency upon the earnings of their husbands;
- measures that loosen the link between contributions and pension amount, for example through a 'best years' formula;
- specific protection to cover periods of caring.

To explain these more fully:

Derived Pensions

Social protection through reliance on a spouse's contribution record is becoming increasingly 'clumsy and obsolete'.[26] This is due to changes in patterns of family formation, especially the decline in legal marriage as the context for motherhood. Moreover, since 2005, derived pensions for partners and survivors in Britain will be available to registered same-sex civil partners in state pensions and defined-benefit occupational pensions (accruing from 1988), but not to the significant numbers of heterosexual cohabitees, with and without children. One-third of British women aged 16–59 with dependent children are not married.[27] Births outside marriage, due to divorce, cohabitation, or unpartnered pregnancy, rose from 7 per cent in the early 1970s to 38 per cent in 1998, with over 60 per cent of these births registered by cohabiting couples.[28] Cohabitation, which carries no derived rights, has dramatically increased. Between 1979 and 2001, the proportion of women aged 18–49 who were never married doubled to over one-third, while the divorced and separated nearly doubled from 7 to 13 per cent.[29]

The decoupling of marriage and motherhood makes derived benefits both ill-targeted and inequitable, due to the substantial cross-subsidies involved. For example, British wives can receive 60 per cent of the basic

[25] L. Luckhaus, 'Equal Pension Rights for Men and Women: A Realistic Perspective', *Journal of European Social Policy*, August (1997).
[26] E. Schokkaert and P. van Parijs, 'Social Justice and the Reform of Europe's Pension System', *Journal of European Social Policy*, 13, 3 (2003), 245–63.
[27] ONS, *Living in Britain: Results from the 2001 General Household Survey* (London, 2002), www/statistics.gov.uk/.
[28] ONS, *Population Trends 98*, Winter (London, 1999).
[29] ONS, *Living in Britain: Results from the 2001 General Household Survey.*

state pension, and 100 per cent as widows, without paying any contributions at all.[30] Widows also receive 50 per cent of their deceased husband's State Second Pension. In contrast, lone mothers and other lone carers must qualify for their state pensions through contributions, Home Responsibilities Protection, or carer credits. Similarly, widows may receive a 50 per cent pension from their deceased husband's occupational pension scheme, a benefit partly funded by the contributions of lone mothers who contribute to the scheme. Crucially, derived pension rights apply irrespective of whether the beneficiary's employment opportunities have been constrained by family caring. Thus the derived pensions of spouses, civil partners, and survivors are subsidized by other scheme contributors, including non-married mothers, who are a particularly financially disadvantaged group. It is doubtful whether this form of redistribution to married women remains justifiable given the social changes of the twentieth century. Instead, it may be simpler and fairer to individualize pensions—phasing out derived pensions for younger cohorts and replacing them with improved pension rights for those with caring commitments.

Relaxing the Link between Contributions and Benefits

A flat-rate pension, especially if the years required for the full amount are relatively few, helps to redistribute towards women. The British basic state pension now largely removes the effect of the gender gap in earnings, although many older women have only a partial basic pension because they opted to pay the married women's 'small stamp' and because pension protection for carers was not introduced until 1978.

Residence-based citizen's pensions break the link between contributions and pensions completely, providing equal amounts to men and women as well as to carers and those who have never had caring commitments. In Denmark and the Netherlands, a citizen's pension is payable to all individuals fulfilling residence requirements, at age 67 in Denmark and 65 in the Netherlands. Provided citizen's pensions and flat-rate pensions are inclusive and set at a generous level; they go a long way to compensate women (and men) for time spent in unpaid caring work. To fund the more costly state pensions in most of the EU-15 countries, income tax is generally higher than in Britain.

[30] R. Cuvillier, 'The Housewife: An Unjustifiable Burden on the Community', *Journal of Social Policy*, 8, 1 (1979), 1–26; M. Jepsen and D. Meulders, 'The Individualization of Rights in Social Protection Systems', in H. Sarfati and G. Bonoli (eds), *Labour Markets and Social Protection Reforms in International Perspective* (Aldershot, 2002).

In earnings-related pension schemes, the pension may be based on average earnings over the whole working life (Belgium, Germany, Italy, Luxembourg, Sweden, Britain), during last or later years (Finland, Greece, Spain) or for the best years (Austria, France, Portugal).[31] Using average earnings over the working life, or 'last years', leaves most women at a disadvantage compared with men. A 'best years' formula is more helpful to women, because of their typically fluctuating earnings over the lifecourse. The British State Second Pension helps women by boosting the accrual rate for low earners. Thus those earning between £4,000 and £12,800pa (2006) and those qualifying for childcare or elder-care credits all accrue pension entitlements as though they earned £12,800pa.

Specific Protection for Carers

Most EU state pension schemes recognize family caring for pension entitlement purposes, although this is more common for childcare than for informal care of frail adults.[32] In Britain, Home Responsibilities Protection, introduced in 1978, reduces the years required to qualify for a full basic state pension (BSP) while carer credits are allowed in the State Second Pension (S2P), introduced in 2002 to replace the State Earnings-related Pension Scheme (SERPS). These provisions will increase the proportion of women retiring with a full basic state pension in their own right and will enhance their second-tier pension entitlements relative to SERPS. When the replacement of SERPS by S2P is completed in 2050, the boost to low earners will be maximized. However, if the basic pension continues to decline, the low level of state pensions will undermine this women-friendly provision. Falkingham and Rake[33] estimate that, to obtain state pensions that exceed the threshold for means-testing, a British woman retiring in 2050 would need to have earned above women's average wages and to have been employed full-time for forty-seven years—an unlikely scenario for most women.

[31] S. Leitner, 'Sex and Gender Discrimination within EU Pension Systems', *Journal of European Social Policy*, 11, 2 (2001), 99–115.
[32] *Ibid.*
[33] J. Falkingham and K. Rake, 'Modelling the Gender Impact of British Pension Reforms', in J. Ginn, D. Street, and S. Arber (eds), *Women, Work and Pensions* (Buckingham, 2001), pp. 67–85.

Towards Fairer Pensions for Women

Achieving gender equality in employment and earnings requires policies to reconcile family caring with paid work, including provision of affordable, good-quality childcare and elder-care services, as well as regular equal pay audits. Equal sharing of domestic and caring work between women and men is also needed. However, while women remain the chief providers of family care at the expense of earnings, inequality in state pensions can be minimized in several ways, as outlined above. In Britain, the problem is that gender equality in state pensions will be futile unless these pensions provide an income well above poverty level.

Under current British pension policies, this is not the case. The BSP, already low at about 15 per cent of national average earnings, is projected to decline to only 7 per cent in 2050. For an individual with a full employment record on average earnings, the total amount from the BSP and S2P will decline from 37 per cent of average earnings in 2000 to only 20 per cent in 2050.[34] Those with employment gaps or lower than average earnings, mainly women, will receive even less.

Ignoring women's disadvantages in private pensions, policy-makers in the past twenty-five years have aimed to increase the role of private pensions. Evidence of the vulnerability of private pensions to stock market conditions and increasing longevity might have prompted reconsideration of this objective. Instead, the Pensions Commission, set up in 2002, was asked to review the adequacy of private pension saving and to recommend whether increased compulsion was needed.

Wisely, the Commission recognized that it needed to consider the interaction of private with state pensions and with means-tested benefits. It provided a comprehensive analysis of British pensions, including acknowledging women's longstanding pension disadvantage.[35] The proposals, while representing some improvement on current policy, fall far short of what is needed to improve women's pensions. It is proposed that the basic state pension (BSP) be relinked to average earnings from 2010, increasing the full BSP (above inflation) by £1.36 per week in that year.[36] But, since the full BSP is some £25 per week below the means-tested minimum, this provides little or nothing for women pensioners receiving

[34] Government Actuary Department, *Government Actuary's Quinquennial Review of the National Insurance Fund*, Cm 6008 (London, 2003).

[35] Pensions Commission, *First Report*.

[36] Pensions Commission, *A New Pensions Settlement for the Twenty-first Century. The Second Report of the Pensions Commission* (London, 2005).

means-tested benefits and only a trivial gain for those who are not. It is suggested that, if and when feasible, the government might consider making the BSP universal for those aged over 75, which again would bring very little to those receiving means-tested benefits.

For working-age women, the Pensions Commission's recommendations would bring slightly more gains relative to current policy. First, earnings-linking the BSP from 2010 would halt its otherwise projected decline, making a significant difference in the medium to long term. Second, a proposal to base future accruals of BSP on residence instead of employment would eventually bring equality between men and women in the BSP without the need for Home Responsibilities Protection. Third, the State Second Pension (S2P) would become more inclusive of carers. However, the proposal that S2P should gradually become flat rate (by 2030) would have mixed effects for women. It would benefit the low paid, who are mainly women. But it would also deprive those with moderate earnings (£12,800–£32,000pa) of a state-run defined-benefit earnings-related pension. This is a significant loss, since private pension schemes are increasingly based on defined contributions, placing all the risk of stock market falls and reduced annuity rates on the individual. Such pensions have additional drawbacks for women: disproportionately heavy pension losses for missed contributions in the early years, a lower annuity rate than for men, and relatively high charges in individually arranged personal pensions (up to 1.5 per cent of the accumulated fund).

The proposed new National Pension Savings Scheme (NPSS) would be a voluntary, private defined-contribution scheme, but with low charges, auto-enrolment, and the right to an employer contribution of 3 per cent of relevant earnings. An advantage for women is that the NPSS would be additional to S2P, unlike other private pensions where the employee is contracted out of S2P. Thus women could benefit from S2P throughout their working life, but could also make extra contributions to NPSS if and when they could afford to do so. A danger is that those employed in small and medium enterprises (mainly women) could be pressured by their employer to opt out of the NPSS, thus losing the benefit of employer contributions. For those contributing to NPSS, the drawbacks of defined-contribution schemes for women, noted above, would apply. Reduced market risk, probably advisable for low earners, could be achieved through investing in government bonds, but only at the cost of poor returns on contributions. As with other types of private pension, women would typically obtain lower amounts than men from NPSS.

The proposed rise in state pension age to 67–9 could create additional difficulties for women in their sixties providing informal care for ageing relatives. Moreover, gendered ageism among employers reduces job opportunities for older women.

Overall, the Pensions Commission produced an excellent analysis but disappointingly cautious proposals. Despite the rhetoric of paying attention to women's needs, the pensions problem for women—how to build adequate independent pensions while undertaking the socially important tasks of childrearing and elder-care—persists because of the continuing inadequacy of state pensions. And older women, one of the poorest groups in Britain, would gain almost nothing from the recommendations.

A wide range of organizations—including think-tanks, academics, charities concerned with older people, trade unions, pensioner organizations, women's organizations, and representatives of the private pensions industry—advocate raising the basic pension to the level of the Guarantee Credit (£114pw from April 2006) and making it more inclusive. Most recognize that linking the basic pension to some measure of national prosperity is fair and necessary if older people are not to be socially excluded.

Affordability of Better State Pensions

Paying a universal pension at the 2005 threshold for means-testing (£109pw, or 22 per cent of national average earnings) would cost an extra £7.3 billion net in the first year.[37] Although this would require increased spending on state pensions, not all of it has to come from increased National Insurance (NI) contributions.

The increase in cost is only one-third of the amount spent to incentivize saving through private pensions. In 2005 the net cost of tax relief on private pension contributions was £21 billion or 1.8 per cent of GDP.[38] Tax relief is highly regressive, with half the benefit received by the top 10 per cent of taxpayers and one-quarter by the top 2.5 per cent.[39] It is mainly men who benefit from tax relief whereas for the majority of women state pensions are their only source of pension income.

Rebates for contracting out of the State Second Pension are also a costly subsidy to private pensions, with men as the main beneficiaries. Every pound paid as rebate incurred a net cost to the National Insurance

[37] N. Churchill and M. Mitchell, *Labour's Pension Challenge* (London, 2005).

[38] Pensions Policy Institute (PPI), *Facts on Pensions* (London, 2005).

[39] P. Agulnik and J. Le Grand, 'Tax Relief and Partnership Pensions', *Fiscal Studies*, 19, 4 (1998), 403–28.

Fund of 22p in the 1990s.[40] NI receipts could be increased by restoring the upper earnings limit on contributions to its original (higher) level or abolishing it altogether. Costs of raising and extending the basic state pension would be partly offset by lower spending on means-tested poverty relief.

The NI Fund has a swelling surplus, due to paying price-linked benefits while collecting earnings-linked contributions. By March 2006 the surplus is projected to be £34.6 billion, of which some £25 billion can be treated as usable surplus, above the prudent reserve that must be kept. This usable surplus represents 58 per cent of current spending on the basic pension (£43 billion). Government actuary figures show that annual surpluses of income over spending in the NI Fund will rise from £3.4 billion in 2005 to £7.4 billion in 2009. On current policies the balance will be about £60 billon by that time. Using the NI surplus to buy government bonds provides the Treasury with a convenient extra source of revenue for general spending, one that it is reluctant to forgo. Britain's state pension spending, at about 5 per cent of GDP, is only half the EU average and its meagre state pensions reflect this.

Recently, a business-led group has challenged the doom-laden orthodoxy among policy-makers—that better state pensions are unaffordable in an ageing population. Its report points out that rising productivity will dwarf any effect of an ageing population and that economic activity rates are more relevant than age ratios.[41]

Conclusions

This chapter has shown how pension schemes that tie benefits closely to lifetime earnings disadvantage the majority of women—those who raise children or care for older relatives—placing them at a higher risk of poverty than men in later life. Relying on derived benefits paid to spouses and widows to compensate women is becoming increasingly ineffective, due to changing family forms. Despite increases in women's employment rate, their caring roles continue to reduce their lifetime earnings, and hence private pension accumulation.

International trends to cut state pensions will tend to reinforce gender inequality in pension income, yet debate about these reforms has been gender-blind. Recent acknowledgement by British politicians that the pension system has failed women is welcome. But belated recognition of

[40] Pensions Provision Group (PPG), *We All Need Pensions—The Prospects for Pension Provision* (London, 1998).
[41] P. Sadler, *The Ageing Population, Pensions and Wealth Creation* (London, 2005).

the need to be fair to carers has yet to be matched by the commitment and the policies required. A substantial improvement in the inclusivity and generosity of state pensions would do much to tackle the gender gap in pensions for women of all ages. This would be affordable if the National Insurance Fund surplus were used to finance benefits, instead of being used as a convenient source of borrowing by the government; if NI were payable on all earnings, without an upper limit; and if regressive subsidies for private pensions were redirected towards state pensions.

The Pensions Commission's proposals fall far short of the reforms required to close the gender gap in pension income. Although bringing modest gains for working-age women, they fail to tackle the low pension income of older women and those nearing retirement. The Commission appears to have accepted the government's preference for increasing private, rather than state, pension saving. Yet the argument that population ageing requires a shift to private funded pensions has been widely refuted, given that all pensions are ultimately paid from current production and that funded pension schemes are so clearly vulnerable to the effects of demographic change.[42]

The stark reality for most women is that, unless redistribution is designed into the pension system, it is very difficult both to raise children and to accumulate an adequate independent pension in later life. Yet it is bearing and nurturing children that ensures a new generation of wealth creators, on which all pension schemes depend. As Himmelweit argues, the paid economy depends on the unpaid work of women, since it requires a healthy, educated workforce. 'If insufficient time and resources are devoted to [unpaid care], productivity will suffer as human resources deteriorate and the social fabric is inadequately maintained.'[43] If caring for children is 'a socially-relevant duty'[44] then failure to protect carers' pension entitlements through adequate state pensions is clearly unjust as well as counter-productive.

[42] D. Mabbett, *Pension Funding: Economic Imperative or Political Strategy*, Discussion Paper 97/1 (Uxbridge, 1997); Merrill Lynch, *Demographics and the Funded Pension System* (London, 2000).
[43] S. Himmelweit, 'Accounting for Caring', *Radical Statistics*, 70, 1–8, Winter (London, 1998).
[44] Schokkaert and van Parijs, 'Social Justice and the Reform of Europe's Pension System', 254.

Bibliography

Items that provide a useful introduction to the issues discussed in this chapter are marked with an asterisk.

Agulnik, P. and J. Le Grand, 'Tax Relief and Partnership Pensions', *Fiscal Studies*, 19, 4 (1998), 403–28.
Arber, S. and J. Ginn, 'Ageing and Gender: Diversity and Change', *Social Trends*, 34 (London, 2004), 1–14.
Berthoud, R., *The Incomes of Ethnic Minorities* (Colchester, 1998).
Churchill, N. and M. Mitchell, *Labour's Pension Challenge* (London, 2005).
Cuvillier, R., 'The Housewife: An Unjustifiable Burden on the Community', *Journal of Social Policy*, 8, 1 (1979), 1–26.
Darton, D. and K. Hurrell, *People Working Below Their Potential* (Manchester, 2005).
*Davies, H., H. Joshi, and R. Peronaci, 'Forgone Income and Motherhood: What Do Recent British Data Tell Us?' *Population Studies*, 54 (2000), 293–305.
Department of Work and Pensions (DWP), *Simplicity, Security and Choice*, Green Paper (London, 2002).
——, *Women and Pensions: The Evidence* (London, 2005).
Dex, S., *Women's Occupational Mobility: A Lifetime Perspective* (Basingstoke, 1987).
European Commission (2003), *Joint Inclusion Report*, Statistical Annex, http://europa.eu.int/employment_social/soc-prot/soc-incl/sec_2003_1425_final_en.pdf.
*Evason, E. and L. Spence, *Women and Pensions* (Belfast, 2002).
Falkingham, J. and K. Rake, 'Modelling the Gender Impact of British Pension Reforms', in J. Ginn, D. Street, and S. Arber (eds), *Women, Work and Pensions* (Buckingham, 2001), pp. 67–85.
*Ginn, J., *Gender, Pensions and the Lifecourse: How Pensions Need to Adapt to Changing Family Forms* (Bristol, 2003a).
——, 'Pensions and Poverty Traps: Is Saving Worthwhile for Women?', *Journal of Financial Services Marketing*, 7, 4 (2003b), 319–29.
——, 'Parenthood, Partnership and Pensions: Cohort Differences Among Women', *Sociology*, 37, 3 (2003c), 493–510.
Ginn, J. and S. Arber, 'Gender, Class and Income Inequalities in Later Life', *British Journal of Sociology*, 42, 3 (1991), 369–96.
—— and ——, 'Patterns of Employment, Pensions and Gender: The Effect of Work History on Older Women's Non-state Pensions', *Work Employment and Society*, 10, 3 (1996), 469–90.
—— and ——, 'Changing Patterns of Pension Inequality: The Shift from State to Private Sources', *Ageing and Society*, 19, 3 (1999), 319–42.
—— and ——, 'Gender, the Generational Contract and Pension Privatization', in S. Arber and C. Attias-Donfut (eds), *The Myth of Intergenerational Conflict: The State and Family Across Cultures*, (London, 1999), pp. 133–53.
—— and ——,'Pension Costs of Caring', *Benefits*, 28, May/June (2000), 13–17.
—— and ——, 'Women's Pensions and the Impact of Privatization in Britain', in INSTRAW (ed.), *Ageing in a Gendered World: Women's Issues and Identities* (Santo Domingo, 2000), pp. 49–74.

—— and ——, 'Ethnic Inequality in Later Life: Variation in Financial Circumstances by Gender and Ethnic Group', *Education and Ageing*, 15, 1 (2000), 65–83.

—— and ——, 'Pension Prospects of Minority Ethnic Groups: Variation by Gender and Ethnicity', *British Journal of Sociology* (2001).

—— and ——, (2002), 'Degrees of Freedom: Can Graduate Women Avoid the Motherhood Gap in Pensions?' *Sociological Research On-line*, www.socres online.org.uk/7/2/.

—— and D. Price, 'Can Divorced Women Catch Up in Pension Building?', *Child and Family Law Quarterly*, 14, 2 (2002), 157–73.

Ginn, J., D. Street, and S. Arber (eds) *Women, Work and Pensions: International Issues and Prospects* (Buckingham, 2001).

*Gornick, J., M. Meyers, and K. Ross, 'Supporting the Employment of Mothers: Policy Variation across Fourteen Welfare States', *Journal of European Social Policy*, 7, 1 (1997), 45–70.

Government Actuary Department, *Government Actuary's Quinquennial Review of the National Insurance Fund*, Cm 6008 (London, 2003).

*Groves, D., 'Financial Provision for Women in Retirement', in M. Maclean and D. Groves (eds), *Women's Issues in Social Policy* (London, 1991), pp. 141–62.

Harkness, S. and J. Waldfogel, *The Family Gap in Pay: Evidence from Seven Industrialised Countries*, CASEpaper 29 (London, 1999).

Himmelweit, S., 'Accounting for Caring', *Radical Statistics*, 70, 1–8, Winter (1998).

Jepsen, M. and D. Meulders, 'The Individualisation of Rights in Social Protection Systems', in H. Sarfati and G. Bonoli (eds), *Labour Markets and Social Protection Reforms in International Perspective* (Aldershot, 2002).

Leitner, S., 'Sex and Gender Discrimination within EU Pension Systems', *Journal of European Social Policy*, 11, 2 (2001), 99–115.

Luckhaus, L., 'Equal Pension Rights for Men and Women: A Realistic Perspective', *Journal of European Social Policy*, August (1997).

Mabbett, D., *Pension Funding: Economic Imperative or Political Strategy*, Discussion Paper 97/1 (Uxbridge, 1997).

McConaghy, M., C. Hill, C. Kane, D. Lader, P. Costigan, and M. Thornby, *Entitled but not Claiming? Pensioners, the Minimum Income Guarantee and Pension Credit*, Research Report 197 (summary) (London, 2003), www.dwp.gov.uk/asd/asd5/rrs2003.asp.

Merrill Lynch, *Demographics and the Funded Pension System* (London, 2000).

OECD, *Employment Outlook* (Paris, 2001).

Office for National Statistics (ONS), *Population Trends 98*, Winter (London, 1999).

——, *Living in Britain: Results from the 2001 General Household Survey* (London, 2002), www/statistics.gov.uk/.

——, *Social Trends 2002* (London, 2003).

——, *Social Trends 2003* (London, 2004).

*Peggs, K., 'Which Pension? Women, Risk and Pension Choice, *Sociological Review*, 48, 3 (2000), 349–64.

Pensions Commission, *Pensions: Challenges and Choices. The First Report of the Pensions Commission* (London, 2004).

——, *A New Pensions Settlement for the Twenty-first Century. The Second Report of the Pensions Commission* (London, 2005).
Pensions Policy Institute (PPI), *Facts on Pensions* (London, 2005).
Pensions Provision Group (PPG), *We All Need Pensions—The Prospects for Pension Provision* (London, 1998).
Price, D., 'Marital Status, Money and Pensions: A Sociological Perspective on Women's Pension Scheme Participation', paper presented at the Work, Pensions and Labour Economics Study Group Conference, 18–20 July 2005.
Price, D. and J. Ginn, 'Sharing the Crust? Gender, Partnership Status and Inequalities in Pension Accumulation', in S. Arber, K. Davidson, and J. Ginn (eds), *Gender and Ageing: Changing Roles and Relationships* (Buckingham, 2003).
Sadler, P., *The Ageing Population, Pensions and Wealth Creation* (London, 2005).
*Sainsbury, S., *Gender, Equality and Welfare States* (Cambridge, 1996).
Schokkaert, E. and P. van Parijs, 'Social Justice and the Reform of Europe's Pension System', *Journal of European Social Policy*, 13, 33 (2003), 245–63.
Sohrab, J., 'An Overview of the Equality Directive on Social Security and Its Implementation in Four Social Security Systems', *Journal of European Social Security*, 4, 4 (1994), 163–27.
Women and Equality Unit (WEU), *Women's Income over a Lifetime* (London, 2000).
——, *Key Indicators of Women's Position in Britain* (London, 2002).

7. How to Address Gender Inequality in British Pensions

PATRICIA HOLLIS (BARONESS HOLLIS OF HEIGHAM)

Pensions have been constructed by men in full-time work for other men in full-time work; but most pensioners, two-thirds of them, are women. The basic state pension (BSP) still assumes that women will derive their state pensions as dependants of their husbands. And modern occupational pensions (OP) still assume that women will derive private pensions from full-time work and full-time saving continued without interruption over forty years. Neither the model of the BSP nor of the OP fits the world women inhabit.

Adair Turner, chair of the Pensions Commission, told us in his first report[1] what we need to do. Work longer. Save more. Raise taxes. Or accept reduced income in retirement. But his injunctions are very hard to apply to women. It is hard to ask them to work longer—they are not going to be able to do so easily, given their responsibilities. They are least likely to be able to work still harder; least likely to be able to save; and, accordingly, least likely to have adequate provision in their own right. So women largely cannot do what Turner demands—except perhaps to follow the one path that is indecent, which is for women (though not necessarily men) to accept a lower standard of living in retirement.

Why are women so at risk of poverty in retirement? There are three main drivers pressing them towards poverty—fluid family forms, flexible labour markets, and increased longevity.

Take fluid family forms. In Beveridge's day, most men were in forty-year jobs and forty-year marriages, and women got their income from their husbands on both counts. No longer. Women are increasingly unable to rely on the protection drawn from a husband's pension. In 1976, there were 400,000 marriages; in 2001, 286,000. Four in ten of first marriages,

[1] Pensions Commission, *Pensions: Challenges and Choices. First Report of the Pensions Commission* (London, 2004).

and seven in ten of second marriages, end in divorce. Some 50 per cent of women between 45 and 64—that is, older rather than younger women, for whom the figures will be higher—will by 2030 not be married. They may be single, widowed, divorced, or cohabiting. Married, they would get a 60 per cent addition to a husband's pension; unmarried, they will not. Yet caring responsibilities remain: 64 per cent of women between 25 and 45 have dependent children; one-quarter of women between 45 and 60 are carers and one-quarter of these have dependent children. Motherhood has indeed become detached from marriage; half of all births are now outside marriage.

The second driver is flexible labour markets. Pensions are attached to the labour market. Yet fewer women work than men (under 70 per cent, compared to over 80 per cent for men). They work fewer hours (44 per cent of women work part-time, compared to 10 per cent of men), fewer years, and for far less pay. The median hourly wage for men in full-time work in 2005 was £11.31, for women £9.84, a 13 per cent gender gap. But women's median part-time pay was £6.67 an hour, 41 per cent less than that of men.

The third driver is increased longevity. In Beveridge's day, pensions were an insurance against the risk of old age. They are now—for those who can, mostly men—a way of saving for the certainty of old age, and most women face a longer old age than most men. Women, while rightly being urged to save for their own retirement, also face the need to care for those who have already retired and have become increasingly frail.

So, as a woman approaches pension age now, what sort of landscape does she see? First, she will not have, for the most part, a national insurance (NI) pension in her own right. Men will: 92 per cent of them. Barely 20 per cent of women enter retirement with a full national insurance pension in their own right. She will also find that if she has have worked part-time, as women mostly have, and for small, private, non-unionized companies without pension schemes, she will enter retirement with no private pension either. If she has been married, there is a fifty-fifty chance that it will have ended in divorce. If she is in an unmarried couple relationship she will have no dependency pension from her partner and probably no pension credit from the state as his income will probably float them off it, however uneven the apportionment of income within the household between them. If she then goes on to become widowed (over half of all women over the age of 65 are single, largely widowed) that is likely to happen in her eighties when any annuity he has is likely to die with him. She will then come into the reach of means-tested benefits, and, as we know from our experience of pension credit, may very well hesitate to claim them.

For women are up against the fact that the contributory national insurance pension is meant to be ring-fenced. It is designed to keep some people out. That is the point of it, presumably because they are regarded as less or undeserving. They have not 'worked' hard enough in ways that society (literally) counts, i.e. they may have worked hard in the home, supporting children, partner, and perhaps others also, but they have done too little paid work. The excluded are of course mainly women.

So, as a woman goes into retirement, currently at age 60, she (and we) might note some of the anomalies that the present contributory system has delivered for women.

If she has been married, has never worked, and has had no children, taken on no further caring responsibilities—the so-called idle, wealthy, married woman—she will get a 60 per cent basic state pension as an addition to her husband's as of right. If she is an unmarried partner, with children, and working fifteen hours a week she will get nothing from his basic state pension. The first woman effectively gets something for nothing; the second gets nothing for what we would all regard as something. A company director can retire at 60 with a handsome private pension, to play golf, and gets 'free' NI contributions for the next five years. The working-class woman of 60, who carries on cleaning full-time for several more years, cannot earn or acquire any NI contributions after the female pension age of 60. She cannot earn a higher state pension by working longer. Something for nothing, certainly—against nothing for something?

If, to give another example, she is a stay-at-home mum with a 15-year-old she will still get a home responsibilities payment (HRP). Fine. If a lad is unemployed and he is on Jobseeker's Allowance, he will get an NI credit. Fine. But if a woman has been holding down two or even three fifteen-hour jobs at minimum wage she will get nothing: no credit, no contribution. The job-hours cannot be added together for NI purposes, even though her forty-five hours per week may exceed her partner's forty-hour week. The unemployed son gets the stamp. She does not.

Still further anomalies. If she is a carer looking after someone for thirty hours per week the disabled person she is caring for will almost certainly get a national insurance credit; the female carer doing the unwaged work—and almost certainly denying herself the opportunity of earning a decent wage—will get nothing at all. Waged work counts. Unwaged work, mostly, does not.

We have a contributory system which, as new needs are recognized, decently, has been patched and stretched with credits—for children, for unemployment, for disability—while still nominally described as contributory. Only some 60 per cent of NI years are actually 'earned' and paid for; the rest are credits. Each credit has different rules, qualifications, time constraints, client groups. Consequently, few people know who is entitled to what, how to get it, or what it will amount to until the day after they retire. The anomalies, the lottery, and frankly the injustices, are unacceptable—but they remain, largely because they are opaque. The consequence is that, over their lifetimes, women have on average three-quarters of the earnings, about half the income, and barely one-third of the pensions of men in retirement.

The three contributors to this volume who discuss women's pensions share this analysis. The preceding chapters have described the past and the present state of pensions. Let us turn to the future. Where do we go? We are told, and there is some truth in it, that the situation is getting better and that the problem may diminish over time. The reasons for this, I would suggest, are threefold: first, more women, both married and unmarried, are in work; second, there are as many women as men in occupational pension schemes now; third, the belief that the roll-forward of HRP will eliminate women's penalties for caring. The statistics do at first sight seem to suggest this. But that is because they significantly underestimate the countervailing trends which are worsening women's pension situation.

Four points: first, it is true that women are indeed entering the labour market, but this is essentially a part-time (and very low-paid) labour market. According to the Labour Force Survey (2005), 1.8 million women are working fewer than sixteen hours a week.[2] If they are working fewer than sixteen hours a week they have no NI entitlement and almost certainly no occupational pension. We are, rightly, encouraging women to work more flexibly. We are encouraging them to do part-time work, again rightly so, and that is their choice. But in the process they are likely to take an earnings hit, and a pensions hit, possibly on national insurance, certainly on occupational pensions. In any case, the women who have occupational pensions are very heavily concentrated in the lower pay end of the public sector, especially health workers. In the private sector, work is heavily gendered and occupational pensions there remain as elusive for women as ever.

Second, if they are mothers, since 1978 they rightly get HRP, which is simple to award because it automatically tracks the child benefit book; HRP does not in itself contribute to a pension, it merely reduces the number of qualifying years she has to work to get one. But, of course, from

[2] Office for National Statistics, *Quarterly Labour Force Survey, June–August 2005* (London, 2005).

2010 the pension age for women will rise (a factor that has hardly been mentioned in the current pensions debate) which will substantially reduce the value of HRP as it now is.

Third, just at the point when her children grow up and HRP runs out, and she might start building her contributions, her elder-caring work may come into play. Only 400,000 out of 6 million carers receive a carer's allowance and an NI credit to accompany it. The reason is the need when paying out carer's allowance to audit-trail public monies. We do this by requiring a carer to work thirty-five hours a week for a person on at least middle-rate Disability Living Allowance to qualify. We audit the carer's work essentially by auditing the disability of the person cared for. This assumes a regular waged-work type of model. But, in practice, caring responsibilities vary widely and can change quite rapidly. Illnesses fluctuate; they may go into remission for a week or a year; terminal conditions become more onerous; and mental health needs may change by the day. There is no way a woman can fit in regular waged work around disability and frailty which is seldom so tidy in its demands. Worse, if you care for two people each for twenty hours you get no credit for national insurance. You can no more add your hours of caring together for a credit than you can add together your hours of part-time waged work. How exactly could an agency track the hours spent by one woman caring in one week for a frail mother, an elderly uncle, and a wheel-chair bound neighbour? Especially if the carer and the person cared for think they need more hours of care than the agency deems appropriate? There is no way we can bring fluctuating conditions, multi-caring, the disparate assessment of need, into the NI credit system. It cannot be done. Yet there are now more people over 80 than under 5 years of age; their care needs cannot be captured by NI; and the work of (mainly) women looking after them goes unacknowledged. This is a problem which will become more acute as longevity increases.

My fourth point: twenty years ago, men at 65 were expected to live a further fourteen years until 79. Now at 65 they can expect to live to 85, and by 2030 to 88. Add a couple of years to that for women, and the average life expectancy could be 90. Already one-quarter of women living now will survive to 93. At the moment, life expectancy is growing by a year to eighteen months every decade, and one to two months for every year. We hear a lot about longevity; how actuaries miscalculated; how pensions (men's pensions) will not last long enough to support them until death; that there will be too few workers per pensioner. That is entirely true. But what is barely mentioned at all is the differing impact of longevity on women compared to men. The very pressure of longevity on the actuarial soundness of men's pensions is likely, when translated into a more extended need for carers, to reduce women's capacity to build a pension at all. This is a connection few people choose to make. At the very time she might be moving from childcare into full-time work, a woman is increasingly likely to be caring for a parent or even a grandparent. She can choose between her own financial well-being and supporting theirs. It is unlikely she can do both. A woman in her forties can have teenage-children, parents retired, and a grandparent in their nineties: four generations, three of them potentially pivoting around her health, her work, and her care.

And, although women fondly believe that a husband or partner will look after their pension, increasingly, given divorce patterns, he won't; or, having taken out a single-life money purchase scheme, he can't because the pension will die with him.

What is going on? Why is there such a problem? It is because we are failing, in my view, to read women's lives as a narrative. The more we encourage, rightly, work–life balance in early years (and I am proud of what my government has done in that field) the more women may take a pension hit for it. The more we encourage women to take on the role of carers, which they want to do, the more they are likely to take a pension hit for it. Women as mothers and women as workers need to be connected in a narrative with women as carers and women as pensioners. We are not doing it. Women are doing what they, we, and society want, and they get punished for it.

At the moment an increasingly flexible labour market, increased longevity, and fluid family forms together produce a triple hit on women's pensions. If Joanne were Joe, none of this would affect his capacity to work. Joe and Joanne may equally partner, marry, have two children, divorce a decade later, be single for a few years, and then repartner, while his or her mother becomes increasingly frail. At each of these changes in his personal life, Joe would carry on working, carry on building a pension, both state and private. None of these events would affect his public life, except perhaps to make him miserable.

For Joanne, most of these life changes—children, divorce, single parenthood, repartnering, frail mother—will affect her capacity to work and build a pension. One set of statistics sums it all up: 52 per cent of men are building a pension before they have children; the same percentage builds a pension after they have children. Yet, 31 per cent of women are building a pension before they have children, but, as Scottish Widows has reported, just 15 per cent continue when children come.[3] Because Joe's

[3] Scottish Widows, *UK Pensions Report* (2005).

situation is a steady state we can look at his life almost in snapshots. His pension is predictable. Joanne, however, could not possibly predict at 27 what her work and family life would look like at 37 or 47 or 57—and whether therefore she should try to build a pension. Her future life is riddled with risk and uncertainty. She will know what the right choice to make would be only when it is too late to make it. Men in a full-employment economy can mostly predict their work life, short of a mid-life crisis. But women, who face greater poverty, more insecurity, and longer lives, have the least capacity to pool risk and least knowledge of what that risk may entail. Joanne's life, unlike Joe's, cannot be seen as a set of prospective snapshots, but a narrative with an uncertain ending.

So most women will enter old age without a full BSP from waged work, unable to obtain one from unwaged work, without a full BSP from their husbands, and without a penny of BSP from their partners. But how could they have known what was best to do twenty or forty years before?

What are the options? Turner has analysed them in his first and second reports.[4] Basically, there seem to be three. We can extend, or seek to extend, the NI contributory system to bring more women in, even though the contributory 'something for something' principle is clearly a myth. The patching and tweaking and mending have made it pretty threadbare. Whatever pattern the post-Beveridge design might have had, is now obscure and baffles most observers. The difficulties of incorporating elder-care into a decent credit have been indicated. In any case women's not untypical portfolio of some caring, a couple of part-time jobs, and sustaining family life, is inherently unstable—no basis for a pension structure which takes forty years to roll up. The national insurance principle is a profoundly unfair and unsatisfactory basis for women's pensions in retirement.

The second option is pension credit, or means-testing, which has indeed transformed the income of our poorer women pensioners. But the need for income-related benefits usually kicks in when elderly women have lost their husbands or partners, usually in their eighties, and it is going to be seriously hard to raise the current take-up figure for pension credit of 75 per cent. Pension credit currently covers 40 per cent of pensioners. If nothing much changes, it will reach 70 per cent of them in due course. Pension credit is indeed admirably designed to relieve poverty that has already occurred. It is, in my view, ill-suited to relieve the poverty of future pensioners, precisely because its means-testing is perceived as a

[4] Pensions Commission, *First Report*; Pensions Commission, *A New Pensions Settlement for the Twenty-first Century. Second Report of the Pensions Commission* (London, 2005).

disincentive to save and to build a pension of one's own. Women on low incomes think they are being selfish if they put £20 aside into a work pension for themselves when the children want new trainers. If, in addition, they learn they will be little better off as a result, either because they have an incomplete BSP or because of the withdrawal rates of means-tested benefits, then they will not unreasonably ask, 'Why bother?'

So women are reluctant to save and many employers are reluctant to press pensions on women because they fear mis-selling. If, for example, a low-paid woman working in a supermarket would by retirement have a BSP of just £55 (rather than the full BSP of £82) but has put away £8,000 or so of her wages into a pension, matched by the employer, generating a small second pension of £25 a week, she will not be a single penny better off. She has wasted £8,000 which she can ill afford. Unless employers know that a woman has a full basic state pension, they cannot be sure what proportion if any of that pension she will retain; and therefore they fear they could be accused of mis-selling. Some of the fears about auto-enrolment, or Turner's 'soft compulsion', cannot be overcome in an NI-plus-pension credit landscape. You cannot both means-test, and safely urge people to save. Perversely we have built an interface between the BSP and occupational pensions that not only does not encourage a woman to make good any shortfall in her BSP by building her occupational pensions; rather it actively penalizes her for it. That cannot be sound public policy.

Finally, there are proposals to abandon the NI basis for the state pension altogether. Some, led by the National Association of Pension Funds, have called for a citizen's pension. The term 'citizen's pension', as conventionally used, brings together the BSP and the state second pension (S2P) into one state pension pitched at pension credit level (currently £111pw) But there are difficulties with this, as Turner made clear. We would lose the contributory nature of the S2P and its attachment to the world of work, a move acceptable perhaps for the BSP but not perhaps for a second 'default' pension. The S2P at the moment is more redistributive (and therefore of greater value to low-paid women) than a citizen's pension would be. And ending contracting-out (a necessary consequence) could have destabilizing consequences for final-salary schemes. That may be where industry wants to go in time, as money-purchase schemes become more dominant; and it may be that in ten or twenty years time the S2P will have become more generous, increasingly mirror the BSP, and can be rolled together. But not now and not yet.

In my view, the only way forward that is fair to men and women alike, to the waged and unwaged, to the employed and the self-employed, to existing and to future pensioners, is to have a universal basic state pension. Each individual would get a full basic state pension, based on residency, in their own right. It would not be connected to the contributions or credits of NI; it would not be derived from relationships, with some privileged over others. People would still pay into NI when in waged work, but it would fund a common entitlement at retirement. The S2P, the contributory pension, would continue with whatever modifications were thought appropriate.

There are no losers. A married couple would get two times 100 per cent instead of the current 160 per cent. So would partners. So would same-sex partners. We would have fairness between genders; a recognition that unwaged work which you can't audit can be as valuable as waged work that you can. It would offer simplicity and transparency of administration. People would know what they could expect. It would reduce means-testing. And, because a universal BSP is predictable, it would take the risk out of saving for a pension for those women who might otherwise come within the trap of income-related benefits.

Turner's second report has broadly followed the path of a universal BSP. His Commission seeks to reduce poverty, increase savings, reduce means-testing, and increase simplicity. To ensure that the state pension is a secure platform for retirement, he proposes that future accruals to the BSP should be based on residency, and that ideally a full BSP should be paid automatically to those aged 75 and over.

These proposals are highly desirable. He would keep the S2P as a separate pension though making it more generous for carers. He would then index-link the BSP to earnings to retain its value, part of the cost of which would be met by raising the state pension age with the growth in longevity.

These proposals would, however, take some forty years to roll through, and older women aged between 45 and 75 would remain relatively unprotected. We need to get to Turner's universal BSP faster than that.

The net cost of a universal BSP for all by 2030 would be around £3 billion at a time when the proportion of pensioners in our society is increasing rapidly, and the share of GDP to which they might be entitled could be expected to rise with it. It is, coincidentally, the same additional money as would be generated by a rise in the Upper Earnings Limit to £50,000pa. Or, to put it another way, it would cost one-third of the £10 billion savings garnered by raising women's state pension age from 60 in 2010 to 65 in 2020. By these criteria, it is affordable.

And the legacy? In the first term of the Labour government, 1997–2001, we made work pay for women. We introduced the minimum wage, two-thirds of whose beneficiaries are women. We introduced tax credits, which for the first time ensured that a lone parent, working twenty hours a week on £5 an hour, took home effectively a man's wage of £10 an hour. In the second term, we made work possible for many women, by introducing the right to pursue part-time work, supporting lone parents' re-entry into the labour force, and by extending childcare. Our legacy for women in our third term should be a full state pension when they enter retirement, honouring their unwaged work and their standing as full citizens of our society. We are addressing the poverty of women's working-age lives. It is time to address the poverty of their old age, by ensuring they enjoy a state pension as of right.

Bibliography

Department of Work and Pensions, *Women and Pensions: The Evidence* (2005).

Office for National Statistics, *Quarterly Labour Force Survey, June–August 2005* (London, 2005).

Pensions Commission, *Pensions: Challenges and Choices. First Report of the Pensions Commisssion* (London, 2004).

——, *A New Pensions Settlement for the Twenty-first Century. Second Report of the Pensions Commission* (London, 2005).

Pensions Policy Institute, *The Under-pensioned Women* (2003).

Scottish Widows, *UK Pensions Report* (2005).

Women and Work Commission, *Shaping a Fairer Future* (2006).

Occupational Pensions and Finance

8.

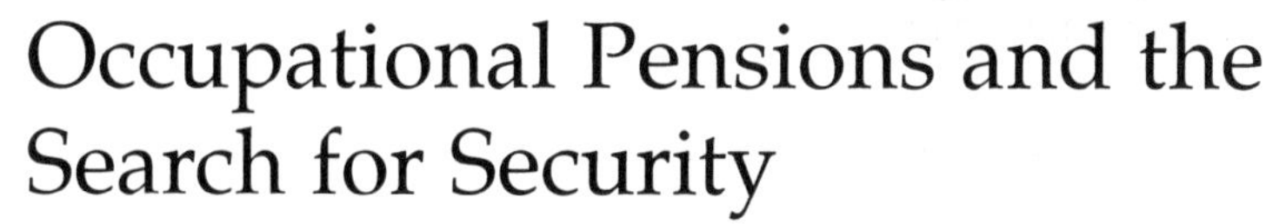

Occupational Pensions and the Search for Security

NOEL WHITESIDE

Introduction

Occupational pensions, linking previous earnings to pensioner income, have long been understood as an essential supplement to a state pension in retirement—particularly in Britain, where state provision as of right is the lowest in the western world. Since the Second World War, policy initiatives in Britain have made sporadic efforts to increase the coverage of occupational or personal pension supplements. The Turner Commission's proposals represent the most recent in a long line of reports and recommendations designed to achieve this end. It could be that the auto-enrolment put forward by the Commission's second report would offer a solution. For one is badly needed: occupational pension cover peaked in the UK (at around 50 per cent of the working population) in 1967.[1] The advent of personal pension plans in the mid-1980s failed to gain much ground. Scandals of mis-selling by commercial insurance companies, problems with what Turner calls persistence coupled with a severe downturn in global financial markets in 2001–3 have all damaged both the extension of cover and public confidence in such schemes. As Beveridge noted in 1942, insecure employment or reduced earnings damages the commitment of the poorest to long-term savings and raises the cost of collecting voluntary contributions. Britain has made little progress for over half a century.

This chapter makes a short evaluation of the role occupational (or earnings-related) pension provision has made to policy during this period, contrasting the British experience with other continental European and Scandinavian economies. The following section offers some introductory remarks about the origins of occupational schemes.

[1] L. Hannah, *Inventing Retirement* (Cambridge, 1986), p. 67.

The next examines their influence on policy developments during the decades after 1945. The last draws some conclusions, specifically addressing the issue of pension security and whether past and present policy strategies in Britain have paid it sufficient regard.

Security and the Working Life: The Genesis of Occupational Provision

The earliest pension schemes stemmed from public-sector employment, varying over time in accordance with the nature of the occupation, the state of the labour market, obligations inscribed within work contracts as well as by national context. The point at which advanced age becomes associated with incapacity for work has reflected the law of the land, the nature of previous occupation, levels of skill and adaptability, and personal states of health. Such factors shape the working life, which in turn is influenced by family obligations, changing technologies, the security available when embarking on new projects. Equally, the apparently uniform nature of pensions is illusory: their purposes are highly diverse. Pensions may represent deferred salary (on a socialized or individual basis), the means to secure long and better service from essential employees, a necessary investment in industrial restructuring, a source of venture capital, as well as protection against destitution in old age.

Current occupational schemes have a long history. Through the prism of pension provision, we can read how normative assumptions structured employment in various occupations. The earliest covered the public sector (the civil service, local government, the armed forces, and state-owned industries), taking the form of an annuity or generous lump sum. These were offered at the end of a pre-specified period, or when the recipient reached a predefined age, or (in the case of the military or emergency services) when the serviceman was disabled or killed in action. Their objective was to persuade the skilled, the strong, and the literate to enter state service: a pension offset a more disciplined (or more dangerous) life and lower earnings than might be gained elsewhere. Its eventual receipt signalled termination of the contract, payment of deferred salary, and a withdrawal from state service. Those leaving the armed or emergency services could use their state annuity as an investment in the next stage of their working lives: in retraining, or adapting skills for the private sector, or acquiring a small business. A financial settlement facilitates a transition. It does not necessarily herald retirement, but the means to secure another life; as deferred salary it is guaranteed under the initial employment contract. The French public-sector workers' recent defence of their *droits acquis* (acquired rights), terms associated with property and proprietorship, reflects this perspective. Attempts by French governments to restructure this contract unilaterally provoked public-sector strikes in France in 1953, in the winter of 1995–6, and in the spring of 2003. Rumours that the British government intended to follow suit stimulated similar union hostility in 2004–5. This occupational benefit for state employees has been immensely influential, spreading to colonial dependencies, a legacy still reflected in pension provision in some African and east Asian states.

During the nineteenth century, pension provision spread beyond the public sector. Major firms in industrializing countries developed schemes to reward company servants with a lump sum or an annuity in their declining years. Commonly confined to skilled technical and white-collar staffs, the company pension allowed employers to discipline the insubordinate, reward the diligent, attract (and retain) the skilled, and lay off the incapacitated and incompetent as required. Such schemes were encouraged by the state: tax concessions and other fiscal incentives became commonplace. The company pension was a lure to the independent artisan or journeyman, who otherwise had to save to acquire his own business or property, using quasi or actual rents as a safeguard against old age poverty. Such pensions helped promote fidelity, persuading the young to follow a career with a single firm, by offering a pension as security. Once again, advancing years led to an adjusted working life: personal savings or a formal pension facilitated transitions from one type of income to another. The alternative for blue-collar workers (who were not usually covered) lay in mutuality, but such funds embodied a different logic. They offered protection to contributors faced with the failing health and infirmity associated with advancing years, forcing the reduction or cessation of waged work. Pooling of risk was popular and, in many European countries, traditions of mutual aid played a prominent role in shaping twentieth-century state welfare. However, such funds were highly vulnerable to the impact of trade fluctuation: the preference of employers for the young and fit determined the age at which a worker was deemed 'too old'. (In 1892, men over 40 in the Belfast shipyards who wore spectacles were dismissed as 'infirm'.) So-called 'early retirement', witnessed in Western Europe in the 1980s and 1990s, has long characterized periods of poor trade or industrial restructuring.

None of the systems described above tackled the problems of old age for the very poor, those in insecure jobs on low earnings and unable to contribute to a fund or accrue personal savings, notably women. The advent of state pensions, albeit pensions targeted on poorer workers, established important precedents. The age at which a state pension might first be claimed became increasingly specified; policy began to establish the 'normal' working life. Following the Second World War, the first obligation to retire from the labour market at a pre-specified age became attached to the receipt of a state pension; occupational or professional pensions, widespread in newly expanded state sectors, followed suit. The notion of retirement changed expectations. Now a pension was to guarantee the subsistence of all, once recourse to earned income had disappeared. In the post-war era when welfare states were at their zenith, pensioner poverty re-emerged as a central problem to face governments in many major European economies. In response, politicians in various countries sought to adapt occupational provision to meet the challenge.

Occupation and Security[2]

In Europe, state-funded pensions formed part of a post-1945 settlement characterized by a standardized working week, solid family structures that divided waged (male) employment from unwaged (female) family care, and faith in the efficiency of state welfare. These varied schemes were less an economic than a political product: a compromise reached between industrial, labour, and national economic interests underwritten by collective agreements and social legislation.[3] The agreements reflected specific historical circumstances: an urgent need to rebuild war-shattered economies, to modernize industrial production, to secure democracy, and to establish universal security following the destructive impact of the Slump years and total war. American paradigms, stressing economies of scale and the commercial merits of large, integrated production systems, influenced how modernity was conceived. Post-war labour shortages encouraged firms to develop company pensions to foster worker loyalty, a development equally evident in the professional protection already established in fast-expanding public sectors. This drive to rationalize labour distribution and to secure worker cooperation for an agenda based on a specific vision of the future represented an apogee in state-sponsored

[2] See also N. Whiteside, 'Adapting Private Pensions to Public Purposes: Historical Perspectives on the Politics of Reform', *Journal of European Social Policy*, 16, 1 (2006), 43–54.
[3] N. Whiteside and R. Salais, 'Comparing Welfare States', *Journal of European Social Policy*, 8, 2 (1998), 139–54.

security.[4] As post-war living standards rose, so demand increased for the socially dependent—particularly pensioners—to share in rising prosperity. To protect public expenditure from future growing burdens, some European governments decided to promote earnings-related pensions by turning to the extension of company and occupational schemes to meet rising expectations.

Post-war welfare states have been extensively documented in both historical and social policy literature; less attention has been directed to developments in earnings-related occupational pensions in the 1950s and 1960s. Here, we should note fundamental differences between continental West European and Scandinavian welfare and pension policies and their Anglo-Saxon counterparts. This is reflected in traditions of joint or tripartite decision-making and the government's role in guaranteeing (and extending) basic employment contracts.[5] Continental European labour law enforces norms and collective agreements underpinning employment contracts, as reflected in rights and obligations of employers and employed (including compliance with social security legislation). Formal agreements establish minimum standards: pension schemes created by collective bargaining, as well as those stipulated by social security legislation, are protected by the law. The apparent divide between public and private pension provision is less profound than in Anglo-Saxon countries, where occupational pension schemes may be collectively negotiated, but are still essentially private arrangements. Moreover, European employers' organizations and trade unions administer occupational or enterprise-based systems as well as state welfare: this reflects long-established conventions of co-determination and corporate governance (strong, for example, in Germany, the Netherlands, and Sweden but less so in France). Such differences are rooted in Bismarckian social insurance schemes, revived after the Second World War.

In the 1950s and 1960s, occupational or complementary pension schemes grew rapidly. In an era of skilled labour shortages, employers cultivated the loyalty of key employees, to offset the attractions of pensions available to public-sector workers and to facilitate internal labour management. Professional and company pensions covered white-collar, professional and technical staffs who were hard to replace; blue-collar, unskilled, or temporary personnel, who were more vulnerable to old-age

[4] R. Salais and N. Whiteside (eds), *Governance, Industry and Labour Markets in Britain and France* (London, 1998), pt 3.

[5] L. Gamet, 'Towards a Definition of Flexibility in Labour Law', in B. Strath (ed.), *After Full Employment* (Brussels, 2000).

poverty, tended to be excluded. While fiscal concessions to promote such schemes were extended, variation in state welfare strategies and sponsorship meant that occupational and professional provision was integrated into the wider sphere of economic and social politics in diverse ways. Legally endowed occupational and professional pension rights formed an institutional heritage highly resistant to change. Post-war processes of establishing (and raising) state pensions necessarily affected previous arrangements. In Europe, the legacy of the war (inflation, industrial devastation, and labour market dislocation) fostered the provision of citizenship pensions (exemplified by Sweden and the Netherlands) to prevent the spread of destitution. These two countries, from the start, thus offered basic pension security to women whose needs were generally marginalized by both occupational pensions and Bismarckian schemes where rights relied on contributory records. The contested solidarity embedded in such public schemes extended to occupational pensions, where risk was also pooled and whose governance was, like its public counterpart, vested in representatives of employers and employed.

The 1950s witnessed the emergence of a pension panic; rising longevity combined with growing prosperity was creating poor pensioners unable to share in rising living standards. West European governments in the 1950s and 1960s sought to adapt existing employment-based, earnings-related provision to solve the problem. This strategy had many advantages. Index-linking contributions and benefits could secure pensioner income against inflation. Contribution income could be used for the purposes of industrial investment and modernization. Finally, higher earnings-related pensions (as deferred salary) helped to contain wage demands. Similar strategies, however, were disguised by the very different roles ascribed to the state (as direct provider, legal guarantor, or participatory administrator) in different national contexts. Even as different governments had constructed different institutional arrangements for the purposes of post-war economic reconstruction, so these precedents helped to shape the nature of state participation in pension reform, creating varied remits of public and private responsibility. A brief historical review of pension politics in this period reveals how such spheres of activity were reconstituted: key cases demonstrate how political processes shaped new public/private divisions that subsequently had a marked impact on guarantees of pension security.

In the late 1950s, Germany and Sweden extended state pension provision to include a universal, earnings-related component on all incomes under a specified ceiling. Norway followed the Swedish example in 1966.[6] Following extensive debate, these countries made the state responsible for pension security, linking pensioner income to current earnings and protecting pensioners against inflation. In Germany, the high replacement ratio guaranteed by the new state scheme[7] did not lead to the complete disappearance of company pensions. On the contrary, German firms continued to promote private schemes. Thanks to the 'book reserve' system, German corporate pensions helped to restrain wage demands while creating funds for the company to invest in future expansion. By the early 1990s, two out of three salaried workers were covered by a complementary company scheme.[8] In Sweden, following the introduction of the state-run earnings-related scheme in 1959 (ATP), additional pension protection was collectively negotiated. A new defined-benefit scheme to cover white-collar workers was collectively agreed in 1960 (ITP), with an additional scheme for blue-collar workers created in 1973 (STP). Finally, defined-benefit pensions were established for central (SPN) and local government (KPA) employees.[9] This created a multi-tiered hierarchy of guaranteed pensions, offering high levels of old-age income replacement and reducing the need for personal saving until pensions were restructured in the late 1990s.[10]

In France and the Netherlands, policy also reinforced and extended occupational pensions: while the state was instrumental in establishing new systems, ownership and management remained with the social partners. In the Netherlands, collectively negotiated post-war welfare, replacing earlier state-subsidized voluntary schemes, was presaged on national strategies for recovery, within which wage restraint was agreed in return for universal protection. The 1947 Emergency Act offered a tax-funded pension to all citizens. This was a temporary measure. In the early 1950s, state-sponsored collective agreements created funded occupational pension schemes in pre-specified sectors (1953); universal state insurance, introduced in 1957, was designed to promote (not replace) these schemes.

[6] K. Hinrichs, 'Active Citizens and Retirement Income', Zes–Arbeitspapier 11 (2004); J. Palme, 'Pension Reform in Sweden: The Changing Boundaries Between Public and Private', in G. L. Clark and N. Whiteside (eds), *Pension Security in the 21st Century* (Oxford, 2003), pp. 144–68.

[7] Following the 1957 legislation, pensioner income rose 70%. Hinrichs, 'Active Citizens', p. 17.

[8] E. Reynaud and G. Tamburi, *Les retraites en France: le rôle des régimes complémentaires* (Paris, 1994), ch. 4.

[9] O. Kangas and J. Palme, 'The Development of Occupational Pensions in Finland and Sweden: Class Politics and Institutional Feedbacks', in M. Shalev (ed.), *The Privatisation of Social Policy* (London, 1996), pp. 211–40.

[10] Palme, 'Pension Reform'.

Sectoral pension funds were invested in post-war reconstruction of the Dutch economy and, from the start, their provision was compulsory for all employers.[11] Coverage grew steadily, reaching 60 per cent of Dutch employees in the 1960s and well over 90 per cent in the 1990s.[12] In France, social security fractured along occupational lines from its very inception.[13] The *cadres* (white-collar and technical staffs in the private sector) supplemented the new state regime of social security created in 1946 with their own earnings-related pension scheme (AGIRC).[14] This formed a precedent for other supplementary occupational pensions in the 1950s, to complement pensions under the *régime général* that remained very low. Many firms committed to such schemes were small: intense economic modernization forced some to disappear or merge with other companies. Larger umbrella associations guaranteed pension protection. For example, AGRR, established in 1951, covered 99,800 firms with 780,000 members in sugar, textiles, wood, and furniture twenty years later. The largest, UNIRS, founded in 1957, covered 298,000 firms, was paying 1.9 million complementary pensioners, and had 4.3 million subscribing members by 1971.[15] In 1961, under official prompting, a collective agreement created ARRCO, an association covering all private complementary occupational pensions below specified earnings.[16] By pooling a proportion of contributions, funds in surplus subsidized those in deficit; employers remained free to offer additional pensions if they wished. By the early 1970s, ARRCO covered all private-sector, blue-collar workers in France and its overseas territories.

These examples show that, through collective agreement and legislative obligation, major West European economies consolidated and extended established occupational pensions. The object was to guarantee pension security while promoting labour mobility during the years of post-war economic modernization: collective provision protected acquired pension rights. In Sweden, the Netherlands, and even France (where ARRCO and AGIRC initially established large reserves), accumulating pension contributions, invested largely in government securities,

[11] B. Van Riel, 'Ageing, PAYG and Funding: Dutch Discussion in the Early 1950s on Financing Public Pensions', unpublished paper (2003).

[12] G. L. Clark and P. Bennet, 'Dutch Sector-wide Supplementary Pensions', *Environment and Planning A*, 33, 1 (2001), 27–48.

[13] B. Palier, *Gouverner la sécurité sociale* (Paris, 2002), ch. 2.

[14] H. Lion, 'La convention du 14 mars 1947 et son évolution', *Droit Social*, 7–8 (1962), 396–403.

[15] ARRCO, *Tenth Anniversary Report* (1972), pp. 27–44.

[16] G. Lyon-Caen, 'La co-ordination des régimes complémentaires de retraites', *Droit Social*, 7–8 (1962), 457–63.

were used for state-sponsored modernization, essentially a public equivalent of what the German book reserve system achieved for the private firm. Equally, pension rights were thereby more firmly anchored to employment; women's pensions, with the exception of Sweden where female labour market activity remained comparatively high, were secured by the contributions of their husbands. Collectively speaking, this arrangement formed a foundation for the European social model. Concordance between public and private was not, however, so visible in Anglo-Saxon economies. Debate over pension reform in the UK illustrates a very different political trajectory.[17]

In Britain, pension reform debates also centred on occupational provision—but here political initiatives were widely (and successfully) opposed. Political dimensions of this opposition have been outlined in Hugh Pemberton's contribution to this volume. Here, the focus is on the economic arguments employed largely by the Treasury that has consistently opposed any state guarantee of earnings-related pension provision outside the public sector: an opposition still encountered by supporters of the Turner Commission's proposals. Unlike other continental economies, initiatives to make occupational provision in Britain compulsory have been successfully resisted; at best, the state has performed a residual role. Instead, every effort has been made to promote voluntary private provision, with singularly unimpressive results.

Evidence of continuing pensioner poverty in the midst of growing affluence, rising earnings-related provision in other European states, and the appearance of Labour's plans for pension reform—all stimulated the introduction of a graduated state pension by the Conservative government in 1959. This earnings-related state scheme was, however, misleading: fiscal incentives and additional insurance contribution rebates gave British employers a public subsidy to contract out of state provision by introducing private company schemes. Thus endowed, occupational cover boomed in the 1960s; pension funds came to represent over one-third of private saving in the UK economy, a proportion higher than that found in the USA.[18] Occupational protection also offered a useful means to bypass official wage-restraint policies, as a higher pension represented a deferred wage rise. This trend was well supported by unions in the public sector, where wage restraint was most effectively enforced; these

[17] For a more detailed account of what follows, see N. Whiteside, 'Historical Perspectives and Pension Reform', in Clark and Whiteside, *Pension Security*, pp. 21–44.

[18] Hannah, *Inventing Retirement*, pp. 48–51.

unions therefore looked askance at plans to universalize occupational cover that would negate hard-won gains for their members. The Labour government in 1964 promised to create a National Superannuation Scheme, to operate on a funded basis, managed by independent trustees, to guarantee an income at 50 per cent of previous earnings. The fund so created would allow government, as in Sweden, to influence investments in the public interest—a powerful tool for national planning.

The scheme provoked opposition from the union movement, from employers, and from the financial services sector. It was also found in Whitehall. One Treasury official condemned the plan as 'nationalization by the back door':[19] a condemnation echoed verbatim by a major fund management activist in recent criticism of Lord Turner's National Pensions Savings Scheme (NPSS).[20] In the 1960s, Treasury antagonism proved fatal. Labour's scheme threatened monetary stability, private-sector investment, and the public finances, officials claimed. Higher contributions (and consumption among the elderly) would prove inflationary and would endanger exports and the balance of payments, thereby damaging international confidence in sterling. Further, the investment of (very substantial) fund balances would prove destabilizing. If placed in equities, this would inflate market prices, forcing up interest rates on gilt-edged and thus the cost of government borrowing for other public modernization programmes.[21] Allowing a state scheme to invest balances in equities would set a precedent for other departments who would demand similar privileges. 'If the government is going to join the rush to get out of gilt-edged', one mandarin noted dryly, ' it is difficult to see who can be expected to stay in'.[22] Conversely, if vested in government securities, the new pension obligations would eventually become just another burden on the public accounts, while simultaneously damaging London's capital markets and internal investment in UK industry. In addition, the Treasury, as head of the civil service, was very well informed about the implications of the new scheme for established public-sector pensions. Here, 500 different administrations covered 1,500 employing

[19] See discussion by the Treasury Economic Section, on file T 227/2223–4: National Archive, Kew (NA).

[20] 'State Pension Fund Could Allow Back-door Nationalisation', *The Guardian*, 6 February 2006, 28. The quote was from Peter Butler, chief executive of Governance for Owners and founder of the Focus funds at Hermes Fund Management.

[21] The Labour administration was planning a programme of new motorways, universities, and industrial restructuring at this time.

[22] Baird, Treasury memo: National Insurance Review Committee, 'National Pensions Fund', 14 Feb. 1966, on file EW 25/219, NA.

authorities and schemes—all embodying different retirement ages, contributory obligations, funding arrangements, and pension rights that varied according to job status, gender, and years of service. The complications induced by the 1959 Act made the possible advent of further legislative intervention infinitely resistible.[23]

Thus public financial interest aligned with its private counterparts to provoke extensive delays. No measures for a national scheme of superannuation reached the statute book during the 1964–70 Labour governments. When a State Earnings-related Pension Scheme (SERPS) was eventually introduced in 1976, it performed a residual role. The primacy of contracting out for employer-based schemes was retained. To guarantee equity and to protect all occupational pensioners from the threat of inflation, the new public scheme offered earnings-related pension cover to those with none and underwrote the 60,000 private schemes in a manner not witnessed anywhere else in Europe. The result in the inflationary years of the late 1970s was enormous administrative complexity and much higher public liability. During the Conservative governments under Margaret Thatcher (1979–90), the strategy was abandoned. In 1986, substantial public subsidies were again used to persuade individuals to contract out of SERPS by buying a personal pension plan sold by the insurance companies. Subsequent scandals provoked by mis-selling of private policies and the mismanagement or misappropriation of funds have provoked more extensive state regulation of UK financial services and occupational pensions, but no return to a state-run scheme. In Britain, the priority of monetary policy objectives has been absolute. Looking at official archival sources, it is hard to find any reference to pensioners themselves at all.

* * *

These limited historical narratives demonstrate how a similar strategy (the promotion of earnings-related occupational pensions) was understood as a potential solution to common problems (pensioner poverty, funding for inward investment, wage restraint) in widely differing combinations of private responsibility and public regulation or provision. From the roots of a common strategy emerges a history of divergent policy trajectories, as political contingency combined with social necessity to generate multiple public–private distributions of responsibility for

[23] Ministry of Housing and Local Government to Government Actuary, Apr. 1966, on file ACT 1/1554, NA; also G. Rhodes, *Public Sector Pensions* (London, 1966), ch. 6.

old-age security. Varied pathways were taken towards a common goal. Different states intervened at different points to promote a common objective. Clear distinctions between Pillars 1 and 2 under the World Bank classification[24] become hard to sustain and identifying public and private spheres of responsibility is rendered problematic. Both Dutch and French occupational systems, for example, were established by legislative enactment, but were regarded as essentially private arrangements—not least by those administering the funds. In both cases, management was vested with a legal responsibility for balancing the books: as and when resources fail to meet demand, so contributions and benefits have to be recalculated.[25] Faced with crisis, pooled systems such as these examples from continental West Europe renegotiate their terms and all share equally in the pain involved. In Britain, by contrast, insecurity and hence uncertainty are much more marked: the closure (or, worse, failure) of the company pension scheme is an occupational hazard against which state regulation still offers minimal protection. For decades governments of varied political complexions have tried to promote pension security through the medium of occupational or personal schemes: yet numbers of workers today with no or inadequate pension protection remain about the same as they were in the late 1960s. Surely it is time to conclude that this policy has failed.

Conclusions

With its greater emphasis on auto-registration, does the Turner Report offer the opportunity to break out of our current dilemmas? In some respects at least, the answer is in the affirmative: under the Commission's recommendations, employers are compelled to offer a minimal contribution towards the provision of a supplementary pension for their workers. The higher state pension offers a foundation on which supplementary personal provision can build: tax incentives are simplified and are rendered more transparent. The advanced role for the state brings the UK more into line with other EU member states, possibly a response to the European Commission's adaptation of the Open Method of Coordination to the comparative provision of pension benefits. All these improvements are very welcome and are desperately needed if a basic minimum pension

[24] World Bank, *Averting the Old Age Crisis: Policies to Protect the Old and Promote Growth* (Oxford, 1994).

[25] ARRCO was obliged to reform its pension scheme in 1993: raising contributions and reducing benefit rights.

is to be assured that does not rely on expensive means tests and to encourage further saving. Even so, we should note that Turner's objective—a combined pension of 45 per cent of median earnings—remains well below continental European pension schemes. Even after recent cutbacks, these still offer pensions in excess of 60 per cent.

However, the Commission's report does not offer a way out of a very British pension feature that invites future problems. In spite of the recent spate of closures and collapses—and in spite of evidence that more are on the cards[26]—the company pension retains its privileged position. Contracting-out survives intact with its customary public subsidies. The problems of company pensions are not confined to their tendency to fail in times of crisis. Their rise to prominence reflected an era of Chandleresque corporate structures embodying values of scale and scope in business enterprise, encouraging those with talent and skill to dedicate their working lives to a single profession, even a single firm. Equally it assumes the stability of family forms that rising divorce rates currently belie. However, life is changing. From the European Commission to the Blair government, we are all required to raise our employability: to train in new skills, to engage in entrepreneurship, and (above all) to be flexible in employment. Future patterns will not entail one job in one firm, but will require individuals to combine multiple types of job—as employees, subcontractors, or independent workers—in the course of their working lives. This is even more true of women who still have somehow to incorporate waged employment into obligations to supply family care.[27] As far back as 1962, French critics pointed out that British company pensions prevented labour mobility, penalized those who changed jobs, while creating horrendous administrative complexities as workers transferred from public to private sector, from contracted-out to non-contracted-out work.[28] With the NPSS designed to add only 15 per cent to individual pension rights, why could not the new proposed scheme be capped at that level and be made universal and compulsory (leaving companies and individuals free to top up the basic 45 per cent that Turner recommends)?

Through the analysis of policy logics and their location within different collective values, this chapter has revealed some of the unwritten (and unspoken) assumptions that guided occupational pension development in different countries. The UK's preoccupation with the value of sterling and the profile of the public accounts, over all considerations of equity or

[26] See, in particular, Gordon Clark's contribution to this volume.

[27] See the contributions of Thane, Ginn, and Hollis in this volume.

[28] J. Doublet, 'Les régimes complémentaires a l'étranger', *Droit Social*, 7–8 (1962), 464–73.

pensioner security, is striking, making even French Gaullist dirigisme appear as almost a model of democratic probity. The reasons for the significance of public finance in British social policy are largely embedded in Britain's imperial past: in the legacy of protecting sterling as a major global trading currency and the role played by the Treasury as guardian of that legacy. In contrast, in continental Europe, politicians and public alike understood occupational pensions less as a potential problem for the public accounts and more as the rightful property of employers and employed. Here government is endowed with a duty to secure such schemes, to guarantee social justice and equity—either by direct involvement (as in Sweden) or by legislation guaranteeing their proper governance (as in France and the Netherlands). The finance ministries play a less prominent role: while recent pension restructuring has provoked extensive protest and debate, none of the countries described here is facing the acute pension crisis currently confronting British politicians. It would be very refreshing if current UK debates were less dedicated to issues of pension finance and more open to questions of pension governance, for—by guaranteeing social justice—public confidence can be restored and trust regained. In this regard, the Turner Commission has taken a step towards creating simplicity and transparency, but there is still a very long way to go.

Bibliography

Items that provide a useful introduction to the issues discussed in this chapter are marked with an asterisk.

ARRCO, *Tenth Anniversary Report* (1972).

*Blackburn, R., *Banking on Death* (London, 2002).

*Bonoli, G., *The Politics of Pension Reform: Institutions and Policy Change in Western Europe* (Cambridge, 2000).

Clark, G. L. and P. Bennet, 'Dutch Sector-wide Supplementary Pensions', *Environment and Planning A*, 33, 1 (2001), 27–48.

*Clark, G. L. and N. Whiteside (eds), *Pension Security in the 21st Century* (Oxford, 2003).

Doublet, J., 'Les régimes complémentaires a l'étranger', *Droit Social*, 7–8 (1962), 464–73.

*Fiedler, M., 'La "rationalisation sociale" de l'entreprise', in MIRE Rencontres et Recherches, *Comparer les systèmes de protection sociale en Europe, vol. 2 Rencontres de Berlin* (Paris, 1996), pp. 87–115.

Gamet, L., 'Towards a Definition of Flexibility in Labour Law', in B. Strath (ed.), *After Full Employment* (Brussels, 2000).

*Hannah, L., *Inventing Retirement* (Cambridge, 1986).

*Haverland, M., 'Another Dutch Miracle? Explaining Dutch and German Pension Trajectories', *Journal of European Social Policy*, 11, 4 (2001), 308–23.

Hinrichs, H., 'Active Citizens and Retirement Income', Zes–Arbeitspapier 11 (2004).

*Kangas, O. and J. Palme, 'The Development of Occupational Pensions in Finland and Sweden: Class Politics and Institutional Feedbacks', in M. Shalev (ed.), *The Privatisation of Social Policy* (London, 1996), pp. 211–40.

Lion, H., 'La convention du 14 mars 1947 et son évolution', *Droit Social*, 7–8 (1962), 396–403.

Lyon-Caen, L., 'La co-ordination des régimes complémentaires de retraites', *Droit Social*, 7–8 (1962), 457–63.

Palier, B., *Gouverner la sécurité sociale* (Paris, 2002).

*Reynaud, E., *Réforme des retraites et concertation sociale* (Geneva, 1999).

Reynaud, E. and G. Tamburi, *Les retraites en France: le rôle des régimes complémentaires* (Paris, 1994).

Rhodes, G., *Public Sector Pensions* (London, 1966).

Salais, R. and N. Whiteside (eds), *Governance, Industry and Labour Markets in Britain and France* (London, 1998), pt 3.

Van Riel, B., 'Ageing, PAYG and Funding: Dutch Discussion in the Early 1950s on Financing Public Pensions', unpublished paper (2003).

*Whiteside, N., 'Security and the Working Life', in R. Salais and R. Villeneuve (eds), *Europe and the Politics of Capability* (Cambridge, 2002), pp. 325–43.

*——, 'Comparing Welfare States: Conventions, Institutions and Political Frameworks of Pension Reform', in J.-C. Barbier and M.-T. Letablier (eds), *Politiques sociales: enjeux épistémologiques et méthodologiques* (Brussels, 2005), pp. 211–29.

*——, 'Adapting Private Pensions to Public Purposes: Historical Perspectives on the Politics of Reform', *Journal of European Social Policy*, 16, 1 (2006), 43–54.

—— and R. Salais, 'Comparing Welfare States', *Journal of European Social Policy*, 8, 2 (1998), 139–54.

World Bank, *Averting the Old Age Crisis: Policies to Protect the Old and Promote Growth* (Oxford, 1994).

9.
Why Has It All Gone Wrong? The Past, Present, and Future of British Pensions

FRANK FIELD, MP

The contribution of the British Academy in promoting this volume documenting the pension debate is immensely important. Big public policy issues need a forum in which people are free to speak the truth as they see it without necessarily feeling that their future research grants might be affected. The fact that we have a large number of research bodies is an undoubted strength of the British political system. However, some of these organizations make their observations with one eye on how their patrons might review their next grant application.

This is not to argue that the political masters will get nasty and actually cancel grants. The pressure in our sophisticated model is much more subtle. Just as Mr Murdoch is unlikely to be in daily contact with his editors influencing the details of his papers' content, those editors nevertheless know what his views are and adapt their messages accordingly. Some research bodies view their government paymasters in the same way. Their stance reminds me of that famous quip at the expense of Arthur Balfour who, as prime minister, on the question of tariff reform, was accused of yet again nailing his colours to the fence. I am sure no contributor to this present volume has felt it necessary to nail their views to the fence.

Another reason for supporting the Academy's initiative stems from the emphasis placed on historical perspectives and the involvement of important academic social policy historians in developing our understanding of the past, thus helping us to understand why discussion of reform of pensions in the UK is so necessary today. The contribution of Patricia Hollis adds an additional historian of note who has changed the debate on the political role of women in the nineteenth century. I shall draw on their collective work while emphasizing the importance of political tradition in devising sustainable political strategies. It is not that difficult to come up with political reforms. The challenge lies in ensuring they will last. And one of the keys to their durability is whether or not they are tailored to a country's political tradition.

I would like to make three comments to guide the debate. First, I want to signal what I see as the political framework within which the debate about retirement income is conducted. I suggest that in this country we are both the willing inheritors but also the unconscious captives of one of the most important political strategies advanced by Sidney and Beatrice Webb. In their great study of trade unions they looked at how the skilled trade unions had advanced the interests of their own members' welfare. They then pondered whether the unions which were then beginning to be formed to represent the semi-skilled and unskilled workers could equal the achievements of skilled workers. They concluded that such an outcome was unlikely and that the role of the state should be to universalize the achievements free collective bargaining had secured for the skilled working class. In this way, semi-skilled and unskilled workers would benefit from the fruits of economic growth in equal measure. The British debate about pensions still sits within this framework. The assumption set long ago, and since all too easily forgotten, has been how can the best occupational pension schemes be universalized?

It is here that I think Noel Whiteside's presentation is particularly useful and interesting. Richard Titmuss led the debate down a cul-de-sac in thinking that governments could somehow devise strategies to universalize through a state-run scheme the very best occupational pension provisions then on offer. We have only to read the final report of the Pensions Commission to realize how this tradition endures.[1] You may remember that he was posing the question whether it would be possible to recreate a funded SERPs-type arrangement. In even posing this question I believe the Pensions Commission is misreading the politics of pension reform.

I tried to use the lessons of this national minimum strategy, but taking into account today's political realities, when drawing up a pensions reform programme. The Pensions Reform Group (PRG)[2] advocates a new basic universal pension which guarantees an income in retirement above means-testing. This is to be achieved by keeping the current pay-as-you-go state pension and building alongside it a funded scheme so that in total a pension between 25 to 30 per cent of average earnings can be paid. This is a collective scheme but is not one run by the state as is today's national insurance retirement pension. The governance of the new scheme is to be housed at the Bank of England. To underline its independent governance,

[1] See www.pensionscommission.org.uk/publications/2006/final-report/final_report.pdf.

[2] See Pensions Reform Group website, www.pensionsreformgroup.org.

the scheme is to be run along the lines of the Monetary Policy Committee. (This welfare reform should therefore also be seen as part of the reform of the constitution by re-establishing civil institutions undertaking national tasks.) But pensions are too big an issue for the government not to be involved. The government will therefore have the right to nominate governors for up to fifteen-year periods but only after Parliament has approved their appointment. The governors will have fiduciary conditions attached to their appointment and it will be for the governors to appoint trustees that have then to be approved by the membership of the entire scheme. Much of the fund management of the scheme will be farmed out under competition to private-sector fund managers.

My second comment is to invite you to stand back and see pensions reform as part of a much wider debate which is influencing not only this country but much of Europe as well. Pensions reform is part of the politics of renegotiating the post-war settlement. There are, I believe, very serious dangers in believing that these renegotiations are taking a uniform pattern. They are not. Voters clearly attach different degrees of importance to different parts of the post-war settlement depending on the circumstances of the country in which the settlement was struck. It would be amazing if, in Germany, which experienced the impact of hyperinflation on savings during the Weimar Republic, the same importance was attached to funding pensions as it is in this country. In France and Germany the most lasting aspect of the post-war settlement has been the active belief that a tax contract between generations can be struck and held to finance pensions. It is much more doubtful that British voters hold a similar view. For our political arrangements, the ownership of capital gives a better claim on future national income than does a statement by today's taxpayers that future taxpayers, some of whom are not yet born, will honour current tax-financed commitments.

A very different picture emerges if we then look at the role health has played in the post-war settlement. In both France and Germany any questioning of the pensions settlement is likely to result in mass demonstrations. However, in both countries the most sane debate can take place over whether health care is best provided by the public or private sector. The reverse is true in this country. The most major changes can occur in state pension provision with little or no political backlash whatsoever. The NHS is, however, sacrosanct and any tinkering with it must be largely invisible to the general public. Political realism led Mrs Thatcher to embark on health reform reluctantly and only then because of the growing financial crisis within the NHS. How well the present Labour government would have fared on this issue if it was not facing a broken-backed opposition is open to speculation. Whether the government would have survived without such large majorities as it began seriously to renegotiate the post-war settlement on health is perhaps a question for another day.

A final comment: while reforming pensions is part of the broader renegotiation of the post-war settlement it is also a debate about renegotiating what we mean by the term 'government'. Most commentators seem to assume that state and government are interchangeable. I do not. Today's debate is about a renegotiation on what we mean by the term 'collective action'. Jose Harris has suggested elsewhere that if we were standing as observers in 1900 and asked to prophesy the kind of welfare provision which would dominate Britain fifty years hence most of us would have prophesied wrongly.[3] As Britain moved into the twentieth century few countries had a more decentralized method of delivering welfare; few had one which relied on greater personal, face-to-face contact; and few countries had a welfare system where charity, let alone mutual aid, redistributed more resources than did the state-initiated Poor Law.

There are a number of reasons why this most decentralized form of welfare provision evolved fifty years later into one of the western world's most centrally directed of operations. Jose Harris herself has emphasized the collapse of the Idealistic tradition which provided Britain with a public ideology. Martin Daunton has emphasized the role a buoyant income tax base played in enabling governments to centralize much of the welfare provision.[4] That centralizing process came to a full stop when the Thatcher governments began responding to voters' disquiet on direct tax levels. Since then, Britain has been floundering around trying to agree a redefinition of what collective provision is without properly realizing that that is the debate in which the country is involved.

In reforming pensions the Pensions Reform Group which I chair has been a market leader in this particular debate. The Group sees the need to ensure an adequate universal minimum pension but is adamant that this is not an attempt to reinvent 1945 statism. Prior to the election of the Attlee government commentators would have easily understood that there were many ways of achieving collective provision which had nothing whatsoever to do with state provision. In proposing a pension reform which combines the current pay-as-you-go basic state pension with a new funded pension, the PRG proposes establishing a form of

[3] Jose Harris, 'Political Thought and the Welfare State 1870 to 1914: An Intellectual Framework of British Social Policy', *Past and Present*, May (1992).
[4] Martin Daunton, 'Payment and Participation: Welfare and State Formation in Britain 1900–1951', *Past and Present*, February (1996).

governance which is at arm's length from Westminster and Whitehall. Serious pension reform is far too big an issue for governments not to be interested in the outcome. That interest is accepted but balanced by the form of governance the PRG is proposing. Governors would be appointed by the government, but for periods of up to fifteen years. Their appointments would require ratification by the House of Commons and governors would have fiduciary commitments tied to their appointment. This governance model builds on that already in operation for the Monetary Policy Committee at the Bank of England. Indeed the governance of the new pension scheme would be similarly housed with the governor of the Bank chairing trustee meetings. This form of governance would have been easily understood by most participants before 1945. One consequence of the Attlee government reform was to give a one-dimensional definition to what collective provision entails. That single model of collective provision was itself the product of middle- and working-class taxpayers having a common interest in allowing taxes to rise to finance a nationalized-type welfare. Voters and taxpayers are less trusting of central government with their money. Hence the attempt to renegotiate part of the post-war settlement on pensions which similarly renegotiates what has for the last fifty years been thought of as collective provision.

Bibliography

Daunton, M. J., 'Payment and Participation: Welfare and State Formation in Britain 1900–1951', *Past and Present*, February (1996).

Harris, J. 'Political Thought and the Welfare State 1870 to 1914: An Intellectual Framework of British Social Policy', *Past and Present*, May (1992).

Pensions Reform Group website, www.pensionsreformgroup.org.

10.
The UK Occupational Pension System in Crisis

GORDON L. CLARK

Introduction

During the mid-1990s, the British political establishment congratulated itself on the robustness and integrity of the United Kingdom (UK) pension system. At the time, debates over the probable costs and benefits of a European single currency identified the prospective, unfunded liabilities of continental European pension schemes as an important reason for not entering the Euro. By contrast, UK pension liabilities were believed to be much less significant through to 2050 due to modest state benefits and the significance of funded occupational pensions.[1] So much for the story told in the 1990s. A decade later, as the Pensions Commission (Turner Report) demonstrates, few commentators are so confident about the prospects for UK pension and retirement income.[2] UK coverage rates are much lower than anticipated, private defined-benefit (DB) or final-salary plans are facing extinction, and the provision of other types of pension plans such as defined-contribution schemes have not made up the difference (as in the USA and Australia).

However, the problems in UK occupational pensions extend beyond coverage rates and benefit levels. Private-sector sponsors of existing defined-benefit plans face an uncertain future notwithstanding the establishment in 2005 of the Pension Protection Fund (PPF). As for the public sector, the unfunded status of many defined-benefit plans raises significant doubts about their long-term viability. There are efficiency and equity issues to be considered when evaluating the prospects of UK occupation pensions. Whatever happens to the Turner Report, the UK pension

[1] G. L. Clark, *European Pensions and Global Finance* (Oxford, 2003).

[2] Pensions Commission, *A New Pension Settlement for the Twenty-first Century* (London, 2005).

crisis has just begun; it is bound to dominate domestic politics for another generation.

As calibration of the future costs of employer-sponsored pension benefits has become a recognized industry here and abroad, and as the actuarial profession has become more attuned to the market price of those future benefits, financial markets have become wise to the previously hidden costs of defined-benefit pensions.[3] As well, the modern corporation has undergone profound long-term changes: occupational pension schemes are much less significant for human resource management programmes. What remains unclear is why, in the UK private sector, the decline in defined-benefit plans was not matched by early growth of coverage in defined-contribution or hybrid plans as in the USA.[4] And yet, defined-benefit pension plans are not about to evaporate overnight: for many of the FTSE100 firms, the scale of pension obligations is likely to constrain corporate strategy and the market for corporate control. There remain significant efficiency costs for UK society in sustaining private-sector defined-benefit pension obligations just as there are likely to be significant equity costs with unfunded public-sector pension plans.

The Turner Report rightly recognizes the retreat of private plan sponsors from the institution. But is the solution to be found in a national savings system designed to mimic the features of a quasi-compulsory private, multi-employer pension scheme? The average value of supplementary pension benefits is unlikely to be significant and may create considerable inequality of benefits. The scale of such an institution is daunting, and reference to the experience of small countries such as New Zealand and Sweden simply amplifies their differences with the UK. Most importantly, the Turner Report promotes an institutional arrangement that will last a century but which lacks the capacity to change form and innovate in the light of changing national, European, and global financial circumstances. Turner has found a way back to social democracy rather than promoting innovation in the private sector.

[3] A number of large investment and advisory companies have made calibration of DB obligations an important part of their business—see, for example, the websites of Credit Suisse, Bear Stearns, and Standard & Poors. Recent estimates of the funding shortfall of UK private pension benefits by Mercer Human Resource Consulting, *FTSE350—Pensions Scheme Deficits and Trends*, 5 January 2006 (London, 2006) puts the cost at £93 billion. Many similar estimates reflect revised estimates for longevity, the equity premium, and the rate of interest if pension benefits were to be capitalized (among other issues).

[4] A. Munnell, 'Employer-sponsored Plans: The Shift from Defined Benefit and Defined Contribution Plans', in G. L. Clark, A. Munnell, and M. Orszag (eds), *The Oxford Handbook of Pensions and Retirement Income* (Oxford, 2006), pp. 359–80.

Pensions and Modern Capitalism

In various forms, occupational pensions have been with us for centuries. The provision of old-age and invalid pensions has been motivated by various considerations including gratitude, a paternal concern for welfare, and the orderly transfer of long-serving employees from work to non-work dependency.[5] Of course, relatively few 'loyal servants' survived through to what we now count as retirement age. Retirement as we understand the term was rare; early national pension systems relied on this fact of life when estimating likely obligations.[6] Over the nineteenth century, public and private institutions began to establish formal administrative procedures designed to manage the assessment of pension claims and the allocation of benefits of certain value and duration. By the early twentieth century, some of Britain's largest employers, including railways and manufacturing companies, had established pension systems based upon the inherited common-law trust institution.[7]

The rapid growth of pension coverage in the public and private sectors in the years following the Second World War can be explained in a variety of ways.[8] A set of interrelated forces together raised coverage rates to just about 50 per cent of working people by 1970. Reconstruction of industry following wartime destruction precipitated its greater concentration, in some cases, nationalization, and the formation of near-monopoly public corporations. The scale of these institutions encouraged the management of internal labour resources as a profession in its own right; the principles of scientific management covered all forms of compensation including pensions. Pension benefits were conceived as deferred wages being included in negotiated wages and salaries by class of employee and were therefore less subject to the whims of employers. Competition for labour resources was such that attracting and retaining labour through defined-benefit pensions was believed to be consistent with the interests of firms.[9]

[5] P. Thane, 'The History of Retirement', in Clark, Munnell, and Orszag, *Oxford Handbook*, pp. 33–51.

[6] A deliberate policy consideration of the UK Treasury when considering the costs of various pension reforms discussed at the turn of the 20th century (see Clark, Munnell, and Orszag, 'Pension and Retirement Income in a Global Perspective', in Clark, Munnell, and Orszag, *Oxford Handbook*, on Treasury estimates of the likely costs of the 1908 Old Age Pension).

[7] G. L. Clark, *Pension Fund Capitalism* (Oxford, 2000).

[8] G. L. Clark, 'Re-writing Pension Fund Capitalism 1', Working Paper in Employment, Work and Finance, WPG05–08 (Oxford, 2005).

[9] A. Shonfield, *Modern Capitalism: The Changing Balance of Public and Private Power* (Oxford, 1965); J. K. Galbraith, *The New Industrial State*, 2nd edn (London, 1967).

Pension benefits became a standard part of compensation packages, and were diffused from large employers to small employers via the competition for labour. Of significance for the structure and performance of UK securities markets, the forward-funding of pension benefits became established practice and was then codified in statute, contributing to the growth of a vast reservoir of assets that changed the economic structure of the Anglo-American world.[10] With the stability and growth of large employers over several decades, pension funds evolved from immaturity, to maturity and beyond, relying upon the expertise available in the City of London. If established as beneficial institutions, the speculative bubble of the 1990s transformed pension funds into important financial institutions in their own right in the Anglo-American world.[11]

The recent history of UK occupational pensions is shown in Table 10.1. The growth in private-sector pension coverage from 1953 until about 1970 was dramatic, peaking at about 48 per cent of all private-sector employment. By contrast, public-sector occupational pension plan coverage, already significant in 1953, continued to grow albeit relatively slowly to about 90 per cent in 2002. When considered in the light of trade union membership in the United Kingdom, the growth of private pension coverage until 1970 was correlated with the rise and fall of private-sector trade union membership (compare Table 10.1 with Figure 10.1). Behind the correlation, however, lies the decline of manufacturing industries and firms with heavy union representation (and pension plan coverage) and the rise of industries and firms with low rates of unionization (and pension plan coverage).[12]

If work and pensions have been transformed in the private sector, the growth of public-sector employment and the equitable expansion of pension benefits within that sector have sustained overall rates of pension

[10] Clark, *Pension Fund Capitalism*; M. J. Clowes, *The Money Flood: How Pension Funds Revolutionized Investing* (New York, 2000); J. P. Hawley and A. T. Williams, *The Rise of Fiduciary Capitalism: How Institutional Investors Can Make Corporate America More Democratic* (Philadelphia PA, 2000).

[11] G. L. Clark and T. Hebb, 'Pension Fund Corporate Engagement: The Fifth Stage of Capitalism', *Relations Industrielle/Industrial Relations*, 59 (2004), 142–71.

[12] This transformation remains highly contested and its long-term significance disputed: see A. Booth, *The British Economy in the Twentieth Century* (Basingstoke, 2001). As a political issue, it is embedded in inter-regional rivalries (north and south) and is apparent in the tensions within the governing Labour Party. Notwithstanding claims made on behalf of social solidarity in a stakeholder society, it is not obvious that these ideals have the same status in the UK as in continental Europe: compare W. Hutton, *The State We're In* (London, 1995) with D. van Reil, J. De Deken, and E. Ponds, 'Social Solidarity', in Clark, Munnell, and Orszag, *The Oxford Handbook*, pp. 141–60.

Table 10.1. UK occupational pension plans, private and public sectors, 1953–2000.

	Private sector (in millions)		Public sector (in millions)		Total members (in millions)	Total employed (in millions)	Coverage rate (%)		
	Total members	Total employed	Total members	Total employed	Private + public	Private + public	Private sector	Public sector	Total
1953	3.1	16.3	3.1	5.6	6.2	21.9	19.1	54.9	28.3
1956	4.3	16.9	3.7	5.8	8.0	22.7	25.5	63.3	35.2
1963	7.2	17.0	3.9	5.9	11.1	22.9	42.4	66.1	48.5
1967	8.1	16.9	4.2	6.9	12.3	23.2	47.9	60.9	53.0
1971	6.8	15.8	4.3	6.7	11.1	22.5	43.0	64.2	49.3
1975	6	15.8	5.4	7.2	11.4	23.1	38.0	75.0	49.4
1979	6.1	15.7	5.5	7.4	11.6	23.4	38.9	74.3	49.6
1983	5.8	14.3	5.3	6.8	11.1	21.1	40.6	77.9	52.6
1987	5.8	15.2	4.8	6.4	10.6	21.6	38.2	75.0	49.1
1991	n.a.	n.a.	n.a.	5.8	n.a.	n.a.	n.a.	n.a.	n.a.
1995	n.a.	n.a.	n.a.	5.2	n.a.	n.a.	n.a.	n.a.	n.a.
2000	5.7	15.0	4.5	5.1	10.2	20.1	38.0	88.2	50.7

Sources: Data of total employed in public sector in the years 1963, 1991, 1995, and 2000, and data of total employed in both private and public sectors in the years 1953 and 1956 from the Office for National Statistics, UK; all other data from the Occupational Pension Schemes Surveys, published by the Government Actuary's Department, London, in various years.

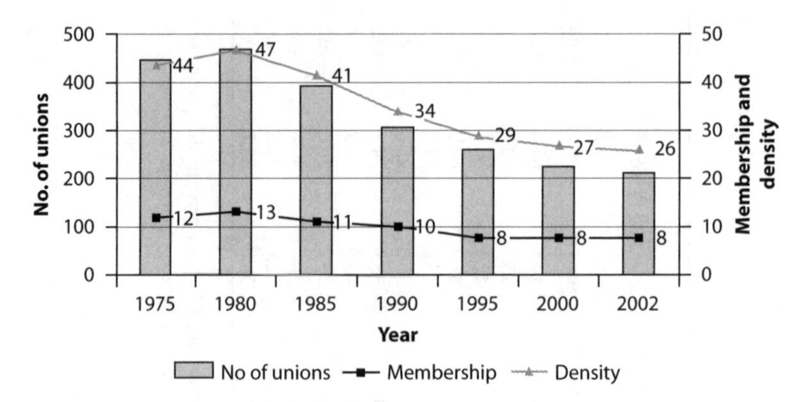

Figure 10.1. Trade union numbers, membership (in millions) and density* (in %) for the United Kingdom, 1975–2002.

* Union density is defined as the ratio of the number of union memberships to the number of total employment; LH (in columns) shows the number of unions, while the RH (in lines) shows the memberships (in millions) and density (in %).

Sources: Data of total union memberships and number of unions from the Annual Report of the Certification Officer, published by the Department of Trade and Industry, London, in various years; data of total employment from the Office for National Statistics in various years.

plan coverage particularly among women.[13] These trends carry significant implications for understanding current circumstances and future prospects.

Corporate Capitalism in a Global Environment

Reading commentaries on post-war capitalism, the contemporary belief that capitalism had found a settled form of organization and production that would last a century is striking.[14] The form of capitalism inherited from the post-war era has now evidently become the object of corporate and industrial restructuring. In play in the market for corporate control are the managerial systems such as defined-benefit pensions that played important roles in buying industrial peace in the years following the Second World War. The corporation is neither a constant nor is it necessarily homogeneous. The challenge is to design a private pension system that is neutral in relation to the evolution of the changing forms and func-

[13] D. Hill, C. Davis, and L. M. Tigges, 'Gendering Welfare State Theory: A Cross-national Study of Women's Public Pension Quality', *Gender and Society*, 9 (1995), 99–119.
[14] O. E. Williamson, *The Economic Institutions of Capitalism* (New York, 1991).

tions of the corporation.[15] To illustrate, consider four corporate 'models' and their implications for the nature and value of pension benefits.[16]

Firm A is a large market-leading corporation that has been around for many years having dominated its home market before spreading its wings to the rest of the world. Firm A was known as a progressive firm; it provided its employees with defined-benefit pensions whatever their tasks or functions. But now, let us introduce three points of contention. With the rise of the market for corporate control, senior managers are encouraged to take up stock-options as part of their compensation packages. The management of brand-name products moves from the corporation's traditional home in provincial Britain to London and New York and into very different labour markets for talent. New production technologies radically increase productivity while decreasing the demand for skilled labour.[17] Social solidarity between workers is fractured by the changing demand for labour, volatility in the supply of labour, and consequently changed forms of compensation.

Having fostered a well funded defined-benefit pension system, Firm A introduces early-retirement pensions to encourage home-based managers and employees to retire. This strategy has three effects. First, the internal 'market' for defined-benefit pension benefits shrinks as home-based tasks and functions are rationalized. Second, the industry 'market' for defined-benefit pensions shrinks as tasks and functions move to external service providers in other labour markets characterized by higher turnover and defined-contribution, personal pensions, or no plans at all. Third, the national 'market' for DB schemes shrinks as other forms of compensation become more attractive particularly for managers who no longer expect to remain with the firm or industry for their careers. Within a decade, the ratio of active to deferred and retired plan participants dramatically declines with an emerging funding problem compounded by lower-than-expected investment returns in the aftermath of the bubble in the

[15] L. Zingales, 'In Search of New Foundations', *Journal of Finance*, 55 (2000), 1623–53.

[16] Clark, 'Re-writing Pension Fund Capitalism'.

[17] The significance of the geography of industrial structure for the concentration of defined benefits in the UK, and the increasing separation between company sites of production and the executive and financial control of UK firms (north and south), has been noted. These trends resonate with observations made by reformers in the late 19th century that, with increasing geographical separation between where workers lived and worked, the paternal commitment of employers for workers' welfare was discounted. R. L. Martin and R. Minns, 'Undermining the Financial Bases of Regions: The Spatial Structure and Implications of the UK Pension Fund System', *Regional Studies*, 29 (1995), 125–44.

global securities markets and actuarial revisions to the expected longevity of beneficiaries.[18]

Firm B, in contrast, produces its products by contract, relying upon an extensive network of suppliers governed according to specific performance criteria.[19] Given the premium on quality and lower costs, Firm B's suppliers face a trade-off between capital investment and labour's wages and benefits. This is resolved, in almost all cases, in favour of the former: suppliers seek sites of production which are relatively cheap with little in the way of long-term commitments to wages or pensions. To the extent that suppliers offer pension benefits, most offer defined-contribution benefits based upon employee contributions alone. Likewise, Firm B employs part-time workers; many are women and have little commitment to the firm. Few of Firm B's employees are eligible for the company's available defined-contribution pension systems. Perhaps paradoxically, at the most senior level, managers participate in incentive-based compensation schemes that include highly lucrative defined-benefit pensions.[20]

Imagine that a new Firm C enters the market. Assume this company was formed to take advantage of the gap in the market between firms A and B as neither is focused on new products designed to latch-on to emerging tastes and fashions. What kinds of compensation and pension benefit systems are consistent with the interests of Firm C's principals? Human capital is apparently the cornerstone of Firm C's competitiveness: by buying into the market knowledge and quality control experience of senior executives, investors place bets on their capacity to conceive and implement a competitive strategy that cannot be replicated by large competitors. The time horizon for such a bet is longer than many public capital market investors would accept; but a series of sign-posts indicating positive progress could result in investors being carried through to an

[18] R. Shiller, 'Bubbles, Human Judgement, and Expert Opinion', *Financial Analysts Journal*, 58, 3 (2002), 18–26.

[19] Here, firms that rely upon their own resources and organizational infrastructure for scale and scope are distinguished from firms that rely upon supplier networks for scale and scope. The former have a huge inventory of tangible assets, the latter are dominated by intangible assets such as brand image and corporate reputation: see B. Lev, *Intangibles: Management, Measurement, and Reporting* (Washington DC, 2001), and D. Teece, *Managing Intellectual Capital* (Oxford, 2000). Corporations can become just governance systems, dispelling claims made about virtues of the embedded firm: compare G. Grabher, *The Embedded Firm: On the Socio-economics of Industrial Networks* (London, 1993) with G. L. Clark, 'Global Interdependence and Regional Development: Business Linkages and Corporate Governance in a World of Financial Risk', *Transactions, Institute of British Geographers*, 18 (1993), 309–25.

[20] L. Bebchuk and J. Fried, *Pay Without Performance: The Unfulfilled Promise of Executive Compensation* (Cambridge MA, 2004).

initial public offering (IPO). To get that far, however, requires a governance regime that integrates the short term with the long term between the partners and within the firm.

For example, a firm could offer a standard defined-contribution pension to all employees regardless of status. This would have the advantage of treating all employees as equal, building solidarity and commitment around teams of individuals committed to the firm's long-term growth. Because the success of Firm C is doubtful, a defined-contribution pension plan with an external service provider may provide an exit option for workers unwilling to carry the risk of the firm's survival. And given the contingent nature of funding, it is unlikely that Firm C would match individual contributions to the defined-contribution scheme. Indeed, the level of contributions to offered defined-contribution schemes and its variants are much lower than an equivalent defined-benefit scheme. But the firm holds out the promise of significant wealth through stock options should the company be floated through an IPO. Here, employees are required to trade-off short-term insecurity and limited pension benefits with the prospect of wealth or higher incomes in the medium term.[21]

Then there is Firm D. It comes to market from another country that has neither private pension schemes nor comprehensive social security entitlements. Its costs of production are a fraction of those of incumbent firms although it has access to the most recent generation of production technologies that dominate the industry. It enters the market, in the first instance, through Firm B's supply chains. However, once established, Firm A recognizes opportunities to out-source component manufacturing of brand-name products and Firm C gambles on a relationship with Firm D to cover short-term limitations in its own capacity. The unit of retirement income is neither the firm nor the state. It is the family, the village community, or the prospective life-time opportunities of the city.[22]

[21] These types of firms were lauded for their innovativeness at the peak of the 1990s speculative bubble, especially in North America. One aspect of their compensation schemes that has attracted attention is the use of company stock or stock options as matching contributions to individuals' contributions to DC pension schemes. The consequences of such schemes in terms of concentrating risk can be highly deleterious for those involved. There is little data on such schemes in the UK; but they do exist (especially as supplementary bonus and incentive schemes).

[22] In effect, my argument joins together immanent tendencies of change in corporate form and functions with the consequences of globalization for western markets and third-world producers. See Clark, 'Global Interdependence'. This resonates with argument in political science and sociology over welfare state futures and whether variations in state-market formations can survive global competition: see F. W. Scharpf and V. A. Schmidt (eds), *Welfare and Work in the Open Economy 1: From Vulnerability to Competitiveness* (Oxford, 2001).

Lessons for Public Policy

Recognition of the social and economic transformation of western societies from manufacturing to diversified commercial and financial economies is widespread. For example, Esping-Andersen began with an account of modern welfare states referencing traditional industry and then reformulated his argument to take account of changes in the nature of work and changes in society including reference to gender, the family, and so-called non-traditional modes of income generation.[23] It is not surprising that defined-benefit pensions have lost their centrality given the decline of related institutions.

Plan sponsors are very different from fifty years ago. Companies have become highly differentiated with multiple links to related organizations at home and abroad. Expectations of a settled corporate form and function based on a hierarchical division of authority and tasks have given way to very different models of the internal organization of the firm with alternative modes of motivation and compensation.[24] Furthermore, what counts as a firm and the identification of its legal borders has changed, driven in part, by capital market expectations and, in part, by the core competencies of managers.[25] In many ways, the leading firms of the FTSE100 are iconic representations of a past era; if we want to know more about the future form of corporate capitalism we should look closely at the firms that enter and leave the FTSE100 lower down the ladder.

These observations offer four lessons for the framing of public policy relevant to occupational pensions in the private sector. First, there must be positive incentives to encourage both the demand and supply of private-sector occupational pensions. If left to the market, employers and employees need not necessarily see the relevance of an occupational pension for their long-term welfare. Table 10.2 shows the coverage of occupational

Notwithstanding the intellectual attraction of concepts such as path dependency, we show in G. L. Clark and D. Wójcik, 'Path Dependence and Financial Markets: The Economic Geography of the German Model, 1997–2003', *Environment and Planning A*, 37 (2005), 1769–91, for Germany, at least, that the rewards of financial markets can undercut corporate commitment to national and regional social and political regimes: compare P. Hall and D. Soskice (eds), *Varieties of Capitalism: Institutional Foundations of Comparative Advantage* (Oxford, 2001).

[23] G. Esping-Andersen, *The Three Worlds of Welfare Capitalism* (Oxford, 1990) and *Social Foundations of Postindustrial Economies* (Oxford, 1999).

[24] Williamson, *Economic Institutions of Capitalism* and J. Roberts, *The Modern Firm: Organizational Design for Performance and Growth* (Oxford, 2004).

[25] M. Orszag and N. Sand, 'Corporate Finance and Capital Markets', in Clark, Munnell, and Orszag, *Oxford Handbook*, pp. 399–414.

Table 10.2. Participants (millions) in UK occupational plans, 1995–2004.

	Defined-benefit plans		Defined-contribution plans		Hybrid		
	Private sector	Public sector	Private sector	Public sector	Private sector	Public sector	Grand-total
1995	5.2	4.1	0.9	0.0	0.1	0.0	10.3
2000	4.6	4.5	0.9	0.0	0.1	0.0	10.1
2004	4.0	5.0	1.4	0.0	0.0	0.0	10.4

Sources: The Occupational Pension Schemes Surveys, published by the Government Actuary's Department, London, in various years; Pension Policy Institute, *Occupational Pension Provision in the Public Sector* (London, 2005); Office for National Statistics, UK.

pension plans for millions of employees by sector and by type of plan (including defined-benefit, defined-contribution, and hybrid plans). Given the decline of defined-benefit plans noted above, defined-contribution and other types of plans have made only a modest difference to *trends* in coverage. Compared to the USA, defined-contribution plans remain a surprisingly small segment of the market not withstanding recent developments.[26]

A second lesson is that any policy designed to encourage the provision of occupational pensions must be neutral with respect to prospective corporate structure. In the UK, occupational pensions were so intimately linked with particular industries and particular forms of the firm that new industries and new forms of corporate organization have found the existing incentives and regulatory apparatus either an enormous burden or irrelevant to their market prospects. This is likely to be even more important in the future than it was over the past fifty years because of accelerating levels of global competition. How firms are organized over time and space is rapidly changing, especially in those firms and industries that encounter competing forms of corporate organization from jurisdictions that share neither liberal democratic traditions nor a commitment to social and economic justice.[27]

The third lesson is that any policy designed to encourage the provision of occupational pensions must be flexible with respect to its design and implementation. Defined-benefit pensions do not match the interests of many employers in providing flexible but targeted retirement savings options and, unsurprisingly, corporations have sought to withdraw from such plans. If important as an institution of public policy, defined-benefit pension plans constrain the variety of corporate compensation practices. At another level, public policy should recognize the varying objectives of employees and other would-be plan participants and beneficiaries. None of this should license adverse discrimination between different classes of employees: government has an interest in setting minimum standards of provision and retirement saving (as suggested by the Turner Report).[28]

[26] A. Munnell and A. Sundén, *Coming-up Short: The Challenge of 401(K) Plans* (Washington DC, 2004).

[27] E. Schoenberger, 'The Management of Time and Space', in G. L. Clark, M. Feldman, and M. S. Gertler (eds), *The Oxford Handbook of Economic Geography* (Oxford, 2000), pp. 317–32.

[28] Having promoted private pension plans to supplement modest national pension entitlements, governments had to regulate eligibility and standards of provision transforming private pensions from contractual arrangements into national institutions. See Clark, 'Regulation of Pension Fund Governance', in Clark, Munnell, and Orszag, *Oxford Handbook*, pp. 483–99 and A. Laboul and J. Yermo, 'Regulatory Principles and Institutions', in *ibid.*, pp. 501–19 for further discussion.

Fourth and most important, any public policy designed to encourage the provision of occupational pension benefits must do so in a manner that neither compromises the compensation objectives of the firm nor introduces conflict between the objectives of the firm and the welfare of different generations of workers. Unfortunately, one of the legacies of defined-benefit pensions has been conflict between managers and workers over the distribution of retained earnings (between investment and pension contributions) and conflict between shareholders and workers over the distribution of corporate profit (between dividends and pension contributions). There is also conflict between younger workers, older workers, and retirees within firms offering defined-benefit pensions: between workers wishing to promote corporate investment (income growth), workers with an interest in higher prospective benefits (older workers), and retirees with an interest in maintaining the real value of benefit entitlements.

The significance of such trade-offs was muted by the speculative bubble of the 1990s when all interests could apparently be met without compromise for any party. So, for example, plan sponsors could take contribution holidays (thereby diverting financial resources to other goals), expand benefits for current workers, and meekly accept UK government policy mandating automatic inflation-adjusted retirement benefits.[29]

For some observers, these lessons for public policy may so favour corporate interests that they are dismissed without serious concern. In effect, these implications suggest that the weight be taken off the corporation as an instrument of government policy for providing supplementary retirement income. This is also an important conclusion of the Turner Report. The Turner solution is, moreover, entirely social democratic: by arguing for greater significance to be attached to an enhanced state pension sustained by a longer working career, the Turner Report would both reduce the relative significance of supplementary pensions and would provide an institutional regime whereby the provision of such pensions would compensate for the declining workplace provision of such schemes.

By emphasizing neutrality both with respect to current and prospective corporate structure *and* the profit-making objectives of the corporation, Turner reconceptualizes the corporation as a means to an end (i.e. promoting growth in workers' incomes) rather than as an instrument of

[29] See D. Bergstresser, M. Desai, and J. Rauh, 'Earnings Manipulation and Managerial Investment Decisions: Evidence from Sponsored Pension Plans', Working Paper 10543 (Cambridge MA, 2004) on the effects of the speculative bubble for reporting corporate earnings, and D. Zion, *Pension Reform: It's a Cash-flow Issue* (New York, 2005) on the aftermath of the bubble for pension funding (in the USA but with the same implications for the UK).

social progress (i.e. provision of retirement income). At the same time, the current regime has fundamentally failed to deliver adequate private pension coverage with the prospect of further decline in pension provision of any kind.

Legacy Costs: Capital Market Efficiency

Even so, thousands of pension funds remain and a significant number of these are quite large. Any future pension regime must deal with what has been inherited. For instance, most of the largest firms listed on the London Stock Exchange carry defined-benefit pension plans some of which remain open, some are closed to new members, and some have been effectively terminated. Over the past five years or so, these plans have been the object of government policy—including reviews of their governance, investment practice, and their integrity with respect to the 'pension promise' exemplified by the recent establishment of the PPF.[30]

Some of the largest UK pension funds are sponsored by firms that were once in the public sector: for example, British Telecom, British Petroleum, and British Airways (ranked by size of total assets of all UK funds as 1, 8, and 12 respectively).[31] Many of the largest pension funds are effectively the residual institutions of denationalized industries such as coal, electricity, railways, and the national power grid. Four other types of fund appear significant: those of banks, quasi-public-sector funds (the BBC and the Universities Superannuation Scheme) and especially local government authorities, the pension funds of companies that were once household names such as Marconi Corporation and Cable & Wireless, and a mix of retail companies and service companies such as Tesco and Royal SunAlliance. Outside the top 100 funds, there appears to be a myriad of large and small plan sponsors; most are listed on the London Stock Exchange.

[30] For recent government legislative initiatives on pension fund governance, see G. L. Clark, 'Pension Fund Governance: Expertise and Organization Form', *Journal of Pension Economics and Finance*, 3 (2004), 233–53. Many in the industry have been preoccupied with initiatives designed to improve the competence of pension fund trustees and private pension fund management. See G. L. Clark, E. Caerlewy-Smith, and J. C. Marshall, 'Pension Fund Trustee Competence: Decision-making in Problems Relevant to Investment Practice', *Journal of Pension Economics and Finance*, 5 (2006), 91–110 for an assessment of the competence of the average trustee.

[31] G. L. Clark. and Y.-W. Hu, 'Rewriting Pension Fund Capitalism 2: The UK Pensions Crisis and Pension Plan Coverage Rates', Working Paper in Employment, Work and Finance, WPG05–09 (Oxford, 2005).

Following the 1990s speculative bubble, and (notwithstanding the recent performance of UK, US, and global stock markets) the revaluation of pension fund assets and liabilities according to more restrictive international accounting standards, most of the larger UK pension funds appear underfunded.[32] Whereas plan sponsors were able to claim contribution holidays on the back of advancing stock market returns in the 1990s, recently many have had to dramatically increase their contributions even if those contributions still fall short of that needed to bring plans to fully funded status. Many corporate plan sponsors have been reluctant to make such contributions, recognizing competing claims by shareholders for increased dividends, and the volatility of pension funding implied by current market valuation. In this context, unsurprisingly, more than 50 per cent of FTSE100 corporate plan sponsors have closed their defined-benefit pension plans to new entrants and, in some cases, have even limited the accrual of benefits of existing participants.

There are reasons to be concerned about the long-term viability of such funds. In Table 10.3, the largest pension funds are classified by size and relative maturity where maturity is defined in terms of the ratio of

Table 10.3. Distribution/number of UK's top 100 pension funds by size (in £), maturity,* and sector, 2004.

	>4bn	2–4bn	1–2bn	Total
Very mature	Public: 0	Public: 0	Public: 0	0
	Private: 9	Private: 12	Private: 12	33
Mature	Public: 0	Public: 1	Public: 0	1
	Private: 4	Private: 5	Private: 9	18
Immature	Public: 1	Public: 6	Public: 7	14
	Private: 5	Private: 5	Private: 3	13
Very immature	Public: 4	Public: 0	Public: 6	10
	Private: 2	Private: 3	Private: 3	8
Total	25	32	40	97**

* Very mature is defined as the ratio of the difference between the number of pensioners and the number of active members to the number of active members greater than 100%; mature as the ratio between 0% and 100%; immature as the ratio between –50% and 0%; and very immature as the ratio less than –50%.

** Three pension funds, i.e. Coal Pension Trustees, Church Commissioners for England, and the Royal London Mutual Insurance, were dropped from the survey due to lack of information.

Source: *Pension Funds and Their Advisers 2005*, published by AP Information Services Ltd, London.

[32] G. Whittington, 'Accounting Standards for Pension Costs', in Clark, Munnell, and Orszag, *Oxford Handbook*, pp. 521–37.

active pension plan participants against non-active plan participants including deferred beneficiaries and retirees. Many private pension plans can be characterized as 'very mature' or 'mature' whereas very few private plans could be characterized as 'immature'. By contrast, many public pension funds are relatively 'immature'.

Three implications can be drawn from these patterns. First, the combination of shortfalls in funding and increasing levels of maturity means that in future private plan sponsors will face greater calls on corporate assets and revenue. Second, as private plan sponsors close their plans to new participants, the maturity of those funds will accelerate. Third, as maturity accelerates private pension funds will inevitably shift their asset allocations towards less risky investments including government bonds. But lower rates of returns, the product of changing the allocation of assets to less risky investments, will raise pressure on plan sponsors to meet funding shortfalls. The largest UK private pension funds will be less secure in five and ten years than they currently appear.

For plan sponsors and their shareholders, pension liabilities may be very onerous. There are few plan sponsors able or willing to renegotiate with stakeholders the promised pension benefit values. So far, large UK plan sponsors have been unwilling to use bankruptcy to rebalance claims by creditors, including pension plan beneficiaries, on the assets of the firm.[33] With greater awareness among financial analysts of the potential costs of defined-benefit pensions, and with the prospect of only modest returns from securities markets over the foreseeable future, there appears to be every chance of another crisis in UK occupational pensions: where many large plan sponsors renege on their pension promises notwithstanding claims made about the PPF's insulation from 'moral hazard'.

As the numbers of those that benefit or would benefit from a private pension become a relatively small subset of the UK working population, the government may be forced to reassess the balance of costs and benefits of holding plan sponsors to account for past promises. Ultimately, these liabilities may impede capital market efficiency especially where large pension plan liabilities are reported on the balance sheets of plan sponsors. If pension plan beneficiaries are privileged debt holders (as implied by the actions of the PPF), and if pension plan trustees are required to exclusively represent the interests of beneficiaries (as implied by the actions of the Pension Regulator), some plan liabilities may be so significant that they

[33] G. L. Clark, *Pensions and Corporate Restructuring in American Industry: A Crisis of Regulation* (Baltimore MD, 1993) and T. Ghilarducci, *Labor's Capital: The Economics and Politics of Private Pensions* (Cambridge MA, 1992).

become an anti-takeover 'poison-pill' limiting corporate rationalization through capital markets.

Considering the collective interest in encouraging the competitiveness of the private sector in the global economy, this may be too high a price for protecting the interests of a privileged minority. The lack of mechanisms for renegotiating the distribution of pension liabilities between interested parties prior to plan termination at the PPF or bankruptcy is a significant efficiency issue: the Dutch have better institutional mechanisms for managing current and prospective pension liabilities.[34]

Legacy Costs: Public-Sector Privilege

Private-sector occupational pensions face an immediate crisis in terms of coverage and a long-term crisis in terms of the viability of past pension promises. By contrast, the evidence presented in Table 10.1 suggests that public-sector occupational pensions have a long-term future. Coverage rates are very high including an important component related to gender equity such that both men and women share in the benefits of public-sector occupational pensions which is much less the case in the private sector. Furthermore, recent public-sector pension coverage has grown to levels hardly contemplated in the private sector. Public-sector trends reflect a commitment to the equitable treatment of different classes of employees whatever their status.

Public-sector occupational pensions include lucrative early-retirement benefits at a high level of income replacement, occupation-specific clauses and benefits relevant to the emergency services, and generous benefits for surviving spouses and dependants. Even so, UK public-sector occupational pensions are not as lucrative as similar types of benefits in some continental European countries; the nature and scope of benefits remain more consistent with private-sector benefits than with European customs and conventions. Nevertheless, public-sector occupational pensions have tended to lead private-sector occupational benefits in terms of their scope and value. In many cases individual contributions are only loosely related to promised benefits; commonly, employer and employee contribution rates are not high enough when compared to the value of benefits.

As noted above, of the 100 largest UK pension funds, a significant number come from the public sector. One of the largest funds is from the tertiary education sector: the Universities Superannuation Scheme (USS)

[34] Clark, *European Pensions*.

is rated the second largest fund in the United Kingdom and among the largest in Europe. Also important are a number of large local government pension funds; many are relatively immature compared to private-sector counterparts. For example, on current estimates, the USS fund will continue to grow for fifteen to twenty years before the net inflow of contributions becomes a net outflow of benefits. The significance of these large funds goes beyond their accumulated assets. They represent a core part of the market for financial services, and are often the most aggressive funds in terms of holding UK, European, and global corporations to account for their standards of governance and social responsibilities.[35]

For all their virtues, public-sector occupational pensions face an uncertain future. Public-sector employees are privileged compared to their private-sector counterparts in terms of access to occupational pensions at high levels, especially as many private-sector employees cannot participate in employer-sponsored pension schemes. This is a political issue. Debate over pension equity and social justice is likely to include debate over the privileges of one sector of society in terms of access to defined-benefit pensions (and occupational pensions of any kind). In recognizing these issues, however, the Turner Report does not provide an easy way forward.

Of even greater significance for the future of public-sector occupational pensions is the fact that many are either underfunded or unfunded.[36] See Figure 10.2 for summary details. If public-sector pension schemes were subject to the same exacting accounting standards facing private-sector plan sponsors, many would be so underfunded that plan trustees would be justified in calling upon government to increase contributions. The consequences for local government taxes, already subject to considerable political debate and highly publicized instances of non-compliance, would be far-reaching. The situation facing central government concerning the unfunded nature of occupational pensions in the emergency services sector and in the National Health Service is also alarming. In Table 10.4, the basic parameters of NHS pension plans are summarized, including the number of employees who will have a claim on central government revenue for occupational pension benefits.

Unfunded or underfunded public-sector occupational pensions are a form of pay-as-you-go social security. The government faces the prospect

[35] Clark and Hebb, 'Pension Fund Corporate Engagement'; Hawley and Williams, *The Rise of Fiduciary Capitalism* on the significance of pension funds as institutional investors in the global marketplace.
[36] Pensions Policy Institute, *Occupational Pension Provision in the Public Sector* (London, 2005).

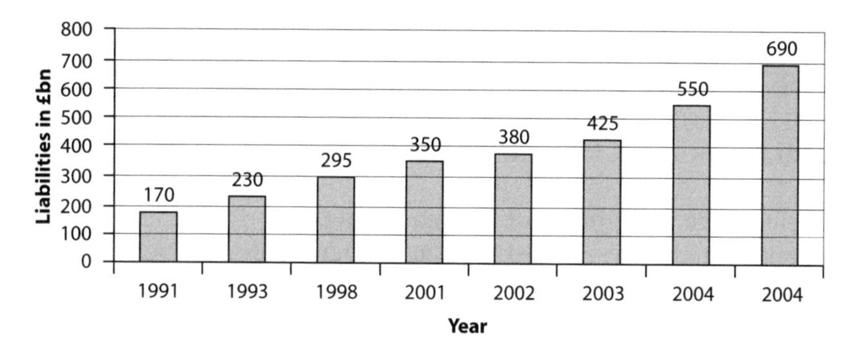

Figure 10.2. Pension liabilities of the unfunded public sector schemes (£bn), 1991–2004.

Sources: Data for 1991—House of Commons Hansard (HCH), 26 Apr. 1993; for 1993—HCH, 26 Feb. 1996; for 1998—HCH, 2 July 1998; for 2001—HCH, 22 Apr. 2002; for 2002—HCH, Jan. 2004. Data for 2003 and 2004 from the PPI, *Occupational Pension Provision in the Public Sector* (2005) and Watson Wyatt, 'Unfunded Public Sector Pension Liabilities Close to £700 Billion' (2005), http://www.watsonwyatt.com/news/press.asp?ID514248. There are two estimates for the year 2004: one at £550bn from the UK government (PPI, 2005), the other at £690bn from Watson Wyatt.

Table 10.4. National Health Service (NHS) pension plans, 1962–2004.

	1962	1974	1984	1994	1999	2004
Participants ('000)*	392.6	600.0	979.5	1,086.2	1,404.2	2,075.1
Total employed ('000)	575.0	911.0	1,223.0	1,177.0	1,422.0	2,975.1
Coverage rate (%)	68.3	65.9	80.1	92.3	98.7	69.7
Total assets (£m)**	951	2,437	n.a.	44,062	57,500	n.a.
Total liabilities(£m)	882	3,440	n.a.	51,616	71,300	104,200
Funding ratio (%)***	107.9	70.8	n.a.	85.4	80.6	n.a.

* Participants are the sum of plan contributors plus pensioners.
** Total assets are the net present value of future contributions from employees and investment income.
*** Funding ratio is total assets/total liabilities.

Source: *Report by the Government Actuary on the National Health Service Superannuation Scheme*, published in various years.

of increasing liabilities over time driven by a combination of past pension promises only loosely related to employee contributions, increasing longevity upon retirement, and the costs of early retirement. Not surprisingly, attempts have been made to reform these pension schemes, to introduce older-age thresholds and longer work-histories for maximum benefits. In some emergency services, where early retirement on high levels of income replacement has been the norm, these reform initiatives could carry significant political costs. Central government faces the prospect of a level of public-sector union opposition to pension reform more often associated with France and Italy than the United Kingdom.[37]

Implications and Conclusions

Current and future prospects of occupational pensions form an important component in the present crisis. For all the significance attributed to these institutions in terms of supplementing modest social security entitlements, most private-sector employees do not have access to such benefits while public-sector employees may see their entitlements passed back to central government to become yet another liability on an already overburdened state.[38] The decline in coverage rates in the private sector can be traced to changes in corporate form and functions that make traditional occupational pensions appear largely irrelevant in terms of corporate compensation practices. The significance of these institutions for the retirement income of future generations of working men and women is coming to an end.

A significant number of public-sector employees participate in underfunded pension schemes, or in unfunded schemes that are really old-fashioned pay-as-you-go pension systems, not viable stand-alone financial institutions. The UK crisis of occupational pensions is not just a private-sector phenomenon. Just prior to the publication of the Turner Report in November 2005, the government effectively withdrew public-sector pensions from the reform agenda guaranteeing current workers their benefits and contribution rates. While the relationship between public-sector unions and the Labour government has been fraught with controversy, the government's interest in union quiescence prompted a deal that left the Turner Report irrelevant to the issue. There seems little prospect, at present, of realigning public-sector pension entitlements with what is deemed appropriate for the private sector.

The UK government faces a significant challenge in resuscitating occupational pensions as a viable institution for private-sector employees. If occupational pensions are to remain crucial retirement income institutions, government policy may have to respond by allowing employers

[37] Clark, *European Pensions.*

[38] In the long run, as the retirement of the baby-boom generation hits government balance sheets and as governments come to recognize the limits of fiscal policy in a world of global competition, there may be unpalatable trade-offs between support for the elderly and the education of the young. Some analysts, such as V. Tanzi and L. Schuknecht, *Public Spending in the 20th Century: A Global Perspective* (Cambridge, 2000), argue that these issues already appear on western governments' balance sheets.

and employees to recraft these institutions in ways that distinguish between different classes of employees. The regulatory burden and the public interest in private pension provision must be both discounted while retaining a judicious mix of oversight and scrutiny with regard to pension security. By this account, the private sector is unlikely to make up the apparent decline in coverage, whatever the claimed significance of new kinds of pension benefits such as defined-contribution and hybrid schemes, unless these types of benefits are directly related to corporate compensation practices. If so, increasing levels of inequality in the nature and value of benefits will reflect how different classes of employees have different value and commitment to their employers.[39]

Recognizing the decline of private pensions, the Turner Report recommends structural changes to the UK pension system, not least improving the long-term value of state-pensions by linking benefits to average income growth in the economy. This would be paid, in part, by increasing the retirement age at which workers could claim maximum benefits. Turner also recommends the establishment of a National Pension Savings Scheme (NPSS), a quasi-compulsory earned-income pension contribution system. By creating such a system, by regulating the available choice of investments, and by setting cost constraints on investment options, the Turner Report argues that UK workers could have the benefits of supplementary pensions without having to rely upon employers to sponsor such plans. At the same time, Turner would allow employer-sponsored schemes to offer an alternative, as long as they are as inexpensive to administer as the NPSS.

These reforms would effectively bypass the market for individual pension products. Individual purchasers of pension and retirement income products are not well-informed consumers in a marketplace that is highly differentiated with enormous (often opaque) costs associated with seeking and finding the best solutions.[40] Furthermore, contracts to supply retirement income carry with them inadequate incentives or obligations with respect to protecting the welfare of intended beneficiaries compared to the underlying ethic informing occupational pension funds.[41] Finally, the average consumer is not well equipped to act consistently in their own best interests when compared to institutions of long-term mutual benefit. In rejecting the market for private pension savings products, the Turner

[39] E. Lazear, *Personnel Economics* (Cambridge MA, 1998).

[40] S. Venti, 'Choice, Behaviour and Saving', in Clark, Munnell, and Orszag, *Oxford Handbook*, pp. 603–17.

[41] Clark, 'Regulation', in Clark, Munnell, and Orszag, *Oxford Handbook*, pp. 483–99.

Report eschews a return to nineteenth-century liberalism in favour of a twentieth-century social market solution.

This chapter cannot mount a critique of the Turner Report, but there are some points of concern. First, is the NPSS cost-effective *and* capable of delivering a risk-adjusted rate of return above the long-term government bond rate? Second, will NPSS governance be efficient *and* adaptive to changing financial circumstances nationally and internationally? Third, how would it be innovative in terms of the nature of offered investment products *and* responsive to the interests of more or less skilled participants? In effect, the question is: can such a saving scheme match the qualities of a well managed large, multi-employer occupation pension plan?

The NPSS may be so limited in terms of allowed costs and consequent investment options that it becomes isolated from the never-ending quest for financial innovation in the global marketplace. Furthermore, it may dampen the capacity of employees and employers to develop compensation schemes that are truly responsive to the labour market conditions of the twenty-first century. A third problem, noted above, is that, given the parameters of such a scheme, the rate of return may not be much better than holding a government bond which is a proxy for national economic growth. Consequently, for many people, the supplementary savings regime will not take the weight off their dependence upon an enhanced state pension; in fact, it may be perceived as just another tax on earned income. Those that have the great fortune of remaining with an employer-sponsored scheme, however, may have access to much greater benefits than those offered by the supplementary savings regime.

Note: This paper was sponsored, in part, by the French Government Ministère des Solidarités de la Santé et de la Famille. I am grateful for the interest and advice of Michele Lelièvre and Najat El Mekkaoui de Freitas. The paper bears the imprint of conversations with a number of colleagues, including Tessa Hebb, Ashby Monk, Hugh Pemberton, Kendra Strauss, and Noel Whiteside as well as my collaboration with Alicia Munnell and Michael Orszag on the *Oxford Handbook of Pensions and Retirement Income* (2006). Research assistance was provided by Yu-Wei Hu and help on data sources was provided by the UK Government Actuary, the Office for National Statistics, the Institute of Fiscal Studies, the Pensions Policy Institute, and the US Employee Benefits Research Institute. None of the above should be held responsible for errors or omissions or for that matter the opinions contained herein.

Bibliography

Bebchuk, L. and J. Fried, *Pay Without Performance: The Unfulfilled Promise of Executive Compensation* (Cambridge MA, 2004).

Bergstresser, D., M. Desai, and J. Rauh, 'Earnings Manipulation and Managerial Investment Decisions: Evidence from Sponsored Pension Plans', Working Paper 10543 (Cambridge MA, 2004).

Booth, A., *The British Economy in the Twentieth Century* (Basingstoke, 2001).

Clark, G. L., *Pensions and Corporate Restructuring in American Industry: A Crisis of Regulation* (Baltimore MD, 1993).

——, 'Global Interdependence and Regional Development: Business Linkages and Corporate Governance in a World of Financial Risk', *Transactions, Institute of British Geographers*, 18 (1993), 309–25.

——, *Pension Fund Capitalism* (Oxford, 2000).

——, *European Pensions and Global Finance* (Oxford, 2003).

——, 'Pension Fund Governance: Expertise and Organization Form', *Journal of Pension Economics and Finance*, 3 (2004), 233–53.

——, 'Re-writing Pension Fund Capitalism 1', Working Paper in Employment, Work and Finance, WPG05–08 (Oxford, 2005).

——, E. Caerlewy-Smith, and J. C. Marshall, 'Pension Fund Trustee Competence: Decision-making in Problems Relevant to Investment Practice', *Journal of Pension Economics and Finance*, 5 (2006), 91–110.

—— and T. Hebb, 'Pension Fund Corporate Engagement: The Fifth Stage of Capitalism', *Relations Industrielle/Industrial Relations*, 59 (2004), 142–71.

—— and Y.-W. Hu, 'Rewriting Pension Fund Capitalism 2: The UK Pensions Crisis and Pension Plan Coverage Rates', Working Paper in Employment, Work and Finance, WPG05–09 (Oxford, 2005).

——, A. Munnell, and M. Orszag (eds), *The Oxford Handbook of Pensions and Retirement Income* (Oxford, 2006).

—— and D. Wójcik, 'Path Dependence and Financial Markets: The Economic Geography of the German Model, 1997–2003', *Environment and Planning A*, 37 (2005), 1769–91.

Clowes, M. J., *The Money Flood: How Pension Funds Revolutionized Investing* (New York, 2000).

Esping-Andersen, G., *The Three Worlds of Welfare Capitalism* (Oxford, 1990).

——, *Social Foundations of Postindustrial Economies* (Oxford, 1999).

Galbraith, J. K., *The New Industrial State*, 2nd edn (London, 1967).

Ghilarducci, T., *Labor's Capital: The Economics and Politics of Private Pensions* (Cambridge MA, 1992).

Grabher, G., *The Embedded Firm: On the Socio-economics of Industrial Networks* (London, 1993).

Hall, P. and D. Soskice (eds), *Varieties of Capitalism: Institutional Foundations of Comparative Advantage* (Oxford, 2001).

Hawley, J. P. and A. T. Williams, *The Rise of Fiduciary Capitalism: How Institutional Investors Can Make Corporate America More Democratic* (Philadelphia PA, 2000).

Hill, D., C. Davis, and L. M. Tigges, 'Gendering Welfare State Theory: A Cross-national Study of Women's Public Pension Quality', *Gender and Society*, 9 (1995), 99–119.

Hutton, W., *The State We're In* (London, 1995).

Lazear, E., *Personnel Economics* (Cambridge MA, 1998).

Lev, B., *Intangibles: Management, Measurement, and Reporting* (Washington DC, 2001).

Martin, R. L. and R. Minns, 'Undermining the Financial Bases of Regions: The Spatial Structure and Implications of the UK Pension Fund System', *Regional Studies*, 29 (1995), 125–44.

Mercer Human Resource Consulting, *FTSE350—Pensions Scheme Deficits and Trends*, 5 January 2006.

Munnell, A. and A. Sundén, *Coming-up Short: The Challenge of 401(K) Plans* (Washington DC, 2004).

Pensions Commission, *A New Pension Settlement for the Twenty-first Century* (London, 2005).

Pensions Policy Institute (PPI), *Occupational Pension Provision in the Public Sector* (London, 2005).

Roberts, J., *The Modern Firm: Organizational Design for Performance and Growth* (Oxford, 2004).

Scharpf, F. W. and V. A. Schmidt (eds), *Welfare and Work in the Open Economy 1: From Vulnerability to Competitiveness* (Oxford, 2001).

Schoenberger, E., 'The Management of Time and Space', in G. L. Clark, M. Feldman, and M. S. Gertler (eds), *The Oxford Handbook of Economic Geography* (Oxford, 2000), pp. 317–32.

Shiller, R., 'Bubbles, Human Judgement, and Expert Opinion', *Financial Analysts Journal*, 58, 3 (2002), 18–26.

Shonfield, A., *Modern Capitalism: The Changing Balance of Public and Private Power* (Oxford, 1965).

Tanzi, V. and L. Schuknecht, *Public Spending in the 20th Century: A Global Perspective* (Cambridge, 2000).

Teece, D., *Managing Intellectual Capital* (Oxford, 2000).

Williamson, O. E., *The Economic Institutions of Capitalism* (New York, 1991).

Zingales, L., 'In Search of New Foundations', *Journal of Finance*, 55 (2000), 1623–53.

Zion, D., *Pension Reform: It's a Cash-flow Issue* (New York, 2005).

11. Paying for Our Futures: The Political Economy of Pension Reform in the UK

PAUL JOHNSON

Introduction

The almost complete absence of serious discussion of pensions in the 2005 election campaign is perhaps the clearest sign that politicians regard the issue as economically challenging and politically intractable. Politicians like good news stories, but pensions are associated with quite the opposite: Maxwell, mis-selling, under-saving, crisis, demographic time-bomb—a depressing litany. Even the good news stories—for example, the reduction in pensioner poverty over recent years associated with the introduction of the minimum pension guarantee and pension credit—become mired in debate about the complexity and disincentives associated with an extension of means-testing. Yet the development of pension provision in Britain since January 1909, when the first public old-age pension was paid, should really be celebrated as one of the greatest achievements of collective action in the twentieth century. Millions of people have pooled risks and resources—by individual choice in the private pension sector, by electoral choice in the public pension sector—in order better to provide for their own and other people's old age. Why has the story of pensions, and particularly public pensions, changed from being something that politicians can celebrate—as it was for Lloyd George in 1909 and Attlee in 1945—to being something they evade?

There are, I believe, two possible empirical explanations for this shift in political attitudes towards pensions:

1 a change in underlying *demographic* conditions and knowledge that has created circumstances which are now very different to those that existed in the past; and

2 a change in underlying *economic* conditions and knowledge that has created circumstances which are now very different to those that existed in the past.

In fact, as I show below, neither of these propositions holds; the pensions knowledge base, though it has evolved over time, has not been subject to fundamental change or innovation over the past several decades. What can be seen instead is the development and embedding, in both political decision-making and in popular perceptions, of a delusional consensus that our pension futures will take care of themselves. The result is a twenty-first-century pension system in which there are strong incentives for individuals and groups to favour jam today instead of jam tomorrow.

In this chapter I sketch what has and has not changed in terms of demographic and economic knowledge of pension systems, before moving on to consider the causes and consequences of this delusional consensus. Finally I make some suggestions about how a more responsible set of political and popular attitudes to pensions might be created, beginning with a fundamental reform to the state pension system.

Demography and Pensions

The demographic imperative which drives current concern about pensions was clearly and directly articulated in the first (2004) report of the Pensions Commission:

> Life expectancy is increasing rapidly and will continue to do so. This is good news. But combined with a forecast low birth rate this will produce a near doubling in the percentage of the population aged 65 years and over between now and 2050, with further increase thereafter. The baby boom has delayed the effect of underlying long-term trends, but will now produce 30 years of very rapid increase in the dependency ratio. We must now make adjustments to public policy and/or individual behaviour which ideally should have been started in the last 20–30 years.[1]

This statement begs the question of why the implication of these demographic trends for pension systems seems to have been misperceived and miscalculated for many decades. Have the trends been hidden or concealed? Have the necessary techniques of analysis been unavailable? Has the technical expertise been lacking? To each of these questions the unequivocal answer is 'no'.

[1] Pensions Commission, *Pensions: Challenges and Choices. The First Report of the Pensions Commission* (London, 2004), p. 1.

The potential impact of low birth rates on the capacity of an economy to support a public pension scheme has been known for at least fifty years. The 'dismal science' of economics has long held that population change can have adverse effects on both welfare and economic activity. The initial intervention by the Reverend Thomas Malthus in 1798 argued that excessively *rapid* breeding would exhaust the capacity of an economy to feed its population. But, ever ready to see gloom where others see progress, by the 1930s economists were lamenting that excessively *slow* breeding, manifested by a sharp fall in birth rates after the First World War, would jeopardize economic growth. The 1949 Royal Commission on Population continued this theme when remarking:

> A society in which the proportion of young people is diminishing will become dangerously unprogressive, falling behind other communities in technical efficiency and economic welfare.[2]

As well as the potential impact of low or declining birth rates on economic growth, there has also been a long-running concern about their impact on the financing of pension systems; since, in the absence of any countervailing changes, an increase in the ratio of pensioners to contributors in any pension scheme, whether public or private, will inevitably increase costs. This point was recognized by Beveridge when he was developing his plans for a comprehensive post-war welfare state. One of the reasons he recommended that the full National Insurance pension should be phased in over a twenty-year period was so that a reserve fund could be accumulated to cover the future pension cost of the large birth cohorts of the late-Victorian and Edwardian periods when they entered retirement from around 1960.[3]

Despite this early recognition of the sensitivity of pension systems to demographic change, policy-makers over the last thirty years appear to have paid little attention to this issue. The failure to pay due attention to the impact of population change on pension systems is particularly striking given the growing knowledge of demographic trends during this time. Although there are inevitable uncertainties about future trends in fertility and life expectancy, there is much that is certain and well known—such as, every person who will reach the age of 65 in 2070 is already born. Even the uncertainties about future demographic trends are predictable within broad limits. Furthermore, there exists a group of

[2] *Report of the Royal Commission on Population* (London, 1949).

[3] See the chapter by Harris in this volume, for a discussion of the financial implications of Beveridge's pension proposals, and that by Pemberton for a discussion of the implications of dropping the twenty-year transition.

professional experts—demographers and actuaries—whose job it is to provide forecasts about future population trends, and the resulting economic and financial implications. They have not been idle in producing just these forecasts and projections, though it has to be said that they have a fairly consistent track record in under-predicting improvements in life expectancy at older ages. For example, forecasts of the mortality rates for 65-year-old males in 2014 made in 1983 by the Government Actuary's Department were 46 per cent higher than similar estimates made in 2003; the 1983 projection of an additional fifteen years of life for men at 65 had become, by 2003, a projection of an additional nineteen years of life.[4] This reflects an acceleration in the rate of mortality improvement at older ages over the past three decades. However, even on the basis of the 1983 projections it was apparent that the cost of public pensions would rise by more than 1 per cent of GDP over the first two decades of the twenty-first century as the post-war 'baby-boomers' moved from paid employment to retirement.[5]

Thus the expertise and necessary knowledge about demographic trends, and how these trends might affect the future financing of pension systems—both public and private—have existed for several decades. The failure adequately to use this knowledge to implement timely reform of these pension systems requires explanation; an appeal to collective self-denial here seems inadequate. The issue calls for detailed investigation beyond the scope of this chapter, but one element of the answer may lie in an inherent degree of economic short-termism that might be labelled 'the tyranny of the discount rate'. The economic effect of demographic change works slowly; a fall in the birth rate today cannot begin to impact on pension finances for at least two decades when the infants of 2006 enter the labour force in significant numbers, and other major effects will be further deferred. The relevant time horizon is even longer when reforms to pension systems interact with demographic shifts; if new pension scheme rules apply only to new entrants, then they will not affect the entire contributor population for almost fifty years, and will not affect the great majority of the pensioner population for more than seventy years. Even twenty or thirty years is a *very* long time in economics; in fact with an annual discount rate of, say, 3 per cent, the present value of expenditure which will occur thirty or more years in the

[4] Pensions Commission, *A New Pension Settlement for the Twenty-first Century. The Second Report of the Pensions Commission* (London, 2005), appendix E, pp. 179–91.
[5] OECD, *Reforming Public Pensions* (Paris, 1988), pp. 35, 138–41.

future dwindles into insignificance, and is therefore barely worth serious economic consideration.

Economic short-termism has been compounded by the tendency of actuaries—including the government actuary—to produce detailed population projections that look only thirty—or sometimes fifty—years ahead. This has encouraged policy-makers to assume that if a thirty-year projection indicates a benign financial outcome, then there is no need to worry about, or even consider, the longer run. It was just this sort of outlook that led to a fundamental misrepresentation of the long-run financial implications of the State Earnings-related Pension Scheme (SERPS). Initial projections made at the time of implementation in 1975 did not look beyond 2009, on the grounds that anything beyond that date would be highly speculative. These projections therefore failed to take account of both the retirement of the post-war baby-boomers, which could be expected from the beginning of the second decade of the twenty-first century, and the maturing of SERPS at around the same time. It did not take long for analysts to recognize this error; official estimates that SERPS would require an additional National Insurance contribution of no more than 4 per cent were countered by longer-run forecasts of a necessary contribution level of over 13 per cent.[6] Indeed, a primary motivation for the SERPS reforms proposed in the 1985 green paper on social security reform was the huge projected growth in its long-run costs.[7] The fact that this reform was proposed (and partially implemented) shows that both the technical capacity and the data necessary for a long-run evaluation of the impact of demographic change on pension system outcomes have existed and have been acted upon (if only in rare cases) at particular moments in the past. It is therefore not credible to suggest that a misperception or miscalculation of the impact of demography on pension finances has been the direct result of inadequate data, inadequate analytical techniques, or a lack of technical expertise.

Economics and Pensions

Could it be a failure in the economic analysis of pension systems, rather than inadequacy in demographic knowledge, that accounts for the three decades of inaction identified by the Pensions Commission? Again I think

[6] R. Hemming and J. A. Kay, 'The Cost of the State Earnings Related Pensions Scheme', *Economic Journal*, 92 (1982), 300–19.

[7] Department of Health and Social Security, *Reform of Social Security: Programme for Action*, Cmnd 9691 (London, 1985).

the answer must be a resounding 'no'. A formal theoretical exposition of the impact of demographic change on the underlying economic logic of a pay-as-you-go pension system was published by Paul Samuelson in 1958, and further elaborated by Henry Aaron in 1966.[8] Their work demonstrated that the implicit rate of return in a pay-as-you-go pension system is determined by the rate of growth of the public pension tax base, which can be represented by the rate of growth of real earnings per worker (h) and the rate of population growth (g). In a funded pension system, by contrast, the rate of return is established by the long-run market yield on investments (i). It can then be shown that pay-as-you-go dominates (in the sense of being able to provide every contributor with a higher internal rate of return on their pension contributions, and thus being the preferable option) if $g + h > i$, but funding dominates if $g + h < i$. During the 'golden age' of post-war growth up to the mid-1970s both g and h were high and pay-as-you-go pensions were attractive, but the slowdown in both population growth and economic growth in the western economies over the past twenty-five years has reversed this position.

The impact of an adverse movement in demographic conditions on the financing of a pay-as-you-go pension can be demonstrated with a simple hypothetical example. In Table 11.1 each cohort lives for two periods, the first being a period of contribution, the second a period of benefit. Each member of each generation contributes £10 to the public pension system while working, and each generation draws a pension funded from the contributions of its successor generation (cohort B pays for cohort A's pensions, C pays for B, and so on). When the population is growing, each generation enjoys pension benefits greater than its pension contributions. Larger individual gains are enjoyed by the earlier cohorts because of their small size relative to the working population, and the greatest gains are captured by the initial generation which pays no contributions but receives windfall benefits. However, when the population begins to decline (from generation E), the pension funds available for each generation become smaller than its net contributions when working; per capita contributions now exceed benefits. If this negative rate of return induces generation H to abandon the public pension scheme, then members of generation G receive no benefits, despite having made contributions throughout their working life.

[8] P. A. Samuelson, 'An Exact Consumption-Loans Model with or without the Social Contrivance of Money', *Journal of Political Economy*, 66 (1958), 467–82; H. Aaron, 'The Social Insurance Paradox', *Canadian Journal of Economic and Political Science*, 32 (1966), 371–4.

Table 11.1. Contributions and benefits of successive cohorts in a hypothetical pay-as-you-go pension scheme.

Contributions									
Cohort	A	B	C	D	E	F	G	H	
Cohort size	2	3	4	5	6	5	4	3	
Contributions per capita	0	10	10	10	10	10	10	0	
Total contributions	0	30	40	50	60	50	40	0	
Benefits									
Cohort		A	B	C	D	E	F	G	H
Total benefits		30	40	50	60	50	40	0	0
Benefits per capita		15	13.3	12.5	12	8.3	8	0	0
Net individual gain (loss)		15	3.3	2.5	2	(1.7)	(2.0)	(10)	0

This hypothetical example demonstrates that an ageing of the population which first reduces the ratio of workers to pensioners, and then leads to an absolute decline in the number of workers, can progressively reduce, and ultimately render negative, the real rate of return produced by a pay-as-you-go pension. There is little that is surprising about this; the result has been known to (at least some) economists for more than forty years.

The economic theory is clear, but the practical experience of the UK public pension system less so. The pensioner share of the UK population has been rising (though not at a constant rate) since the beginning of the twentieth century, but so far each generation of pensioners in the UK has enjoyed a positive, and often large, implicit rate of return on its public pension (National Insurance) contributions. The reason for this is that at any point in time there are a number of factors other than demography which affect the current-year fiscal balance of a simple pay-as-you-go pension. If there exists a condition of annual equivalence of contributions and benefits (which is more or less the case with the UK National Insurance pension), then the system must operate according to the following accounting identity:

$$L(wt) = P(wr)$$

where L is the number of contributors in the labour force, P is the number of pensioners, t is the average NI contribution (tax) rate, r is the average pension replacement rate (i.e. the value of a pension as a proportion of the average wage), and w is the average real wage. Rearranging this equation we can see that:

$$P/L = t/r$$

so that a demographically induced increase in the ratio of pensioners to contributors must either increase the contribution rate or reduce the relative level of the pension, either of which will reduce the internal rate of return of the pension system.

However, several other things have affected the performance of the UK pension system since the inauguration of the Beveridge social security system after the Second World War. The rise in the rate of female employment has increased the size of the contributor base independently of any demographic change; the National Insurance contribution rate has been raised incrementally—for instance from 14 per cent (employer and employee combined) in 1975 to 23.8 per cent in 2005; the pension replacement rate has declined steadily since 1979 as a consequence of the uprating of the basic state pension being linked to the price index in 1980 rather than to the higher of the increases in prices and average earnings; the low inter-war birth rate has resulted in small cohorts of new retirees throughout the 1980s and 1990s, leading to a twenty-five-year pause in the upward movement of the old-age dependency ratio. These and other factors have worked to diminish the apparent long-run pension cost of ageing, but they have not altered the underlying economic logic of pension systems.

The Delusional Consensus

The fundamental economic and demographic relationships which underpin both pay-as-you-go and funded pensions have been well known to experts, and have been accessible to policy-makers, for many decades. Yet, as the Pensions Commission has noted, at all levels of society from the individual to the government we seem to have wilfully ignored the predictable and clearly predicted implications for pensions of population ageing.

The level of understanding of the basic economics of pension systems among the British population is low, and the level of self-delusion about likely pension outcomes is high. The Financial Services Consumer Panel has reported that only 45 per cent of UK consumers are financially literate, and fewer than two in five are confident about making their own decisions.[9] It is therefore unsurprising that the decisions they make are frequently quite unaligned with their expectations. A survey in 2002 by the Consumers Association found that, on average, respondents desired

[9] Financial Services Consumer Panel, *Annual Report for 2000* (London, 2001), ch. 2.

to retire at age 58 on a pension equal to three-quarters of final salary, yet 46 per cent of them were not making *any* contribution to an occupational or private pension scheme.[10] The reality for these individuals is likely to be retirement at 65 on a state pension that pays less than one-quarter of national average earnings.

The self-delusion of the British public seems to extend to government. Public expenditure plans and current levels of private saving imply that total pension income flowing to retirees will rise by about one-fifth over the next forty-five years from 9.1 per cent to 10.8 per cent of GDP. Meanwhile, the ratio of people aged 65+ to 20–64-year-olds is likely to increase by more than three-quarters, from 27 per cent to 48 per cent.[11] In the absence of any significant change in retirement age (something the Blair government ruled out in 2002),[12] this implies a substantial reduction in average pensioner income. Few commentators, across an ideological spectrum from the IMF to the TUC, believe these official projections to be either credible or deliverable.

How has this self-delusion emerged, and how has it been sustained? The government—or, rather, successive governments since 1945—must take the primary responsibility, even for the position adopted by individuals. As Hugh Pemberton has noted, the incremental manner in which major pension reforms have been implemented at least once a decade has created in Britain the world's most complex pension system.[13] For the consumer, a reasonable personal stance in the face of continual change, growing complexity, and predictive uncertainty, is to do nothing. Furthermore, the maintenance by successive governments of the illusion that the basic pension operates on an insurance principle, in which an individual's contributions over their working life 'pays for' their pension, has embedded a popular belief about both entitlements and about the financial sustainability of the state pension system which does not reflect economic reality. In addition, popular confidence in the private pension sector has been undermined by official inertia in the face of commission-based mis-selling of personal pensions, excessive personal pension administration charges, and inadequate legal protection for pensioners

[10] House of Lords, Select Committee on Economic Affairs, *Aspects of the Economics of an Ageing Population. Volume 2—Evidence*, HL Paper 179–II (2003), p. 163.
[11] Pensions Commission, *First Report*, ch. 4.
[12] Department for Work and Pensions, *Simplicity, Security and Choice: Working and Saving for Retirement*, Cm 5677 (London, 2002), pp. 102–4.
[13] See Pemberton, this volume.

and contributors in occupational pension schemes.[14] Thus, even though survey evidence about whom people trust to honour their pension promises shows that fewer than one in seven trust the government, compared to two out of three people who trust their employer, in fact Britain is experiencing a decline in take-up of employer-based pensions.[15] Somewhat bizarrely we see a growing reliance on the pension provider—the government—whom people trust least.

Politicians have been key actors in the construction of this delusional consensus. They have played—and continue to play—party politics with pensions. A five-year electoral cycle is not ideal for political engagement with policy issues where the effect of today's decisions may not be visible for decades. It is not at all obvious why any vote-seeking politician should choose to compromise current electoral appeal in order to solve some future government's financial problem. Real political engagement with pensions requires both statesmanship—that is, an ability to take decisions in the national interest on the basis of disinterested analysis—and consensus. There has been precious little of the former, and only a chimerical presence of the latter: the supposed political consensus created in 1975 over the State Earnings-related Pension Scheme, for example, had entirely vanished within eleven years.

Responsibility in Pensions

The November 2005 report of the Pensions Commission attempts to address this delusional consensus by offering—in its title, at least—'a new pension settlement for the twenty-first century'.[16] In this report, there is a helpful reiteration of the economic and demographic imperative for reform if Britain is to avoid a pensions future that delivers increasingly inadequate and unequal outcomes. There is also a very clear exposition of the inevitability of an increase in state pension age by mid-century if the public expenditure costs of the state pension are to be contained within a range of 7.5–8.0 per cent of GDP, compared to the current figure of just over 6 per cent. Thereafter, however, the 'new settlement' looks rather familiar. The public pension system remains extremely complicated, with both the Basic State Pension and the State Second Pension running in parallel into the distant future, although various adjustments would reduce the proportion of

[14] The inauguration of the Pension Protection Fund in 2005 can be seen as a belated attempt by government to shore up confidence in the occupational pension sector.
[15] Pensions Commission, *First Report*, p. 215.
[16] Pensions Commission, *Second Report*, chs 3–5.

pensioners subject to a means test in 2050 from a projected 70 per cent under current arrangements to just over 30 per cent. Transparency is compromised by the continuation of complex 'contracting-out rebates' until at least 2030.

The Pensions Commission has, however, proposed two 'big ideas'. The first is 'auto-enrolment' in a National Pension Savings Scheme (NPSS) for all employees not covered by other adequate pension arrangements. Auto-enrolment is not the same thing as compulsion; individuals can opt out if they so wish, but the Commission believes the level of inertia with respect to long-term financial planning is such that most individuals will be prepared to let 4 per cent of their earnings be paid into the NPSS, particularly given matching contributions of 3 per cent from employers and 1 per cent from the government in the form of tax relief. The NPSS is the second 'big idea'; it will be a funded pension saving scheme which will benefit from cost-efficient payroll deduction and the bulk buying of fund management services. The Pensions Commission believes it should be possible to operate this fund with management charges of no more than 0.3 per cent per annum, compared with the 1.5–2.5 per cent common in the personal pensions market.

The rationale advanced by the Pensions Commission for maintaining much of the complexity of the current state system is the cost and disruption that would be entailed by radical change. The huge diversity of public pension rights that have been accumulated by individuals since the introduction of the first graduated public pension in 1959, the introduction of SERPS in 1975, and the establishment of the State Second Pension by New Labour makes the transition to any fundamentally different pension scheme complex and costly if each and every accrued public pension right is fully compensated. On the other hand, as the Pensions Commission found out when it conducted focus groups about SERPS and the State Second Pension, there is 'minimal understanding' of how rights are accrued, and what level of pension might ultimately be paid.[17] This suggests that, as long as a transition to a different type of pension scheme preserves entitlements for all current pensioners, and all those within, say, five years of state pension age, it may not be necessary to preserve all accrued public pension rights as long as the average public pension level in the future will be higher than it is today.

The most fully developed alternative to the Pensions Commission proposal for a slow evolution away from the current delusional consensus is the proposal for a rapid transition to a Citizen's Pension—a tax-financed

[17] Pensions Commission, *Second Report*, p. 67.

pension paid to all citizens who meet a residence qualification. Depending on the way in which existing accrued rights and contracting-out arrangements are treated, it has been suggested that a Citizen's Pension could be introduced at a long-run cost no greater than that required for the Pensions Commission proposals, yet it would have the added benefit of sweeping away most of the complexity that currently binds the state pension system in a web of incomprehensibility.[18] Furthermore, a citizenship entitlement would render redundant the complex, and far from comprehensive, set of contribution credits that is currently necessary to ensure that carers—predominantly women—accumulate pension rights in a system predicated on employment-related National Insurance contributions.

A common argument advanced against the Citizen's Pension is that it would undermine the contributory principle that has underpinned state pensions in Britain since 1928, and which was deemed by William Beveridge to be fundamental to the comprehensive welfare system he designed for Britain. As far as Beveridge was concerned, contribution by every (male) breadwinner would provide the moral, as well as economic, basis for universal entitlement, since it would distance benefits from any element of charitable or Poor Law relief. In practice, however, this contributory principle is far from fair or equitable.

To see just how flawed it is, consider the following: imagine a company pension scheme in which workers can choose whether or not to contribute. Those who join the scheme pay 10 per cent of their income into the scheme; those who do not contribute can enjoy significantly higher disposable income during their working life. Then, at the point of retirement, the workers who have failed to contribute demand that they should receive the same pension as their peers who have paid one-tenth of their lifetime income. And at this point the company agrees to pay the same pension to everyone.

This sounds absurd; the scheme is clearly so unfair it would be unsustainable. Yet this is precisely the basis on which the National Insurance pension system works. Because of its pay-as-you-go nature, the pensions of today's workers are paid not from their contributions, but from the contributions of future workers. These future workers are created through the investments in child-rearing made by today's parents, yet parents receive no privileged treatment in the public pension system compared with non-parents. There is, therefore, a clear bias in the National Insurance pensions

[18] National Association of Pension Funds, *Towards a Citizen's Pension: Final Report* (London, 2005).

system against the economic interests of parents, and particularly, therefore, of women.

What does it cost to rear a child? Table 11.2 gives estimates by Davies and Joshi of the foregone earnings of motherhood at 1998 prices. These figures represent the lifetime loss of earnings incurred by mothers, and are made up of a mixture of fewer years in the labour force, fewer hours when in work, and lower pay due mainly to the negative impact of reduced labour force participation on experience. The estimates are much lower for high-skill couples, because graduate mothers are much less likely completely to withdraw from the labour force; for them the corollary of lower foregone earnings is much higher expenditure on formal childcare.

If we focus on a low-skill couple, who are likely to be in the lower deciles of the income distribution, then we can see that, over a working life, a childless couple is likely to be in receipt of a gross income £176,000 greater than a one-child couple, and £255,000 greater than a two-child couple. This is clearly a non-trivial sum in terms of spending power, but it is also a non-trivial sum in terms of saving power. A capital sum of £255,000 will currently purchase for a couple aged 65 a joint-life pension annuity of £203 per week, including survivor benefits of two-thirds and RPI linkage (by contrast, the current level of pension credit for a couple is £167 per week). Is it reasonable that a childless couple should enjoy significantly higher levels of consumption during their working life to that experienced by parents of a similar background, and then receive exactly the same public pension as these parents who have born the costs of raising the next generation of workers and taxpayers? The analogy drawn above with the operation of a funded pension system would suggest that it is not.

Table 11.2. Foregone earnings cost of motherhood (£000), illustrative couples by number of children and skill level.

	1 child	2 children	4 children
Low-skill couple*	176	255	402
Mid-skill couple**	140	257	460
High-skill couple***	0	39	169

* Couple with no qualifications.
** Couple with post-GCSE schooling.
*** Graduate(s).

Source: Hugh Davies and Heather Joshi, 'Who Bears the Cost of Britain's Children in the 1990s?', Working paper, Department of Economics, Birkbeck College, 1999, table 1.

Can government do anything about this? A radical but practical first step, which would begin to introduce some personal responsibility into the operation of the state pension system, would be to make pension contributions compulsory for all working-age adults, so that even those in the lower parts of the income distribution could expect, over a full working life, to accumulate an adequate capital sum to provide for their own retirement. But this obligation to contribute could be commuted by parenthood. Instead of continuing to contribute to a pension fund, parents would be allowed to cease making these payments, focus their resources on the sustenance and development of their children, and thereby accumulate a public pension entitlement which would be honoured by the tax contributions made when the children of today become the workers of tomorrow. The full, tax-financed state pension entitlement would be earned by parents, while non-parents would receive a capital-funded retirement income based on their accumulated pension savings across their working life.

A 'parental pension' of this sort has many advantages: it is based upon a clear and justifiable reason for the introduction of compulsory pension contributions; it targets contributions on those individuals most able to sustain them; it provides positive financial support for parenthood by removing from parents the obligation of making pension contributions (thereby reducing the gap between parents and non-parents in their lifetime disposable income); it can further target this assistance on active parents (usually mothers) by requiring any parent not participating in the support of offspring to resume the payment of pension contributions. By making clear that pension entitlements are linked to active contribution—whether to childrearing or to saving—this policy would establish the principle that individuals must take direct responsibility for their pension futures—something that a Citizen's Pension clearly fails to do. By making explicit the nature and costs of the intergenerational transfers inherent in a pay-as-you-go public pension it would force politicians to face up to the bad news that the current level of transfer cannot sustain the level of pension most people expect and desire for the future. And, by reducing the net cost of children, it might even increase the birth rate.

Bibliography

Items that provide a useful introduction to the issues discussed in this chapter are marked with an asterisk.

Aaron, H., 'The Social Insurance Paradox', *Canadian Journal of Economic and Political Science*, 32 (1966), 371–4.

Department of Health and Social Security, *Reform of Social Security: Programme for Action*, Cmnd 9691 (London, 1985).
*Department for Work and Pensions, *Simplicity, Security and Choice: Working and Saving for Retirement*, Cm 5677 (London, 2002).
Financial Services Consumer Panel, *Annual Report for 2000* (London, 2001).
Hemming, R. and J. A. Kay, 'The Cost of the State Earnings Related Pensions Scheme', *Economic Journal*, 92 (1982), 300–19.
*National Association of Pension Funds, *Towards a Citizen's Pension: Final Report* (London, 2005).
OECD, *Reforming Public Pensions* (Paris, 1988).
*Pensions Commission, *Pensions: Challenges and Choices. The First Report of the Pensions Commission* (London, 2004).
*——, *A New Pension Settlement for the Twenty-first Century. The Second Report of the Pensions Commission* (London, 2005).
*Pensions Policy Institute, *The Pensions Landscape* (London, 2003), available online at www.pensionspolicyinstitute.org.uk.
Report of the Royal Commission on Population (London, 1949).
Samuelson, P. A., 'An Exact Consumption-Loans Model with or without the Social Contrivance of Money', *Journal of Political Economy*, 66 (1958), 467–82.

12.
Financing UK Pensions

JOHN HILLS

The chapters in this volume do a very valuable job in discussing some of the potential suspects that might be identified in determining just how we ended up where we are today when it comes to pensions. 'Where did it all go wrong?, as the title of the conference from which this book sprang had it. In particular, why, and when, did things begin to go wrong with the financing of British pensions?

A key feature of the pension challenges currently facing Britain is the decline of the system of occupational pensions, particularly the decline of defined-benefit pensions. Here, it is often argued that the villain of the piece, having delivered a series of hammer blows to the system, has effectively been government (in fact a succession of governments). In this view, over the past decades successive governments have delivered a catalogue of regulation and legislation that, though often well intentioned, has ultimately worked to the detriment of occupational pension provision. That catalogue of regulation and legislation has, if you like, steadily blocked all the bolt-holes which occupational pension providers could have used in coping with the risks they were sometimes unaware they were running.

Alternatively, one might argue that we could have seen it all coming. Paul Johnson argues in this volume, for example, that the villain of the piece is not a lack of demographic knowledge, nor a lack of actuarial science, nor a lack of economic knowledge, but rather a continuous political short-termism. A whole series of politicians has shied away from solving problems, the results of which will accrue to unknown political successors at some point in the future. In this view, political shortcomings opened up the opportunity for free-riding on the part of individuals; giving some of the post-war baby boom generation the opportunity to do little about securing their future pensions, and encouraging them to see themselves all right in the end by relying not on prudent provision for the future but on the political muscle that their numbers, and their greater likelihood of voting, would give them in their retirement years. (Although one could note in tempering this that people appear increasingly unconfident as to whether their political muscle will actually achieve that end.)

I have some sympathy with many of these points. However, those who focus on the failures of politicians in general, and of governments in particular, may have drawn their dragnet a little narrowly in their search for villains in the field of pensions. Is it really possible, for example, entirely to exonerate the demographers and the actuaries? For instance, Johnson notes that demographic science has long recognized the potential for changes in birth and death rates to create problems for pensions systems. The point here though is that, while it is certainly true that we *could* have seen it all coming, the fact is that we didn't. Indeed it came as a pleasant surprise to me during my work for the Pensions Commission to find that the government actuary had not previously foreseen the extent of the increase now expected in my own cohort's life expectancy. Nor, I think, did anybody in the private sector who had relied on the output of the wonderfully named Continuous Mortality Investigation. Nor is it entirely evident that the private sector's actuaries were reacting particularly rapidly over the past twenty years, and making the necessary gradual adjustments to mortality tables to reflect increasing life expectancy. Instead, the private sector has tended to move rather as a pack, with adjustments coming in a rush over the last few years. So I personally think the actuaries are still in the frame. And, as Jose Harris suggests elsewhere in this volume, this failure adequately to predict rising longevity, and to make policy-makers and other interested parties aware of the implications of what might to some extent have been predictable demographic change, goes way back to the government actuary advising Beveridge in 1942.

Paul Johnson also argues in his chapter that economists were long able to see all our current problems coming too, going back to Samuelson in 1958.[1] Now, it is true that the long-term economic implications of adopting a pay-as-you-go approach to pensions were foreseeable at the time. So too, indeed, were the long-term consequences for adequacy of moving to price-linking the state pension in 1981 rather than linking it to some measure of average earnings. Thus the long-term implications of these key decisions in the development of our modern system of pensions were all foreseeable. Yet, despite this, what we find when we look back is a persistent assumption that, somehow or other, the private sector would see us all right in the end. You see that assumption most recently in the

[1] P. A. Samuelson, 'An Exact Consumption-Loans Model with or without the Social Contrivance of Money', *Journal of Political Economy*, 66 (1958), 467–82.

government's 1998 green paper on pensions.[2] This referred to a reversal of the then alleged 60 per cent of the financing of pensions coming from the public sector and 40 per cent from the private sector—to 40 per cent coming from the state and 60 per cent from the private sector. In fact, this has not happened, because the private sector has failed to take up the slack in the way that the government hoped.

We also need to look at the evidence that some of this decline in private-sector provision actually predates much of the legislation and regulation that is sometimes seen as having caused that decline.[3] As Pemberton, Whiteside, and Glennerster point out in this volume, membership of occupational schemes peaked in 1967. Contributions going into pension schemes as a share of GDP peaked in 1981 and declined rapidly after then.[4] Clearly, pensions legislation and regulation have served to remove some of the bolt-holes that might otherwise have been used by occupational pension providers when returns deteriorated with the end of the 1990s equity boom in 2000. But I think it is worth remembering, as we were reminded by Lord Hunt in his opening remarks to our conference in July 2005, that some of those bolt-holes weren't actually very good bolt-holes in the first place. For example, schemes were protected by their ability to reduce pension rights for early-leavers, to the detriment of such former employees. Pension funds could also hope for a good dollop of inflation to reduce the real value of people's nominal rights over the long term and thus to contain fund liabilities—this, for example, is exactly what happened when shares crashed in the mid-1970s at a time of high inflation. Limited price indexation is part of what blocked that bolt-hole; but so too is the setting up in 1997 of the Monetary Policy Committee and its success (so far) in subsequently reducing inflation.

In addition, while it is possible to point the finger at governments for the increasing amount of regulatory legislation, and at the people who have called for that regulation, I don't remember many private companies protesting very loudly at the contributions holidays that resulted from some of that regulation in the early-1990s, or at their ability at that time to finance corporate restructuring through raids on their pension funds. So it seems to me to be a little unfair to put all the blame for those changes on government.

[2] Department of Social Security, *A New Contract for Welfare: Partnership in Pensions*, Cm 4179 (London, 1998).

[3] Pensions Commission, *Pensions: Challenges and Choices. The First Report of the Pensions Commission* (London, 2004), ch. 3, annex.

[4] Pensions Commission, *First Report*, fig. 3A.6.

Now, I know that when the first report of the Pensions Commission came out one newspaper columnist accused us of having blamed everybody back to the Venerable Bede for Britain's current pensions problems. At this point it is traditional to say 'like the *Murder on the Orient Express*' when we're looking for culprits responsible for the pensions problems that we now confront, in a sense 'everybody was to blame'. However, I think we should look at the end of Dorothy L. Sayers' much better detective story, *The Nine Tailors*, where it turns out that everybody has done it, that the hammer blows that have done the deed are actually those that have rung the bells in the church tower, but that the victim was killed unwittingly. When it comes to pensions, it seems to me that this is perhaps a better analogy than *Murder on the Orient Express*, where all the protagonists *intended* to kill their victim.

I would like to finish with two points about where that leads us in the future. It is important that future policy should do more than just deal with the increases in life expectancy which we can see coming. It needs also to be set up in a way that is sustainable and robust enough to cope with the huge *uncertainty* around the increase in life expectancy which we are hoping for. This particular problem is greatly compounded by the discrepancy between fixed expectations about pension ages and the increases in life expectancy which we have already had. In 1950, when the male pension age was 65 and when men retiring at that age could expect to live for a further thirteen years, that was a much easier prospect for governments and for private providers to cope with than it is today. Now one must cope with an expected life expectancy of nineteen years at the same pension age of 65. By 2050, on current projections, male life expectancy at age 65 will have risen further to nearly twenty-four.[5] Just the sheer length of time into which we are expecting pension providers to enter the 'funnel of uncertainty' when it comes to future liabilities seems to me to create a problem which is a whole order of magnitude greater than the problem which we faced in the past.

My second point concerns the lack of knowledge and trust in the system that people have. This is clearly very much part of the problem we face at the moment in the pensions arena. But it is also, in another way, an important opportunity. As Paul Johnson points out in his chapter in this volume, at the moment the government is expecting in its long-term spending forecasts to spend an increasing percentage of GDP on pensions, and such projections have indeed increased substantially over

[5] Pensions Commission, *A New Pension Settlement for the Twenty-first Century. The Second Report of the Pensions Commission* (London, 2005), figs 1.44 and 1.38.

the last two years. But a lot of people actually believe that they are in 'Generation G' of Table 11.1 in Paul Johnson's chapter, and thus believe that, despite having paid into the system throughout their working lives, they are likely to get little or nothing back from it when they retire. So, despite the fact that government is tearing its hair out trying to work out how to cope with these future pension pressures, many people in the country at large are expecting to get very little out of the system in their own retirement. With a clearer explanation of what people's entitlements will be, and with a better structure to deliver what we are already planning to provide, there might in fact be an opportunity to give people some sort of pleasant surprise in amongst all the bad news they have been getting when it comes to pensions expectations.

I do, however, agree that a lot of the reason why there is such a lack of understanding on the part of both the public and policy-makers when it comes to the way in which the pensions system currently works, and the way in which our problems with that system might be solved, is a shared lack of appreciation about how the fundamental trade-offs within pensions work. If we can build institutional structures which make those trade-offs more apparent, and if we can find ways of continually keeping those trade-offs in clear view as we move into future funnels of uncertainty, then there will be an opportunity for better decisions all round. There is thus another important potential gain here.

Now, a transition from the current complexity that is highlighted by several contributors to this volume to a more straightforward set of structures, or at least to a situation in which people understand the rules of the game better, will not be without its own complexities—for all the reasons that Hugh Pemberton has outlined in his chapter. But there are potential large gains out there to be had alongside the bad news that will inevitably be highlighted by greater clarity, even if it takes us a little while to get there.

Bibliography

Department of Social Security, *A New Contract for Welfare: Partnership in Pensions*, Cm 4179 (London, 1998).

Pensions Commission, *Pensions: Challenges and Choices. The First Report of the Pensions Commission* (London, 2004).

Pensions Commission, *A New Pension Settlement for the Twenty-first Century. The Second Report of the Pensions Commission* (London, 2005).

Samuelson, P. A., 'An Exact Consumption-Loans Model with or without the Social Contrivance of Money', *Journal of Political Economy*, 66 (1958), 467–82.

Lessons from Abroad

13. Anglo-Saxon Occupational Pensions in International Perspective

STEVEN SASS

Occupational pension plans are today a major 'second tier' in Anglo-Saxon retirement income systems, providing benefits to a significant portion of the elderly population atop the basic 'first tier' benefits provided by the state. In the USA, for example, employer plans provide one-fifth of the income of the elderly—one-quarter if we exclude earnings from work—half the amount provided by public plans. This chapter describes the development of employer plans, their unique role in Anglo-Saxon nations, and their prospects for the future.

The Development of Employer Pension Plans before 1940[1]

Occupational pension plans predate the creation of national old-age income programmes. They were put in place by large organizations—such as governments, railroads, utilities, universities, hospitals, and big business corporations—that emerged over the course of the nineteenth century and came to employ an extensive permanent staff. These organizations put such plans in place because they found them valuable as instruments for shaping their relationship with their workforce in three distinct ways.

First, the pension helped develop career civil servants and managers. These large employers increasingly delegated authority to a special class of workers who oversaw their operations. Such workers had to invest in organization-specific skills and relationships, make decisions and execute responsibilities in the best interest of the organization, and do so with limited oversight over their entire working lives. The British civil service pension plan of 1859 became the model, and, in the USA, governments, utilities, universities, and financial firms adopted similar plans. These

[1] See also the contribution by Clark to this volume.

plans targeting white-collar workers paid a comfortable pension, pegged to salary and years of service, to those workers who remained with the employer to a pre-specified retirement age. Workers who left early typically got only a return of their own contributions. The pension thus functioned as an incentive to remain with the organization and to rise through the ranks. And the substantial value of the pension, net of the worker's accumulated contributions plus interest, reflected the value of a career to the employer.[2]

Pensions also proved valuable in shaping relationships with blue-collar workers. Organizations in industries such as railways, urban public transport, and manufacturing employed large numbers of blue-collar workers to operate their capital-intensive, high-throughput operations. In the USA in particular, these employers typically paid high market wages to attract better workers, win their loyalty, and keep union organization at bay. But beyond a certain point, employers found it more effective to provide 'industrial insurance' rather than ever-higher wages. This insurance protected workers and their families against the loss of earnings due to accident, death, illness, or age. Given the new dependence on wage and salary earnings in industrial economies—and the significant risk of accident, death, illness, and becoming too old to work—workers whose basic economic needs had largely been met valued such protection for themselves and their families. These plans also eliminated the need to take up collections to assist a worker or his family after such events—they discharged a social obligation in a routine and predictable fashion.[3]

Blue-collar industrial insurance programmes replaced a small share of earnings in the event of a 'loss'. Pensions were often 1 per cent of earnings multiplied by years of service—barely half the amount found in white-collar plans—and not enough to offer retirement in comfort. One reason for such low pensions was economy—larger benefits required higher contributions and there was a limit on the amount of insurance, or social obligation, that employers and workers were willing to purchase. A second reason was the need to reduce 'moral hazard'—the risk that the availability of insurance would induce behaviour that increased the like-

[2] Alfred D. Chandler, *The Visible Hand: The Managerial Revolution in American Business* (Cambridge, 1977); Marios Raphael, *Pensions and Public Servants: A Study of the Origins of the British System* (Paris, 1964); Leslie Hannah, *Inventing Retirement: The Development of Occupational Pensions in Britain* (Cambridge, 1986); Edward P. Lazear, *Personnel Economics* (Cambridge, 1995); Steven Sass, *The Promise of Private Pensions* (Cambridge, 1997).

[3] Walter Licht, *Working for the Railroad: The Organization of Work in the Nineteenth Century* (Princeton NJ, 1983); Sass, *Private Pensions.*

lihood of a claim. If benefits were too high, perfectly able workers might feign an illness to claim an old-age or disability pension.

By the end of the nineteenth century, many large employers became concerned about the opposite problem. Their offices, machine shops, and locomotives were increasingly staffed by older workers whose productive abilities had clearly declined. So, beginning in the 1890s in the UK, and at the turn of the century in the USA, some large employers found a third use for pensions. They began to mandate retirement at a specified age. And, to remove older workers without damaging relations with the rest of the workforce, or the public at large, they retired these workers on a pension. As companies with pre-existing white-collar or blue-collar plans saw the number of older employees steadily rise, many introduced compulsory retirement, on pension, and extended their plans to cover all workers.[4]

By the end of the 1930s, employer pension plans had become standard in governments and mature big businesses throughout the industrial world. They had become critical tools for strengthening, then severing, relationships with workers. Employer plans then covered about 15 per cent of the workforce in the USA, and a similar percentage in the UK and other industrial nations.[5]

The Great Divide: Employer Plans in Anglo-Saxon Post-war Systems, 1945–65

The economics of ageing changed dramatically after the Second World War. Governments in essentially all industrial nations had established old-age pension programmes that assured the elderly population a basic income without the need to work. They thus assumed much of the 'industrial insurance' function formerly provided by blue-collar employer plans. The 1946 basic state pension in the UK extended the 1925 social insurance pension plan, which paid about 20 per cent of the average wage, to include white-collar as well as clerical and blue-collar workers. Likewise the critical 1950 Social Security Amendments in the USA restored pre-war replacement rates found in F. D. Roosevelt's social

[4] William Graebner, *A History of Retirement* (New Haven CT, 1980); Sass, *Private Pensions.*

[5] Murray Latimer, *Industrial Pension Systems in the United States and Canada* (New York, 1932); Hannah, *Inventing Retirement*; Commonwealth Treasury of Australia, 'Towards Higher Retirement Incomes for Australians: A History of the Australian Retirement Income System since Federation', *Treasury Economic Roundup Centenary Edition 2001* (Canberra, 2001); Kenneth Bryden, *Old Age Pensions and Policy-making in Canada* (Montreal, 1974).

security programme—about 30 per cent for the model average worker—while easing requirements for the receipt of full pension benefits and expanding coverage to include essentially all workers. And Canada, in 1951, converted its 1927 programme that provided means-tested benefits into its Old Age Security programme that provided demogrants to all long-term residents. In the post-war period, employer plans thus focused on serving middle- and upper-income workers.[6]

Incentives built into both public and employer pension programmes also encouraged withdrawal from the labour force at a specified age. Many employer plans included compulsory retirement provisions. Public programmes and employer plans without mandatory retirement encouraged retirement by not increasing benefits for those who worked past the 'normal retirement age' (NRA). This effectively cut the compensation of anyone who remained employed past the NRA to their wage less their foregone pension.[7] Most public plans also had an earnings test that denied benefits to anyone who earned more than a trivial amount. So workers had to choose between work or retirement, and most chose the latter. As longevity was also rising rapidly in the post-war period, 'retirement' now emerged as an expected, extended, and well defined stage of life.

The elderly nevertheless remained a distinctly poor population. Over one-third of the US elderly in 1959 were classified as poor; in Canada in the early 1960s, the figure approached 45 per cent.[8] As the industrial world was then in the midst of the long post-war boom, the financial standing of the elderly stood in increasingly sharp contrast to the rising prosperity of working-age adults. A consensus emerged: first that the elderly should share in this prosperity and second that income should be spread more evenly across the lifespan, assuring active workers a reasonable continuation of their living standard when they in turn grow old.

[6] Sass, *Private Pensions*; Hannah, *Inventing Retirement*; Noel Whiteside, 'Historical Perspectives and the Politics of Pension Reform', in G. L. Clark and N. Whiteside (eds), *Pension Security in the Twenty-first Century* (Oxford, 2003).

[7] More precisely, the additional income from remaining employed was the worker's wage *plus* non-pension benefits *less* income and payroll taxes on wages, out-of-pocket working expenses, *and* the foregone pension less income taxes on the pension (which were zero on Social Security benefits).

[8] US Bureau of the Census, *Historical Poverty Tables*, table 3, 'Poverty Status of People, by Age, Race, and Hispanic Origin: 1959 to 2001' (2002), at www.census.gov/hhes/poverty/histpov/hstpov3.html; Lars Osberg, 'Poverty among Senior Citizens: A Canadian Success Story', in *International Perspective*, LIS Working Paper 274 (Differdange, 2001).

Nations on the European continent would expand public and quasi-public old-age pensions and crowd out single company employer plans.[9] The Anglo-Saxon nations, such as the USA, the UK, Australia, and Canada, would expand both public and employer plans. The conservative parties in Anglo-Saxon nations had a much more restrictive view of the proper role of the state and vigorously opposed such an expansion of government control. Continental European nations, by contrast, had strong 'statist, 'corporatist', or 'Christian Democratic' traditions that became the political foundation for a wide variety of labour market arrangements, including old-age pensions, negotiated at the national level in policy processes that included the social partners. In addition to these political differences, Anglo-Saxon nations were also spared the worst ravages of the Second World War. So employers in these nations entered the post-war period with far more resources that could be used to provide retirement incomes.[10]

As public pensions remained low through the initial post-war decades, a significant expansion of employer plans was critical to the success of the Anglo-Saxon approach. And employer plans indeed expanded. Government employment shot up in the post-war period, and most government workers were covered by employer plans. More dramatic was the rise in private-sector coverage rates, which reached 40 per cent in the UK and the USA by the 1960s (see Figure 13.1), although somewhat later in Australia and somewhat less in Canada. This rise can be traced to three factors: the growth of large corporate employers; the increased importance of pensions as tax-advantaged compensation; and, most significantly, the growth of collectively bargained plans.[11]

The post-war decades were the heyday of corporate big business. The long boom was largely driven by giant mass-production mass-distribution enterprises—in industries ranging from cars, steel, and consumer goods to telecommunications, banking and insurance, transport, and public utilities. As employer plans had become an essential component of corporate personnel systems, coverage expanded in line with the growth of big business.[12]

[9] See Whiteside's contribution to this volume.

[10] Whiteside, 'Historical Perspectives'; Gosta Esping-Andersen, *The Three Worlds of Welfare Capitalism* (Oxford, 1990); Gordon Clark, *Pension Fund Capitalism* (Oxford, 2000).

[11] Sass, *Private Pensions*; Hannah, *Inventing Retirement*; Commonwealth Treasury of Australia, 'Towards Higher Retirement Incomes for Australians'; Laurence Coward, *Private Pensions in OECD Countries: Canada* (Paris, 1997).

[12] Chandler, *Visible Hand*.

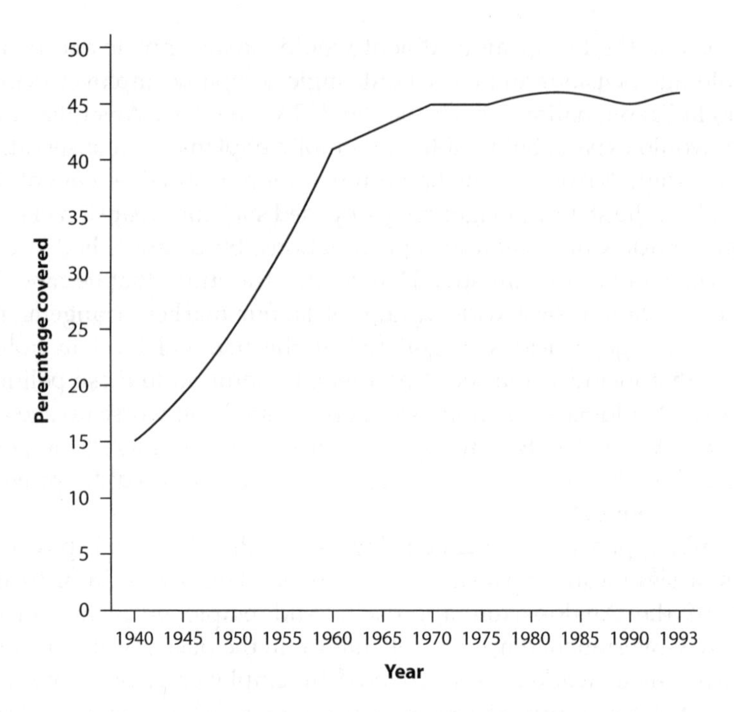

Figure 13.1. US private-sector waged and salaried workers covered by employer plans, 1940–93.

Sources: American Academy of Actuaries, *Financing the Retirement of Future Generations: The Problem and Options for Change* (Washington DC, 1998), p. 10. Data for 1940–70 from Alfred Skolnik, 'Private Pension Plans, 1950–1974', *Social Security Bulletin*, June (1976). Data for 1975–93 based on US Department of Labor analysis of IRS Form 5500.

The special tax treatments of employer pensions also became significantly more attractive in the post-war era. These measures, largely enacted in the 1920s, typically exempted employer contributions and pension fund investment income and taxed beneficiaries only on pensions paid out in retirement. This tax treatment had a limited effect on coverage before the war, as less than 10 per cent of the adult population typically paid tax. Only with the post-war growth of mass income taxation did these treatments have a significant effect on coverage. The government in effect then became a major funder of employer plans, making pensions far less costly to employers and workers and encouraging their spread.[13]

[13] As James Wooten points out, the fact that very few rank-and-file workers paid tax in the 1920s, when these treatments took shape, suggests that they were not enacted as a 'benefit', but to level the playing field between pension and wage compensation—to avoid.

The key factor in the post-war growth of employer pensions, however, was the growth of collectively bargained plans. Labour unions, worker associations, and friendly societies had long sought to provide their members with old-age pensions. But the largely voluntary nature of these organizations and their limited financial resources had restricted their ability to do so. After the Second World War, however, unions throughout the industrial world found themselves in a much stronger position. They had gained powerful collective bargaining rights, represented a significant portion of the workforce, and were closely affiliated with the major left-wing political parties.

Unions used this strength to expand old-age income benefits within the larger post-war political settlement. On the European continent, they successfully pressed for expanded government pensions and/or mandatory, quasi-public employment-based plans that provided supplementary top-ups. In Anglo-Saxon nations, the unions negotiated generous employer plans, often with the help of government. These bargained plans made the employer, not the union, responsible for providing old-age pensions. By making pensions dependent on the success of the employer, these plans helped secure union commitments to industrial peace. They also involved union acceptance of limited government pensions. In the USA, the big industrial unions won generous pension benefits in 1949 and 1950 as part of a political settlement that included long-term labour agreements, controls on labour militancy, and the passage of the 1950 Social Security Amendments. In the decade that followed, pensions became a standard component of labour agreements throughout the unionized sector. In the UK, the unions won generous pensions in nationalized industries from Conservative governments intent on forestalling Labour Party initiatives to expand public pensions.[14]

Employer Plans in the Expansion of Anglo-Saxon Systems, 1965–80

The Anglo-Saxon approach to the old-age income problem had taken root by the mid-1960s. But the results were clearly limited. Employer plans

taxing compensation taken as pensions (at the employer and pension trust level) for workers whose wages would not be taxed. James Wooten, *The Employee Retirement Income Security Act of 1974: A Political History* (Berkeley CA, 2005).

[14] Sass, *Private Pensions*; Hannah, *Inventing Retirement*; Whiteside, 'Historical Perspectives'; Esping-Andersen, *Welfare Capitalism*.

covered just half the workforce. Many covered workers would quit or lose their jobs before gaining a pension. Others would see their plans go bust and their benefits lose much or all of their value. As public pensions provided meagre, barely subsistence-level benefits, old age remained a stage of life generally characterized by a sharp decline in living standards.

In response to these shortcomings, Anglo-Saxon governments launched a series of initiatives to enlarge and strengthen both public and private retirement income programmes. This expansion largely came between 1965 and 1980, at the end of the long post-war boom. The USA, the UK, and other Anglo-Saxon nations raised public pensions to give the 'average earner'—the worker who consistently earned the national average wage and retired at age 65—a pension of about 40 to 45 per cent of the 'average wage' at retirement. These nations also adopted initiatives designed to make employer pensions a more secure and widely distributed component of the national retirement income system.

The US approach involved the imposition of an extensive set of regulations on tax-advantaged employer plans. Government officials had taken note of the large and growing pension 'tax expenditure'—the revenue foregone by the government as a result of the special treatment afforded employer plans. While the precise size of the expenditure is difficult to calculate, most official enumerations put pensions at the top of the tax expenditure list. Such a large revenue loss, these officials reasoned, could be justified only by a comparable contribution to public welfare. And this could be accomplished only if employer plans became a vehicle through which a large portion of the workforce could safely shift income from their years of employment to their years of retirement. So, in exchange for government tax benefits, the Employee Retirement Income Security Act of 1974 (ERISA) imposed the following requirements (which have subsequently been tightened):[15]

1. Vesting standards. Employers were required to vest workers with accrued pension benefits within one of several specified schedules, with full vesting after ten years of service most commonly adopted. Given the turnover in the US labour market, and the difficulty in expanding employer plan coverage beyond large employers and unionized workers, mandatory vesting seemed the

[15] Canada initiated this approach with its Pension Benefits Acts of 1965–6. Coward, *Private Pensions*.

most effective way to increase the share of the workforce that would get at least a small employer pension to supplement their social security benefits.[16]

2 Funding standards. Employers had to contribute the cost of benefits currently accrued (which had been required since 1942) plus the amount needed to amortize any shortfall within thirty years. ERISA also made employers liable for any shortfall up to 30 per cent of their net worth, effectively funding the plan to that level with the equity of the sponsor.
3 Governance standards. The statute required everyone associated with the operation of a plan, from the trustees (typically officers of the sponsor) to their consultants and agents, to act solely in the interest of the beneficiaries. It also listed a series of 'prohibited transactions' that outlawed investments that could advance the interests of corporate and union sponsors, or their officers, but undermine benefit security.
4 Participation in the new Pension Benefit Guaranty Corporation (PBGC), an insurance fund that protected pensions up to a specified level should the plan go bankrupt.

The UK took a different tack to strengthening employer plans.[17] It primarily leveraged the contracting-out provisions in the State Earnings-related Pension Scheme (SERPS), introduced in 1978. SERPS had been enacted with two purposes in mind. First, it was a residual earnings-related pension plan, designed for those not covered by an employer scheme. Second, and more germane to employer plans, the SERPS programme offered employers an incentive to establish a plan. Retaining the provisions of earlier legislation (1959), it provided such employers with a 'rebate' of social insurance contributions if they 'contracted out' and assumed much of the government's newly created pension obligation. Not only would the government fund this tranche of an employer's plan, it also set the rebate above the employer's estimated cost of providing the

[16] ERISA also expanded the number of beneficiaries, specifically to elderly widows who were poorly served by earnings-based retirement income systems, by making a joint-and-survivor annuity the default annuity form. Unless specifically waived, a surviving spouse (nearly always a widow) would receive half the worker's pension, which would be actuarially reduced to pay for this survivor benefit.

[17] See also Pemberton's contribution to this volume.

benefit. In return, the government imposed various requirements on the benefits provided.[18]

Australia took a third approach to expanding employer plans. The government, in 1986, won the inclusion of pension contributions, in lieu of increased cash wages, in the standard labour contract negotiated at the national level by labour and management representatives. These contributions, defined as a uniform percentage of earnings, would primarily go to individual retirement accounts. The Australian national labour bargain did not carry the same authority as similar agreements on the European continent. Nevertheless, coverage reached 72 per cent of waged and salaried workers by the end of the decade. And, to strengthen the new system as a broad-based source of old-age income, the government enacted regulations governing vesting and fiduciary conduct and required worker representation on the boards overseeing such plans.[19]

The Contribution of Employer Plans at the End of the Age of Expansion

By the end of the twentieth century, employer plans had emerged as a critical component of Anglo-Saxon retirement income systems. Because these plans were funded in advance, transferring earnings from the years of employment to the years of retirement, the capital market became a major source of support for much of the elderly population. As shown in Figure 13.2, investment income (about half from employer plans) now provides 40 per cent or more of the income of the elderly in the USA, the UK, and Canada. Only those at the bottom rely on government benefits for nearly

[18] Employers did not have to take on the entire SERPS liability as the government retained the riskier portions of the obligation, such as inflation proofing. To encourage contracting out, the government set the contribution rebate at about half a percentage point above the estimated private cost of providing the benefit. The estimate included administrative expenses, which increased costs above the government alternative; but assumed a significant use of equities in funding the benefit, which reduced costs well below the present value of the benefit discounted at the riskless government rate. Hannah, *Inventing Retirement*; Chris Daykin, 'Contracting Out: A Partnership between Public and Private Pensions', *Pensions Management Institute News* (July 2001).

[19] In addition to advancing retirement income objectives, the government also sought to substitute pension contributions for wages to increase national saving and help achieve more immediate macroeconomic policy objectives: to reduce consumer demand, inflation, interest rates, and the nation's widening trade deficit. Hazel Bateman and John Piggott, 'The Australian Approach to Retirement Income Provision', prepared for the International Seminar on Social Security Pensions (Tokyo, 5–7 March 2001); Commonwealth Treasury 'Retirement Incomes'.

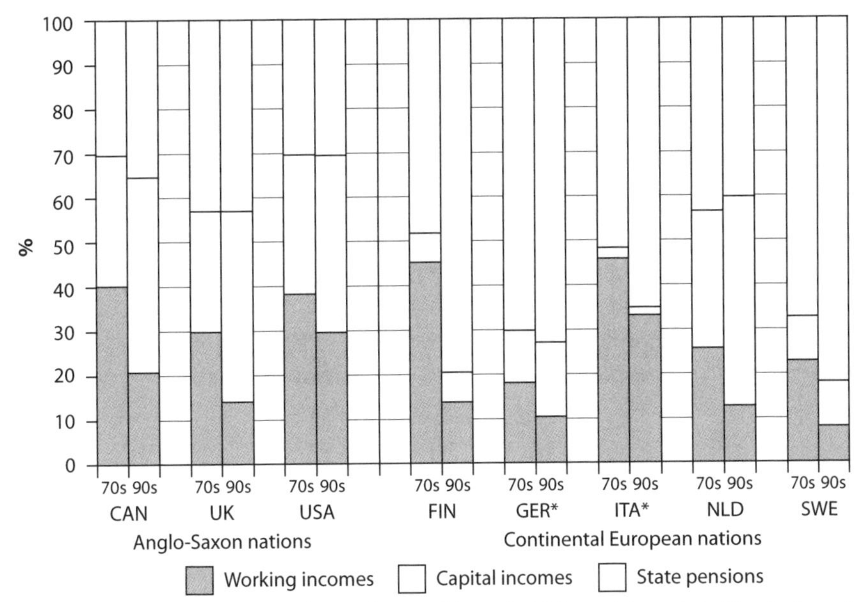

Figure 13.2. Income from employer plans and household financial assets in 'Anglo-Saxon' and 'continental European' nations. Disposable income by source, age 65 and over, 1970s and 1990s.

* Data for Germany and Italy are for the mid-1980s.

Source: Amended from A. Yamada, *The Evolving Retirement Income Package: Trends in Adequacy and Equality* (Paris, 2002).

all their old-age income. Employer plans provide important earnings-related top-ups for middle-income workers, with public pensions functioning as the basic source of financial security. And, for those at the upper end of the income distribution, employer plans and investment income are the dominant sources of support. In nations with continental European retirement income systems—other than the Netherlands—investment income is a minor source of support even for upper income groups (Figure 13.3).

Both Anglo-Saxon and continental European schemes allow the elderly, on average, to maintain a reasonable approximation of their pre-retirement living standard (Figure 13.4). After adjusting for their lower tax burden and smaller household size, the disposable income of individuals aged 65–75 in both systems is not much less than that of working-age adults. And younger adults still have to pay working expenses, save for retirement, and make do with less leisure. Even in the UK, a clear outlier, the disposable incomes of these age groups are reasonably close. Incomes

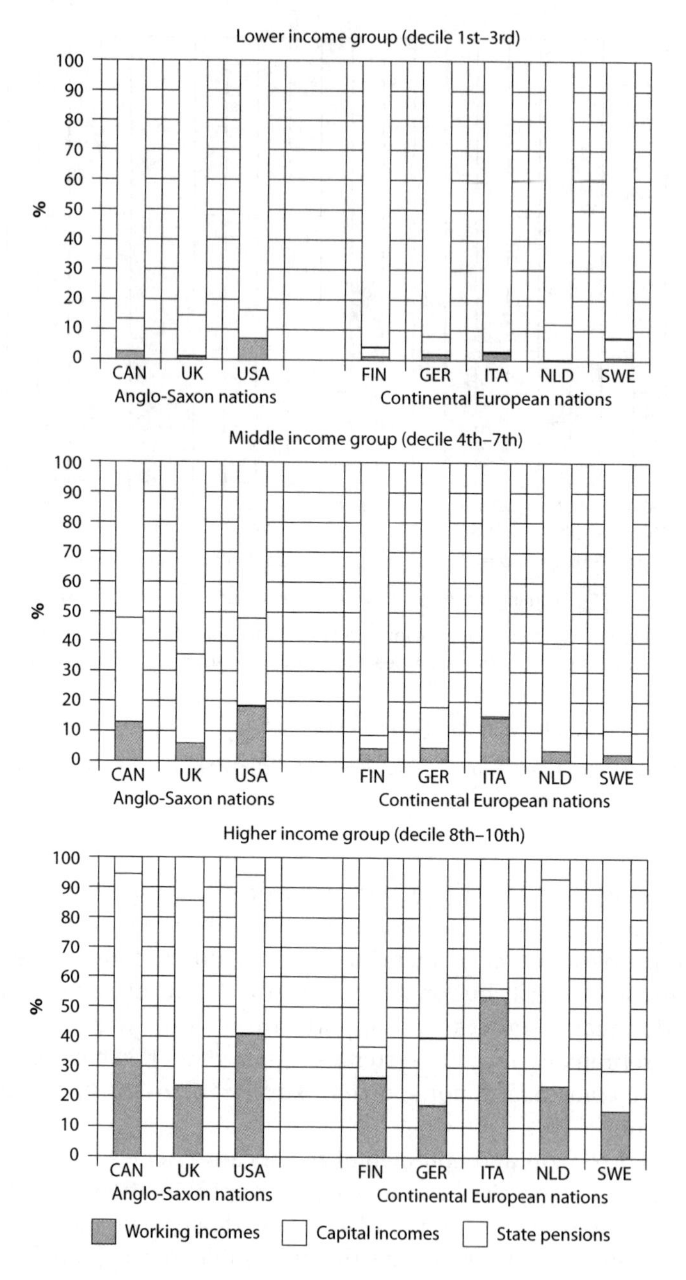

Figure 13.3. Employer plans and other sources of investment income in 'Anglo-Saxon' and 'continental European' systems.

Source: Amended from A. Yamada, *The Evolving Retirement Income Package: Trends in Adequacy and Equality* (Paris, 2002).

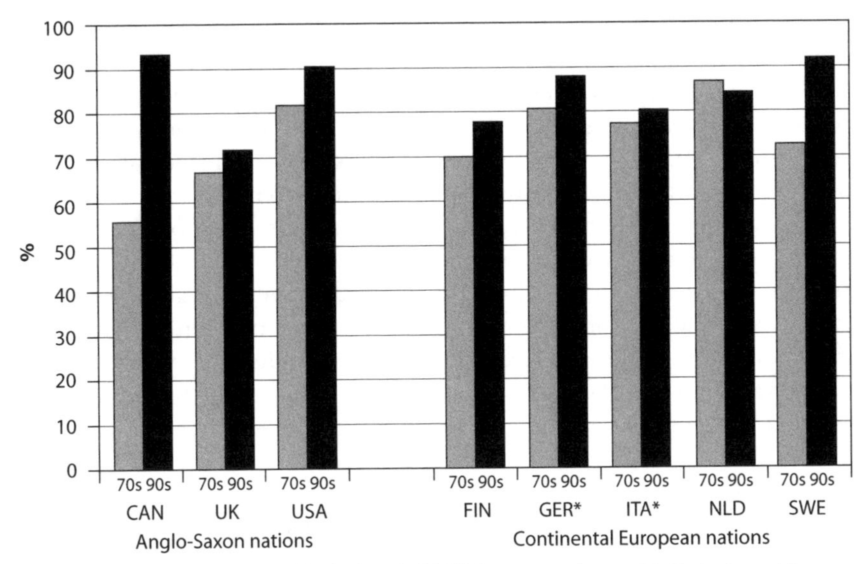

Figure 13.4. Income of the elderly (aged 65–74) in comparison with that of working-age adults. Ratio of income adjusted for taxes and household size of people aged 65–74 to that of people aged 18–64, mid-1970s and 1990s.

* Data for Germany and Italy are for the mid-1980s.

Source: Amended from A. Yamada, *The Evolving Retirement Income Package: Trends in Adequacy and Equality* (Paris, 2002).

in both systems tend to decline over time, and older women, in particular, remain a disadvantaged group. Anglo-Saxon systems also have greater disparities in the distribution of old-age income. Nevertheless, these systems now provide a far more rational distribution of income between the generations and across a worker's lifespan.[20]

The Contribution of Anglo-Saxon Employer Plans in the Future

Almost immediately after the expansion of these national retirement income systems, however, it became clear that rapid population ageing would place enormous pressure on pay-as-you-go government plans in

[20] Atsuhiro Yamada, *The Evolving Retirement Income Package: Trends in Adequacy and Equality* (Paris, 2002).

the early-twenty-first century. Advance-funded employer plans, as a result, appeared increasingly attractive.

But structural economic shifts have seriously weakened employer plans in the years after 1980. Globalization and sharp increases in the educational attainment of the labour force, in the technical level of production, and in the employment of married women have had various corrosive effects. First, these forces undermined the power of trade unions, the major factor in the post-war expansion of employer plans. Second, these forces undermined the financial stability of large corporate employers, making the assumption of long-term pension obligations a more risky undertaking. Third, globalization eroded the ability of governments to tax. As tax rates fell, so did the value of the tax advantages enjoyed by employer plans and their implicit rates of public funding. Finally, globalization, higher education, higher technology, and the entry of married women into the paid workforce changed the nature of optimal employment relationships. These forces diminished the appeal of lifelong careers in favour of intermediate (not spot-market) durations. This is especially so with higher paid workers that employer plans primarily serve. Employers would thus find far less justification for maintaining their traditional defined-benefit pension plans, which rewarded career-long employment, or indeed for continuing any large contribution to employee retirement income programmes.

Just as national retirement income systems had largely addressed a fundamental defect in the modern industrial economy, the continued contribution of employer plans, as well as public programmes, would be called into question. Employers had increasingly little to gain by offering pensions. And the costs of such benefits would continue to rise with the growth of longevity, the imposition of new government burdens, and the volatility of the employer's underlying business and employment needs. So employers are largely abandoning their former role in the provision of retirement income. While they often substitute defined-contribution retirement savings plans, such arrangements require much lower contributions and no risk-bearing or financial management on the part of the sponsor. It is difficult, however, for employers to convert from a traditional defined-benefit pension to a defined-contribution retirement savings plan. In the fluid US economy, the shift from defined-benefit to defined-contribution plans was well advanced by the end of the twentieth century as new firms adopted defined-contribution programmes and subsequently grew rapidly. Meanwhile major economic shocks hit key US industries, specifically steel and airlines, with legacy defined-benefit plans. This led to large pension insolvencies, major deficits at the PBGC, and the imposition of tougher funding requirements on defined-benefit plans with funding shortfalls. The major financial shock at the beginning of the twenty-first century—the slump in the equities markets (producing a fall in the value of pension fund assets) and the decline in interest rates (producing a sharper rise in the present value of future plan obligations)—hit essentially all defined-benefit sponsors. The new funding rules require improved contributions precisely when the economy turns down and cash is at a premium. This financial pressure has intensified employer interest in closing down their defined-benefit plan commitments. In the UK, sponsors of plans that cover half of all participants in defined-benefit plans have closed their plans to new employees. In Canada, a survey of large corporate sponsors found that 30 per cent had either eliminated a defined-benefit plan, converted one to a defined-contribution format, or were planning to do so.[21]

In recent years, debates over retirement income policy have focused primarily on the impending transition to a much older society and the challenge this presents to public pay-as-you-go programmes. Employer plans, which prefund future benefits and reduce current contributions by investing in high-yielding equities, have thus emerged as an attractive alternative. This is clearly seen in President Bush's well publicized Social Security reform initiative. The plan would reduce benefits to fit within the programme's projected revenue stream. It then lets workers direct a portion of their Social Security contribution to an individual account and invest in equities. Workers selecting this option would have their future Social Security benefits reduced at the actuarially appropriate rate, using the yield on government bonds as the discount rate. Because the expected return on stocks is much higher than that on bonds, such workers should gain in the process. And these gains would help offset the initial cut in benefits needed to restore solvency to the programme. While there is broad agreement that Social Security needs reform, President Bush's proposals have thus far gained little political traction.

While retirement income debates have focused on government programmes, policy-makers in Anglo-Saxon nations must also respond to a dramatic transformation in the private sector—the withdrawal of employers as key contributors to the retirement income system.

[21] E. Phillip Davis, 'Is There a Pension Crisis in the UK?', draft keynote address for the Japan Pension Research Council Meeting, Tokyo, 18–19 September 2003; Watson Wyatt Worldwide, *Is There a Crisis? Survey of CFOs on Pension Plan Perspectives, Strategies and Reactions*, Memorandum (June 2004). See also Clark's contribution to this volume.

Employers had contributed to retirement programmes to achieve personnel policy objectives they no longer value, or now find too expensive. In large part due to government requirements, these contributions had to be set aside during the workers' active years and, as a result, prefunded a significant component of the national retirement income system. Because employers were also required to guarantee the solvency of their plans, the system could more safely be prefunded with equities, which carry a high rate of return and reduce the long-term cost of old-age income programmes. With the withdrawal of employers from the retirement income system, policy-makers face a more difficult challenge in securing contributions, in prefunding the coming rise in expenditure on the elderly, and in managing the risks inherent in holding equities in such long-term investment programmes. As evidenced by the difficulties encountered by President Bush's Social Security reform proposals, these difficulties affect not only affect private plans, but also efforts to reform the larger retirement income system.

Bibliography

Items that provide a useful introduction to the issues discussed in this chapter are marked with an asterisk.

Bryden, K., *Old Age Pensions and Policy-making in Canada* (Montreal, 1974).

Chandler, A. D., *The Visible Hand: The Managerial Revolution in American Business* (Cambridge, 1977).

*Clark, G., *Pension Fund Capitalism* (Oxford, 2000).

*Commonwealth Treasury of Australia, 'Towards Higher Retirement Incomes for Australians: A History of the Australian Retirement Income System since Federation', *Treasury Economic Roundup Centenary Edition 2001* (Canberra, 2001).

Coward, L., *Private Pensions in OECD Countries: Canada* (Paris, 1997).

Daykin, C., 'Contracting Out: A Partnership between Public and Private Pensions', *Pensions Management Institute News* (July 2001).

*Esping-Andersen, G., *The Three Worlds of Welfare Capitalism* (Oxford, 1990).

Graebner, W., *A History of Retirement* (New Haven CT, 1980).

*Hannah, L., *Inventing Retirement: The Development of Occupational Pensions in Britain* (Cambridge, 1986).

*Latimer, M., *Industrial Pension Systems in the United States and Canada* (New York, 1932).

Lazear, E. P., *Personnel Economics* (Cambridge, 1995).

Licht, W., *Working for the Railroad: The Organization of Work in the Nineteenth Century* (Princeton NJ, 1983).

Osberg, L., 'Poverty among Senior Citizens: A Canadian Success Story', in *International Perspective*, LIS Working Paper 274 (Differdange, 2001).

Raphael, M., *Pensions and Public Servants: A Study of the Origins of the British System* (Paris, 1964).
*Sass, S., *The Promise of Private Pensions* (Cambridge, 1997).
Watson Wyatt Worldwide, *Is There a Crisis? Survey of CFOs on Pension Plan Perspectives, Strategies and Reactions*, Memorandum (June 2004).
Whiteside, N., 'Historical Perspectives and the Politics of Pension Reform', in G. L. Clark and N. Whiteside (eds), *Pension Security in the Twenty-first Century* (Oxford, 2003).
Wooten, J., *The Employee Retirement Income Security Act of 1974: A Political History* (Berkeley CA, 2005).
Yamada, A., *The Evolving Retirement Income Package: Trends in Adequacy and Equality* (Paris, 2002).

14. Pension Reforms in Southern Europe: The Italian Experience

MAURIZIO FERRERA

South European Pension Systems

The pension systems of Italy, Spain, Portugal, and Greece are organized according to the Bismarckian blueprint: 'corporatist' schemes of compulsory insurance covering different occupational groups, with different regulations. Historically, Italy pioneered developments by introducing compulsory pension insurance in 1919. Portugal and Greece followed suit in the mid-1930s, while in Spain fully fledged compulsory pension insurance arrived in 1947. Between the 1950s and 1980s the South European pension systems were significantly expanded in terms of coverage and improved in terms of benefits. Pay-as-you-go (PAYG) became the dominant form of financing, and very generous earnings-related formulas were introduced (envisaging replacement rates as high as 80–90 per cent), as well as means-tested minimum or social pensions for those elderly who had not contributed sufficiently to gain a social insurance pension.

In the wake of these expansionary reforms, pension expenditure grew rather rapidly in the course of the 1980s and 1990s. In Portugal and Spain, pension expenditure caught up with the EU-15 average by the mid-1990s, while in Greece and especially in Italy the EU-15 average was surpassed by several percentage points (see Table 14.1). Given the prospects of demographic ageing and system maturation, coupled with tighter budgetary constraints, the size and trends of public pensions started to raise increasing worries in the policy agenda. This prompted a number of restrictive reforms aimed at stabilizing spending and at reconfiguring the overall architecture of the pension system. The main ingredients of the reform sequence that started in the early 1990s in all four countries can be summarized as follows:[1]

- restrictive reforms of the pension formula, with a view to reducing replacement rates and tightening the link between contributions and benefits;
- restrictive reforms of wage-indexing mechanisms;
- introduction of penalties for early retirement;
- measures aimed at harmonizing regulations across the various occupational groups;
- improvement of means-tested pensions;
- incentives for a greater reliance on funding through the development of reserve funds and supplementary funded pension pillars.

The latter ingredient is of particular importance. In the European landscape, the pension systems of Southern Europe stand out for having 'invested'—historically—almost exclusively, and very generously, in the first state pension pillar, crowding out supplementary, funded alternatives. Down-sizing the scale of the first pillar has become a top priority in Southern Europe—and especially in Italy and Greece—also with a view to recalibrating the whole welfare state from the (over) protection of old age to the (under) protection of other life-cycle risks, in particular towards the needs of families, women, children, and the frail elderly.

The rest of this chapter illustrates the trajectory of pension reform in the largest country of Southern Europe. Italy's experience is interesting for at least two reasons: the condition of public pensions in the early 1990s was particularly serious, in terms of sustainability and internal imbalances. The period 1992–2005 has witnessed a number of incisive and

[1] On the development and reform of welfare state and pension systems in Southern European countries, see: for Greece, Greek Minister of Economy and Finance and Ministry of Labour and Social Security, *The Greek Report on Pension Strategy* (Athens, 2002), M. Matsaganis, *A Tale of Recurrent Policy Failure? Tackling Retirement Pensions in Greece*, URGE Working Paper 1/2004 (2004), and P. Triantafillou, 'Pension Reform in Greece', paper presented at the 15th SASE Meeting, Aix en Provence, 26–28 June 2003; for Spain, A. M. Guillén, 'Welfare State Development in Spain: A Historical and Explanatory Approach', in MIRE, *Comparing Social Welfare Systems in Southern Europe, Florence Conference, vol. 3* (Paris, 1997), pp. 67–92, Ministerio de trabajo y asuntos sociales, *Report on the Spanish National Strategy for the Future of the Pension System* (Madrid, 2002), and F. Blanco, 'The Spanish Public Retirement Pensions System: Principal Challenges and Recent Developments', *International Social Security Review*, 55, 3 (2002); for Portugal, M. Ferrera, A. Hemerijck, and M. Rhodes, *The Future of Social Europe: Recasting Work and Welfare in the New Economy* (Oeiras, 2000), and Ministère de la Sécurité Sociale, *Rapport national de stratégie sur l'avenir des systèmes de pensions* (Lisbon, 2002).

Table 14.1. Public pension expenditure as a proportion of GDP (%) in Southern European countries, 1980–2001.

	1980	1985	1990	1995	1996	1997	1998	1999	2000	2001
Greece	6.0	9.7	11.5	11.2	11.7	11.8	12.6	12.8	12.7	13.6
Italy	9.1	11.4	12.1	13.3	13.5	14.1	13.8	14.1	13.8	13.9
Portugal	4.1	4.5	5.4	7.7	8.3	8.2	8.2	8.6	9.0	9.4
Spain	6.4	7.7	8.3	8.4	9.5	9.4	9.1	9.0	9.1	8.9
EU-15	8.1	8.9	9.3	9.6	10.2	10.1	10.0	9.9	9.8	9.9

Source: OCSE, *Social Expenditure Database.*

paradigmatic reforms, which have significantly improved the financial situation and laid the conditions of a thorough reconfiguration of the overall pension architecture.[2] The next section illustrates the main reforms of the first pillar; the third section illustrates the efforts for promoting the development of a second, funded pillar; the final section briefly surveys recent developments under the Berlusconi government.

Downsizing the First Pillar: The Amato, Dini, and Prodi Reforms

At the beginning of the 1990s the Italian public pension system witnessed a state of acute crisis. Pension expenditure absorbed around 13 per cent of GDP. Its rapid growth since the 1970s was largely responsible for the country's mounting public debt and budgetary deficits. Spending projections were alarming: in the absence of reform, spending was projected to reach the 20 per cent mark by the year 2015 and the impressive level of 23 per cent of GDP around the mid-2030s—a clearly unsustainable scenario. The internal organization of the system was marked by several inequities, linked to the historical stratification of schemes and regulations for different social groups.

The first important 'modernizing' reform was introduced in 1992. While maintaining the overall architecture of the system (occupational schemes and earnings-related formulas), the 1992 Amato reform introduced a number of significant innovations in a restrictive direction after decades of ameliorations. The main provisions of this reform can be summarized as follows. The retirement age was raised from 55 to 60 for

[2] M. Jessoula and M. Ferrera, 'Italy: A Narrow Gate for Path-shift', in K. Anderson, E. Immergut, and I. Schulze (eds), *Handbook of West European Pension Politics* (Oxford, 2006).

females and from 60 to 65 for males (private employees), to be phased in by 2002.[3] The minimum contribution requirement for old-age benefits was raised from fifteen to twenty years. The reference period for pensionable earnings was extended from the last five years to the last ten years for all workers with at least fifteen of contributions by 1992 (and to the whole career for new entrants in the labour market). Early retirement pensions for civil servants were gradually to become more dependent on longer periods of contribution. Contribution rates were raised and wage-indexation was abolished.

At first the Amato reform faced harsh opposition from the trade unions. However, the climate of financial emergency and Amato's willingness to negotiate eased the reform process. In September and October 1992 a number of strikes were called, in which union leaders were publicly criticized for their willingness to negotiate. Amato's concessions defused this upsurge of protest: in particular, Amato dropped the proposal for elevating the minimum contributory requirement of seniority pensions[4] for private employees from thirty-five to thirty-six years as well as the proposed freezing of indexing for 1993.

The impact of the Amato reform was not insignificant, both in terms of cost-containment and in terms of equity, especially thanks to its provisions on civil servants' 'baby pensions' (i.e. their traditional entitlement to retire with only twenty years' contributions, at very early ages).[5] But the persistent crisis of public finances, the continuing increase of pension expenditure (in spite of the cuts), and the pressures of international agencies such as the IMF, the OECD, and EU institutions convinced the government in the course of 1993/4 that a more incisive reform was needed. In the autumn of 1994 the first Berlusconi government, elected the previous spring, disclosed a new reform plan introducing very severe measures: high penalties for seniority pensions (a 3 per cent reduction for each year of retirement prior to the legal pension age), a reduction of the accrual factor from 2 per cent to 1.75 per cent per year for those workers who had been less affected by the Amato reform (workers with at least

[3] The Dini reform of 1995 equalized the retirement ages of men and women: see below.

[4] Workers are entitled to *seniority pensions* when they have completed a predefined contributory period, regardless of age. By contrast, *old-age pensions* are paid to workers who reach the legal retirement age, having fulfilled a minimum contributory period.

[5] R. Artoni and A. Zanardi, 'The Evolution of the Italian Pension System', in MIRE, *Comparing Social Welfare Systems in Southern Europe, Florence Conference, vol. 3* (Paris, 1997), pp. 243–66; D. Franco, 'Italy: A Never-ending Pension Reform', in M. Feldstein and H. Siebert (eds), *Social Security Pension Reform in Europe* (Chicago IL and London, 2002), pp. 211–61.

fifteen years' contribution seniority in 1992), and a switch from actual to programmed inflation in the indexing mechanism of all pensions. Not previously negotiated with the unions, Berlusconi's plan raised massive protests: on 14 October 1994 a general strike was called and two weeks later as many as 1 million workers crowded the streets of Rome in one of the largest popular demonstrations for decades. The issue of pensions raised unprecedented tensions between the executive and the President of the Republic, Mr Scalfaro, who recommended separating pension reform from the budget for 1995 that needed to be approved by the end of 1994. The issue also created fundamental strains within the parliamentary majority, with the Lega Nord party (opposed to reform) precipitating a cabinet crisis. As an emergency measure, Berlusconi was able to enact a more rapid schedule for phasing in the new retirement age (introduced by the Amato reform) as well as a temporary freeze on all seniority benefits. After the approval of the budget in December 1994, the first Berlusconi cabinet fell and was replaced by Lamberto Dini's technical cabinet. The trade unions agreed to negotiate with this government a new broad reform by the first semester of 1995.[6] In May 1995 the Dini government succeeded in striking an agreement with the trade unions, which was approved by Parliament the following August.

The new cooperative approach of the trade unions can be explained by at least four factors. First, the trade unions had undergone an internal process of maturation: the reform-oriented components of the movement grew stronger, offering an articulate platform of proposals to the national leadership. The second factor was the collective style of policy-making introduced by Dini (who was technically supported in the Parliament by left-wing parties), very different from the adversarial style adopted by Berlusconi.[7] The third factor was the significant number of concessions granted to the trade unions by the Dini cabinet concerning the phasing-in of pension reform. Finally, there were the very sharp spurs of the international markets. As a consequence of the political crisis and the ensuing loss of credibility of the Italian government, interest rates started to soar in the winter of 1995 and the lira suffered an alarming fall against the Deutschmark. The unions thus learnt that refusing the reform was not equal to maintaining the status quo, but made things much worse.[8]

[6] M. Regini and I. Regalia, 'Employers, Unions and the State: The Resurgence of Concertation in Italy?', *West European Politics*, 20, 1 (1997), special issue on *Crisis and Transition in Italian Politics*, ed. by M. Bull and M. Rhodes, 210–30.

[7] Regini and Regalia, 'Employers, Unions and the State'.

[8] M. Ferrera and E. Gualmini, *Rescue by Europe? Social and Labour Market Reforms from Maastricht to Berlusconi* (Amsterdam, 2004); Jessoula and Ferrera, 'Italy'.

The main novelty of the Dini reform is the introduction of a new contributions-related formula in place of the earnings-related formula in force since 1969. The pension is no longer related to pensionable earnings, but to the total amount of contributions paid throughout the working career. Since this change represents a sort of Copernican revolution not only as regards the Italian welfare state, but also within the general context of European pension systems, it deserves closer analysis.

Since 1975 (including the 1992 Amato reform) the Italian pension formula linked pension benefits to previous earnings, counting 2 per cent of the latter for each year of insurance seniority. For example, if pensionable earnings amount to 100 and the years of insurance seniority are 40, the pension amounts to 80 (2 per cent × 40). Thus, what mattered was only the *duration*, not the effective *amount* of contributions paid in. The 1995 Dini reform, on the contrary, has directly linked the pension to this amount. To calculate future pensions, the total amount of contributions effectively paid by an insured worker will be divided by an actuarial coefficient that depends on the age of retirement (the pensionable age can vary between 57 and 65). This coefficient will be revised every ten years in order to take into account demographic and economic trends. Moreover, it is worth noting that the new system provides a mechanism for automatic adjustment of pensions in case of low economic growth: contributions paid by the workers are in fact indexed to the average GDP growth rate over the last five years. After retirement the new contributions-related benefits will be indexed to inflation, and the elderly without sufficient contributory rights and below a specific income threshold will receive a social allowance financed by fiscal revenues. A series of 'credits' is foreseen for contributory interruptions due to parental and care leaves, i.e. such periods count as if contributions had been paid. Even if it simulates the logic of a funded system, the new system will maintain a PAYG type of financing: contributions paid in by active workers will not add up to a cumulative fund, but will be used immediately to pay current pensions. This logic is known internationally as a 'notional defined-contribution system'.

Apart from this new contributory formula, the Dini reform has introduced other important novelties: a new flexible retirement age for both men and women (57–65); the gradual extension to forty years of the contributory period for full seniority pensions; the gradual standardization of rules for public and private employees; the graduation of survivor benefits according to income; and stricter rules on the combination of disability benefits and incomes from work, as well as tighter controls on beneficiaries. Besides changes on the benefit side, the Dini reform also rationalized and raised contribution rates and widened the contribution base by extending compulsory pension insurance to special categories of self-employed workers. According to estimates made at the time of the reform, the Dini provisions were to produce savings in order of 0.6 per cent of GDP per year between 1996 and 2005.

The Amato and Dini reforms represented a major breakthrough with respect to the institutional legacies of the past. They were also, however, the result of social and political compromises in which the government had to make a number of concessions with regard to its own original plans. The most evident concession was the introduction of the new pension formula in 1995. The Dini reform exempted all workers with more than eighteen years of insurance seniority by December 1995 from the application of the new contributions-related system (i.e. the same cohorts that had already been less affected by the Amato reform three years earlier).

But the approach of the EMU deadlines kept Italian authorities under acute budgetary pressures: soon after each one of these compromises, the government relaunched its reformist efforts, ever widening the scope of its ambitions. In this vein, the new centre-left 'Olive Tree' coalition led by Romano Prodi and voted into office in the spring of 1996 made the comprehensive reform of the social security system its highest priority. In January 1997 Mr Prodi appointed a commission of experts to draft a broad plan for reform. An articulate report was submitted by this commission (known as the Onofri Commission, after its chairperson, a Bologna economist). In the field of pensions, this report recommended additional measures of retrenchment and rationalization. Despite a positive evaluation of the basic principles and elements of the Dini reform, the Commission pointed out that the phasing-in of the new system was too slow, burdening younger generations with the costs of change.

The Onofri report was the object of a heated debate in the summer and autumn of 1997. In the budget for 1998 the Prodi government tried to adopt many of the Commission's specific recommendations. The fierce opposition of the Refounded Communists (whose votes were crucial for reaching a majority in Parliament) and the difficult negotiations with the social partners, however, forced the government to substantially scale down its ambitions. Prodi was able to introduce some cuts in seniority pensions, especially for public employees: their contributory requirement for claiming early retirement was fully aligned with that applying to private employees, thus tightening the Amato and Dini provisions. Contributions for the self-employed were raised, a temporary freeze on the indexation of higher pensions was introduced, and some steps were made on the harmonization front. However modest (with respect to the government's original ambitions), these cuts had the advantage of being immediately effective and thus contributed 0.2 per cent of GDP towards reaching the budgetary targets for 1998—thereby gaining admission into the EMU club. The most important recommendation of the Onofri plan, i.e. a much faster phasing in of the new pension formula introduced in 1995, could not be adopted, and by creating a cabinet crisis the Refounded Communists were able to obtain the exemption of blue-collar workers from the cut in seniority pensions.

The three reforms of the 1990s have not fully eradicated the distributive distortions and the structural imbalances of the Italian pension system; but they have significantly reduced them. The significance of the 1992–2000 reforms must be appreciated in contrast with the status quo. According to the estimates of the Italian Treasury, in the absence of reforms, pension expenditure would have reached the impressive peak of 23.4 per cent of GDP by the year 2040, before starting to decline.[9] After the reforms, the peak is expected to reach 'only' about 16 per cent of GDP in the year 2033 (see Table 14.2). The virtual stabilization of pension expenditure may not have been enough to cure the long-standing bias towards pensions (to the detriment of all other social programmes) of Italy's unbalanced welfare state. But it has certainly contained its fatal worsening. The reforms have also significantly enhanced the overall equity of the pension system. This has been achieved in several ways: by eliminating the legal privileges of civil servants and the de facto advantages enjoyed by the self-employed after the 1990 reform; by eliminating the premium enjoyed by workers with more dynamic careers (typically white-collar and managerial staff) under an earnings-related formula that linked benefits to last or best years; and by increasing social and minimum pensions.

Promoting the Second Pillar: The Gradual Transformation of the 'TFR'

As mentioned above, in the European context the Italian pension system has traditionally stood out for the overwhelming preponderance of the first pillar, which still provides for the largest share of pensioners' incomes. The reforms of the 1990s have tried to promote the development of a funded second pillar, whose benefits should make up for the future erosion of the value of first-pillar benefits. It is in fact estimated that the

[9] Ministry of the Treasury, *Convergenza dell'Italia Verso l'UEM* (Rome, 1998).

Table 14.2. Projections of public pension expenditure as a proportion of GDP in EU countries, 2000–50.

Country	2000	2010	2020	2030	2040	2050	Max Variation
Austria	14.5	14.9	16.0	18.1	18.3	17.0	4.2
Belgium	10.0	9.9	11.4	13.3	13.7	13.3	3.7
Denmark	10.5	12.5	13.8	14.5	14.0	13.3	4.1
Finland	11.3	11.6	12.9	14.9	16.0	15.9	4.7
France	12.1	13.1	15.0	16.0	15.8	—	4.0
Germany	10.8	11.1	12.1	13.8	14.4	14.9	4.1
Greece	12.6	12.6	15.4	19.6	23.8	24.8	12.2
Ireland*	4.6	5.0	6.7	7.6	8.3	9.0	4.4
Italy	13.8	13.9	14.8	15.7	15.7	14.1	2.1
Luxemburg	7.4	7.5	8.2	9.2	9.5	9.3	2.2
Netherlands	7.9	9.1	11.1	13.1	14.1	13.6	6.2
Portugal	9.8	11.8	13.1	13.6	13.8	13.2	4.1
UK	5.5	5.1	4.9	5.2	5.0	4.4	-1.1
Spain	9.4	8.9	9.9	12.6	16.0	17.3	7.9
Sweden	9.0	9.6	10.7	11.4	11.4	10.7	2.6
EU-15	10.4	10.4	11.5	13.0	13.6	13.3	3.2

* Percentage of GNP.

Source: European Commission and Council, *Joint Report on Adequate and Sustainable Pensions* (Brussels, 2003), http://ec.europa.eu/employment_social/social_protection/pensions_en.htm#2.

Table 14.3. Projected gross replacement rates (%) for a private employee who retires at 65 with forty years' contributive seniority, 2000–50.

	2000	2010	2020	2030	2040	2050
Compulsory public pensions	76.9	76.7	72.4	66.8	64.0	63.4

Source: Ministry for Labour and Welfare, *Report on National Strategies for Future Pension Systems* (Rome, 2002), http://ec.europa.eu/employment_social/social_protection/pensions_en.htm#2.

actual gross replacement rate for a typical worker (e.g. a private employee retiring at the age of 65 with forty years' contributions) will decline from around 76.9 per cent in 2000 to 63.4 per cent by the year 2050, as a consequence of the Dini reform (see Table 14.3).

The strategy that the various governments have pursued for encouraging the take-off of the second pillar has been that of diverting (on a voluntary basis) towards occupational funded plans the mandatory contributions that Italian employers have to pay for the so called 'end-of-contract-payment' (TFR): a lump sum that employees receive when their contract with an employer ends—typically at the age of retirement. TFR benefits are no trivial component of Italy's income maintenance system, in particular for people who retire: mandatory contributions are set at around 7 per cent of gross earnings; the yearly spending for such benefits amounts to around 1.5 per cent of GDP.

In 1993 the Amato government introduced a new regulatory framework on supplementary funded pension pillars. This framework envisaged the voluntary transfer of the TFR contributions into occupational pension funds, encouraged the formation of 'closed' funds (at the sectoral level) run by the social partners, but also foresaw the possibility of 'open' funds set up by financial intermediaries. In the case of closed funds, the 1993 law envisaged the separation of ownership/control from asset management functions, making the latter subject to competition. To a large extent, we can say that the 1993 law already anticipated the EU approach—formalized by the 2003 pension fund directive.[10]

The transformation of the TFR into a proper funded pension system has proven more difficult and slower than expected. The social partners have in fact a strong vested interest in keeping TFR resources firmly under their control. For employers, TFR contributions are a significant source of cheap credit. They are set aside only notionally in the company's budget, and the interest which must be paid on them (eventually accruing into the final payment to the employee) is much lower than ordinary interest rates levied by financial institutions. The trade unions in turn consider TFR benefits as deferred wages and are not keen on making them available to third parties (e.g. open funds) and on weakening the significance of such benefits in wage bargaining. The 1990s witnessed a long tug of war between the government and the social partners about the transformation of the TFR and its mobilization as a launch pad for second-pillar plans. Looming in the background of this controversy is the issue of openness. If moved into the second pillar, the substantial resources of the TFR would be liberated from their captivity within Italy's industrial relation system and domestic economy and would be up for grabs by other players (insurance companies and other financial institutions) and global financial markets. This scenario might be good for the sustainability of Italian pensions and the security of future cohorts of retirees, but would deprive—in the present—important social actors of crucial financial resources.

In order to make the reconversion of the TFR into a second pillar more palatable for the social partners, between 1992 and 2000 various governments offered increasing financial and regulatory incentives—most

[10] 2003/41 EC.

prominently tax breaks for encouraging the (voluntary) diversion of TFR contributions into pension funds. This strategy has produced some positive effects. Affiliations to second-pillar funds have developed especially in central sectors of the economy, that is the industrial sector. The take-up rate for closed pension funds in the industrial sector grew to over 30 per cent, and some particularly virtuous funds have managed to attract between 60 per cent and 80 per cent of potential beneficiaries. But in the early 2000s it became clear that the transition was proceeding at too slow a pace, while spending trends and projections of the first pillar—even if considerably lower thanks to the 1992, 1995, and 1997 reforms—remained a source of serious strain for Italy's still unsound public finances.

Enter Berlusconi: The 2004 Reform

As mentioned above, when the new system introduced by the Dini reform becomes fully operative (around 2035) the replacement rate of first-pillar benefits will be substantially lower than the current 75–80 per cent for a typical worker. This worker should, however, get an additional second-pillar benefit, ranging from 10 to 20 per cent of earnings and thus compensating for the declining generosity of the first pillar. After reaching the steady state (i.e. when most pensions are based on the new formula, around 2050) the system should be able to sustain itself, with an incidence of pension expenditure on GDP of around 13.5 per cent. There are, however, two serious obstacles to this development. In the first place, the transition to the steady state is going to be very slow. The old, generous pre-Dini formula will be phased out very gradually, i.e. it will continue to operate fully for all those workers who had paid at least eighteen years' contributions in 1995. In combination with demographic trends (the retirement of the baby-boomers) this will produce an increase in the incidence of pensions as a proportion of GDP from 13.8 per cent in 2001 to 16 per cent in 2033: only thereafter will spending start to decline. This *gobba* (hump) in expenditure trends raises serious financial preoccupations, also in connection with the persistent stagnation of Italy's economy. The second problem is the actual take-off of a fully fledged second pillar: a development which cannot be taken for granted given the strong interests of employers and unions in the status quo and the preferences of Italian workers, who are reluctant to abandon the TFR system—despite the incentives introduced during the 1990s.

Soon after being elected, in May 2001, the Berlusconi government strove to tackle both issues through a new pension reform. This aimed, first, at raising the average retirement age within the first pillar to further contain expenditure trends and, second, at making the diversion of TFR contributions into pension funds compulsory, using legal force to accelerate the reconversion of the TFR into a fully fledged second pillar.

After a rather turbulent political process, a broad reform act was passed by Parliament in the summer of 2004.[11] Regarding the age of retirement, the Berlusconi reform has introduced a two-step process. During the first phase (until 2007), the postponement of retirement will remain voluntary, but strongly encouraged by financial incentives. Private employees who have an entitlement to a seniority pension under the Dini formula (57 years of age and thirty-five years of contributions) can elect to continue to work, receiving a bonus equal to 100 per cent of pensions contributions—a bonus that can increase net earnings by up to 50 per cent. The second phase (after 2007) will rest on structural changes: a higher, and fixed, retirement age for old-age pensions (65 years for men, 60 for women, with a minimum contributory period of five years) and tightened eligibility conditions for seniority pensions.

Law 243/04 directly reformed the first pillar, while prescriptions regarding the TFR and supplementary pillars were to be confirmed and specified by a government decree. A lively and prolonged debate started, focusing in particular on the mechanism for the transfer of the TFR to pension funds in the default ('silence') option, the portability of employers' contributions when moving from an occupational to an open fund, and the definition of compensatory measures for firms in case of transfer of the TFR to pension funds. On the first two points, two different views emerged, splitting the governmental majority and social partners. On the one hand, the Finance Ministry (*Forza Italia*) pushed for a bigger role for the financial institutions, which in their turn lobbied for measures aimed at levelling the playing field between open and occupational pension funds. On the other hand, the Ministry of Welfare (*Lega Nord*), with the support of the unions, favoured a more prominent role for occupational funds. The employers' association, in turn, was very concerned about measures to compensate the loss of an important source of financing such as the TFR—especially because the troubled condition of public finances (expected deficit/GDP ratio in 2005: over 4.5 per cent)[12] seemed to leave the government little room to manoeuvre.

After more than one year of debate and negotiations, a final compromise was found. In the case of silence by workers, the TFR is paid into

[11] Law 243/04.

[12] Under the Stability and Growth Pact governing the Eurozone, member states are required to keep this ratio below 3 per cent.

occupational closed funds. The automatic portability of the employer's contribution is not allowed when moving from an occupational to an open pension fund. The reform of the supplementary pillar will become operative only in 2008, in order not to worsen the situation of public finances and to give some time for firms to find alternative sources of financing. The decree was finally issued on 24 November 2005.[13]

The measures contained in the decree may represent an important step for the transition of the Italian pension system towards a fully fledged multi-pillar configuration, though the procrastination until 2008 once more delays the definitive take-off of supplementary pensions. Above all, the final outcome on this front will ultimately depend on workers' choices on the transfer of the TFR to pension funds.

Conclusion

The rapid sequence of pension reforms that started in the early 1990s has definitely had the great merit of defusing a financial crisis that, given the high generosity of the pension formula and demographic trends, risked becoming very dramatic. For British policy-makers, the Italian experience demonstrates how pensions can be radically restructured when this is collectively deemed necessary. Previous policy pathways can be abandoned and new directions established. The almost continuous introduction of restrictive changes and the climate of alarm that accompanied them have, however, left Italian public opinion somewhat disoriented. This is especially true for the younger cohorts, who are the main victims of the cuts. It must be noted that young people have also been affected, over the last decade, by a process of labour market deregulation that has significantly increased work instability for all new entrants.

The issues of adequacy and equity for the future pensions of younger cohorts have already surfaced in the debate. In Italy these problems are going to be less serious than in the UK, thanks to two elements. Even after the cuts, Italian replacement rates (first pillar) will remain much higher than in the UK and career breaks because of various social commitments will not seriously affect the amount of pension provided. The Italian pension system is, however, likely to become more similar to the British system in terms of inequality, in the wake of the development of second-pillar pensions. Most at risk here are not only younger age cohorts, noted above, but also the unskilled (who are also more likely to suffer from unemployment)

[13] Legislative Decree 252/2005.

and women workers, whose earning capacity (and therefore contributory record) tends to be lower than that of their male colleagues. The analysis and recommendations of the UK Pensions Commission's first report regarding the flaws and failures of private pension schemes in the UK should ring a bell for Italian policy-makers, who are now working at designing the specific rules for transforming the TFR into a supplementary pension.[14] And if Italian workers could be made more familiar with the British situation, many of them would probably opt for sticking to the old system.

Bibliography

Artoni, R. and A. Zanardi, 'The Evolution of the Italian Pension System', in MIRE, *Comparing Social Welfare Systems in Southern Europe, Florence Conference, vol. 3* (Paris, 1997), pp. 243–66.

Blanco, F., 'The Spanish Public Retirement Pensions System: Principal Challenges and Recent Developments', *International Social Security Review*, 55, 3 (2002), 57–72.

Bull, M. and M. Rhodes, 'Crisis and Transition in Italian Politics', special issue of *West European Politics*, 20, 1 (1997).

Ferrera, M. and E. Gualmini, *Rescue by Europe? Social and Labour Market Reforms from Maastricht to Berlusconi* (Amsterdam, 2004).

——, A. Hemerijck, and M. Rhodes, *The Future of Social Europe: Recasting Work and Welfare in the New Economy* (Oeiras, 2000).

Franco, D., 'Italy: A Never-ending Pension Reform', in M. Feldstein and H. Siebert (eds), *Social Security Pension Reform in Europe* (Chicago IL and London, 2002), pp. 211–61.

Greek Minister of Economy and Finance and Ministry of Labour and Social Security, *The Greek Report on Pension Strategy* (Athens, 2002), http://ec.europa.eu/employment_social/social_protection/pensions_en.htm#2.

Guillén, A. M., 'Welfare State Development in Spain: A Historical and Explanatory Approach', in MIRE, *Comparing Social Welfare Systems in Southern Europe, Florence Conference, vol. 3* (Paris, 1997), pp. 67–92.

Jessoula, M. and M. Ferrera, 'Italy: A Narrow Gate for Path-shift', in K. Anderson, E. Immergut, and I. Schulze (eds), *Handbook of West European Pension Politics* (Oxford, 2006).

Lapadula, B. and S. Patriarca, *La Rivoluzione delle Pensioni* (Rome, 1995).

Matsaganis, M., *A Tale of Recurrent Policy Failure? Tackling Retirement Pensions in Greece*, URGE Working Paper 1/2004 (2004).

[14] Pensions Commission, *Pensions: Challenges and Choices. The First Report of the Pensions Commission* (London, 2004).

Ministère de la Sécurité Sociale, *Rapport national de stratégie sur l'avenir des systèmes de pensions* (Lisbon, 2002), http://ec.europa.eu/employment_social/social_protection/pensions_en.htm#2.

Ministerio de trabajo y asuntos sociales, *Report on the Spanish National Strategy for the Future of the Pension System* (Madrid, 2002), http://ec.europa.eu/employment_social/social_protection/pensions_en.htm#2.

Ministry for Labour and Welfare, *Report on National Strategies for Future Pension Systems* (Rome, 2002), http://ec.europa.eu/employment_social/social_protection/pensions_en.htm#2.

Ministry of the Treasury, *Convergenza dell'Italia Verso l'UEM* (Rome, 1998).

Pensions Commission, *Pensions: Challenges and Choices. The First Report of the Pensions Commission* (London, 2004).

Regini, M. and I. Regalia, 'Employers, Unions and the State: The Resurgence of Concertation in Italy?', *West European Politics*, 20, 1 (1997), special issue on *Crisis and Transition in Italian Politics*, ed. by M. Bull and M. Rhodes, 210–30.

Triantafillou, P., 'Pension Reform in Greece', paper presented at the 15th SASE Meeting, Aix en Provence, 26–28 June 2003.

15. Perspectives on Pensions in Eastern Europe

KATHARINA MÜLLER

Introduction

The dramatic political and economic changes witnessed by Central and Eastern Europe (CEE)[1] and the Former Soviet Union (FSU)[2] since the late 1980s did not leave the area of old-age security unaffected. While the inherited pension systems were rather uniform, the past seventeen years have brought diversity to the region's retirement schemes. Most transition countries have opted for parametric reforms, thus changing key characteristics of their pre-existing pay-as-you-go (PAYG) schemes. A number of countries in the region have embarked on partial or full pension privatization, thereby following the much advertised Latin American role models.[3] Moreover, some countries have introduced notional defined-contribution (NDC) plans, similar to the schemes of Sweden and Italy.[4] Overall, contributory approaches to old-age security—whether publicly or privately organized—dominate the post-socialist pension reform agenda.

This chapter comes in four parts. The first section outlines the pre-1989 legacy in old-age security and the impact of transformation on the

[1] Albania, Bosnia & Herzegovina, Bulgaria, Croatia, the Czech Republic, Hungary, Macedonia, Poland, Romania, Serbia & Montenegro, Slovakia, and Slovenia.

[2] Armenia, Azerbaijan, Belarus, Estonia, Georgia, Kazakhstan, Kyrgyzstan, Latvia, Lithuania, Moldova, Russia, Tajikistan, Turkmenistan, Ukraine, and Uzbekistan.

[3] K. Müller, *The Political Economy of Pension Reform in Central–Eastern Europe* (Cheltenham and Northampton MA, 1999) and *Privatising Old-age Security: Latin America and Eastern Europe Compared* (Cheltenham and Northampton MA, 2003).

[4] R. Disney, 'Notional Accounts as a Pension Reform Strategy: An Evaluation', World Bank SP Discussion Paper 9928 (Washington DC, 1999); D. Franco and N. Sartor, 'Notional Defined Contribution in Italy: Unsatisfactory Present, Uncertain Future', paper for World Bank and RFV Conference on Notional Defined Contribution Pensions (Sandhamn, September 2003).

existing retirement schemes. Then, the different pension reform paths to be observed in CEE and the FSU are reviewed. These include parametric as well as systemic reforms, i.e. the introduction of NDC plans and prefunded schemes. The final part evaluates the state of pension reform in the post-socialist world.

The Socialist Legacy and the Impact of Economic Transformation

During the decades of socialist rule, retirement schemes in CEE and the Soviet Union were organized along similar lines, without rendering them identical. The creation of a unified pension scheme, integrated into the state budget and cross-subsidizing other expenditure items, was the central policy measure of the socialist era. A major achievement of the postwar years was the gradual expansion of coverage, which turned universal by the 1960s or 1970s. As a rule, the legal pension age was decreased to 60 for men and to 55 for women, while the effective retirement age was several years lower.

Employees' contributions were abolished in most countries, and employers' contributions became the only source of financing. The latter were made as a percentage of the total payroll and were thus interpreted as a wage tax rather than a pension contribution. Contribution records were rarely kept at an individual level. Hence, the contribution–benefit link tended to be weak, with pensions depending on years of service rather than on the level of contributions made on the insured's behalf. In a context of high labour participation rates, this implied scant benefit differentiation. Yet, pension privileges—a lower retirement age and higher benefits—granted for occupations of strategic importance marked an important departure from universalism.

The insufficient adjustment of current pensions to price or wage dynamics implied that newly granted pensions were considerably higher than average retirement benefits, giving rise to problems of inter-cohort fairness and of benefit adequacy. In Poland, this problem came to be known as 'old pension portfolio'—the longer a pension was drawn, the lower its purchasing power.[5] Many pensioners continued their gainful employment to top up low retirement benefits.

[5] M. Zukowski, *Wielostopniowe systemy zabezpieczenia emerytalnego w Unii Europejskiej i w Polsce: Miedzy panstwem a rynkiem* (Poznan, 1997), p. 138.

The early years of economic transformation affected the existing PAYG schemes in different ways. Price liberalization and the curtailment of subsidies on basic goods and services required a shift from indirect to direct transfers, resulting in rising pension expenditure. Later, the restructuring of state-owned enterprises had an effect on both the revenue and the expenditure side of public pension schemes. Privatizing, downsizing, and closing down these enterprises resulted in a mounting number of disability pensions. At the same time, early retirement policies were to disguise the employment effects of structural adjustment. The retirement system was thus used as a substitute for welfare and unemployment benefits. By leading to an increased number of pensioners and a falling number of contributors to the public pension scheme, this policy resulted in a significant destabilization of public pension finances.[6] Moreover, as in all insurance-based schemes, the shrinking number of contributors also translated to plummeting future coverage ratios and thus to a gradual erosion of formerly universal social insurance protection of the elderly.

While the times of full employment are long over in the post-socialist world, intra-regional differences in formal employment rates increased rapidly. In 1997, only one out of three was still employed in the formal sector in Georgia, Yugoslavia, and the Kyrgyz Republic.[7] In comparison, labour market trends were far less dramatic both in the EU accession countries and in those countries with lower degrees of transition, such as Belarus. Most of the countries in the region were unable to create jobs at sufficient pace to replace those that were lost, hence employment-to-population ratios are currently well below the Lisbon target of 70 per cent and often trending downward.[8] In many places, the main source of employment growth turned out to be the informal sector. Given that the self-employed rarely make pension contributions, the percentage of the labour force still contributing has often dropped dramatically, the extreme examples being Armenia with only 27 per cent and Albania with a mere 21 per cent of the labour force still counted as contributors. Some countries even registered fewer contributors than pensioners, most notably Albania, Georgia, and Armenia.[9]

[6] M. Cichon, 'Notional Defined-contribution Schemes: Old Wine in New Bottles?', *International Social Security Review*, 52, 4 (1999), 91, aptly denominates this effect as the 'artificial ageing of a pension scheme'.

[7] World Bank, *Balancing Protection and Opportunity: A Strategy for Social Protection in Transition Economies* (Washington DC, 2000).

[8] A. Alam *et al.*, *Growth, Poverty, and Inequality: Eastern Europe and the Former Soviet Union* (Washington DC, 2005).

[9] World Bank, *Balancing Protection and Opportunity*.

Public pension spending also turned increasingly dissimilar throughout the region. Eight years after the start of economic transformation, only Poland and Slovenia had surpassed the West European average, with pension expenditures amounting to 13.7 and 13.4 per cent of GDP. With expenditure levels between 1.7 and 4 per cent of GDP, pension spending was lowest in the Caucasian and Central Asian republics of Georgia, Azerbaijan, Tajikistan, and Turkmenistan, where replacement rates hovered between 23 and 27 per cent of average wages. Yet, the differences in pension spending are also accounted for by the heterogeneous demographics in the region. In Central Asia, the Caucasus, Albania, and Bosnia, the old-age dependency ratio was only 7–12 per cent, while it amounted to 20 per cent and above in Bulgaria, Hungary, Latvia, Ukraine, Croatia, and Estonia.[10]

Post-socialist Pension Reform Paths

In the course of the 1990s, it had become clear all over the region that the old-age security systems inherited from the socialist past were in dire need of reform, to secure their financial sustainability, to meet the demographic challenges ahead, and to adapt to the new economic order. A rather uniform policy legacy notwithstanding, different types of pension reform can be observed in CEE and the FSU. These include parametric reforms, which alter established features of the existing PAYG schemes, and systemic reforms, i.e. the introduction of NDC plans and prefunded schemes. These different reform paths are presented below.

Parametric Reforms

In the early 1990s, it was relatively undisputed among social security experts in CEE and the FSU that essential pension reform measures included a higher retirement age, the abolition of branch privileges, tighter eligibility for invalidity pensions and early retirement, the separation of pension schemes from other social insurance plans and the state budget, and the introduction of an employee's contribution.[11]

[10] World Bank, *Balancing Protection and Opportunity*; K. Müller, 'Pension Reform Paths in Central–Eastern Europe and the Former Soviet Union', *Social Policy and Administration*, 36, 2 (2002), 156–75.

[11] The division of contributions among employer and employee is largely irrelevant in economic terms. However, post-socialist reformers introduced individual contributions as part of a broader agenda geared towards self-provision and insurance-type arrangements—after 'decades of spoon-feeding', as put by J. Kornai, 'Reforming the Welfare State in Postsocialist Societies', *World Development*, 25, 8 (1997), 1186.

Moreover, benefits often became linked more closely to lifetime earnings in order to introduce more horizontal equity and to improve contribution incentives. For example, Bulgaria, Croatia, Romania, Serbia, and Slovakia introduced German-style points systems[12] in the first tier. Yet in a PAYG scheme, a greater differentiation of benefit levels requires extra financial means to improve the financial position of middle and high lifetime earners, if minimum benefits are already very low and cannot be reduced. Several FSU countries, especially those in Central Asia and the Caucasus, could hardly afford earnings-related pensions and thus spent scarce resources on benefits providing minimal consumption.[13]

The introduction of automatic indexation rules amounts to yet another potentially costly measure presupposing fiscal leeway. Where benefits did not keep up with inflation and/or wage growth, they were often so meagre that they proved insufficient to prevent old-age poverty.[14]

Parametric reform has now been implemented throughout the region.[15] However, a large agenda of outstanding issues remains in most countries—notably the improvement of contribution collection, further revisions of the benefit formulae, and a higher retirement age—thus calling for a second or third round of reforms.[16]

[12] With their contribution payments, German employees acquire pension entitlements in the form of annual earnings points in the PAYG state pension scheme. For each calendar year in which their individual earnings equal the average earnings of all employees, one earnings point is credited to their account. On retirement the sum of all earnings points is assessed in relation to the current trend in wages and salaries, as well as other factors, such as the timing of retirement and the system dependency rate.

[13] D. Lindeman, M. Rutkowski, and O. Sluchynskyy, 'The Evolution of Pension Systems in Eastern Europe and Central Asia: Opportunities, Constraints, Dilemmas and Emerging Best Practices', mimeo., 2000.

[14] J. Braithwaite, C. Grootaert, and B. Milanovic, *Poverty and Social Assistance in Transition Countries* (New York, 2000); P. Castel and L. Fox, 'Gender Dimensions of Pension Reform in the Former Soviet Union', in R. Holzmann and J. E. Stiglitz (eds), *New Ideas about Old Age Security: Toward Sustainable Pension Systems in the 21st Century* (Washington DC, 2001), pp. 424–51.

[15] For an overview, see E. Fultz, 'Pension Reform in the EU Accession Countries: Challenges, Achievements and Pitfalls', *International Social Security Review*, 57, 2 (2004), 3–24; K. Müller, 'Die Rentenreformen in den mittel- und osteuropäischen EU-Beitrittsländern', *Vierteljahreshefte zur Wirtschaftsforschung*, 72, 4 (2003), 555.

[16] M. de Castello Branco, 'Pension Reform in the Baltics, Russia, and other Countries of the Former Soviet Union (BRO)', IMF Working Paper WP/98/11 (Washington DC, 1998); R. Holzmann and R. Hinz, *Old Age Income Support in the 21st Century: An International Perspective on Pension Systems and Reform* (Washington DC, 2005), pp. 150–9.

Notional Defined-contribution (NDC) Schemes

NDC schemes are placed beyond the traditional distinction between defined-benefit (DB) and defined-contribution (DC) plans. All contribution payments are recorded in notional individualized accounts, where capital accumulation is only virtual as the schemes are still financed on a PAYG basis. Individual benefit levels depend mainly on past contributions and their notional rate of return.[17] Moreover, future pension benefit levels are linked to mortality trends for specific age cohorts and to the retirement age chosen by the insured. Years spent in higher education, military service, and childcare can be credited to individual accounts, provided the government assumes contribution payment for these periods. An NDC plan fundamentally changes the rules within the public pension 'pillar' or tier, tying benefits closely to contributions and automatically adjusting the benefit level to a shortening of the period of contributions and/or an extension of the years in retirement.[18]

NDC plans, developed by Swedish and Italian experts,[19] introduce a quasi-actuarial pension formula to the public tier. In 1996, Latvia was the first transition country to introduce an NDC plan. Meanwhile Poland, the Kyrgyz Republic, Mongolia, and Russia have followed suit. The Latvian pension formula can be simplified as

$$P = C / E$$

with P = annual pension, C = total amount of indexed contributions accumulated by the insured, and E = remaining life expectancy at the time of retirement. In the case of delayed retirement, P increases due to both a higher C and a lower E. The insured receive annual statements about paid contributions and on the pension they can expect when retiring at age 60, 65, or 70, to guide their retirement decisions.[20]

Advantages attributed to the NDC approach include a gain in transparency, endogenous adjustment to increases in life expectancy, greater incentives for formal employment as well as later retirement, and reduced

[17] This is a discretionary factor, mostly indexing the virtual pension capital to the growth of the contribution base.

[18] Cichon, 'Notional Defined-contribution Schemes'; R. Holzmann and E. Palmer, *Pension Reform through NDCs: Issues and Prospects for Non-financial Defined Contribution Schemes* (Washington DC, forthcoming).

[19] See contributions by Hinrichs and Ferrera in this volume.

[20] K. Müller, 'Old-age Security in the Baltics: Legacy, Early Reforms and Recent Trends', *Europe–Asia Studies*, 54, 5 (2002), 725–48; I. Bite and V. Zagorskis, 'Country Study Latvia', in GVG (ed.), *Social Protection in the Candidate Countries—Country Studies Estonia, Latvia, Lithuania* (Berlin, 2003), pp. 1–138.

future pension expenditure.[21] As regards disadvantages, NDC plans inherently withdraw the commitment to benefit adequacy and may increase old-age poverty. Since they are essentially functioning on a PAYG basis, NDC plans will run into financial problems when birth rates are falling, unless benefits are indexed to the dynamics of the contribution base. Moreover, as in prefunded schemes, unexpected increases in longevity will affect current pensions from NDC plans. The instant differentiation of benefit levels intended by the introduction of NDC schemes was hampered by the fact that few CEE and FSU countries kept individual contribution records prior to 1989. Finally, early experience highlights that in order to function at all, an NDC plan presupposes the readiness and ability to make significant investments in sophisticated information technology.[22]

The Move towards Prefunded Schemes

In most CEE and some FSU countries, the early 1990s brought a first change in the funding mix, when supplementary private schemes were introduced on a voluntary prefunded basis. Given that this move was intended to strengthen the idea of self-provision for old age, these programmes were largely organized as personal pension funds. Inspired by the West European example, some countries also set up mutual funds or occupational schemes, sponsored by employers. The new voluntary pension funds were expected to provide long-term investment capital, thereby contributing to the development of local capital markets. Yet, in most countries, the amount of pension capital collected on a voluntary basis fell short of expectations.[23] This was due to widespread income constraints and a mistrust of domestic financial institutions after a series of scandals and crises, as well as insufficient tax incentives. In some countries, such as Lithuania, small population size and underdeveloped financial markets have long discouraged private companies from starting funds.

[21] R. Holzmann, 'On Economic Benefits and Fiscal Requirements of Moving from Unfunded to Funded Pensions', University of Saarland Forschungsbericht 9702 (Saarbrücken, 1997); N. Barr and M. Rutkowski, 'Pensions', in Barr (ed.), *Labor Markets and Social Policy in Central and Eastern Europe: The Accession and Beyond* (Washington DC, 2005).
[22] In Poland, however, the IT system, specially designed for the new pension system, was not ready on time, with severe IT problems continuing for several years thereafter. In Kyrgyzstan, the IT system was ready on time but not secure: some insured managed to enter their NDC accounts in order to credit extra contribution amounts.
[23] See, for example, A. T. Werner, 'Poland: Individual Pension Accounts Prove to be Unpopular', *Pensions International*, 74 (October 2005), 9–11.

Since 1998, several CEE and FSU countries—among them six out of the eight post-socialist new EU member states[24]—have opted for a more radical move: full or partial pension privatization, thus following the approach long recommended by the World Bank.[25] The first country in the region to embark on the new approach, Kazakhstan, has remained the only transition country to have substituted its PAYG system entirely with a prefunded scheme. In comparison, Hungary, Poland, Latvia, Bulgaria, Croatia, Estonia, Lithuania, and Slovakia have introduced mixed systems by partly diverting pension insurance contributions from the public PAYG scheme to a mandatory prefunded second tier (see Table 15.1). Similar reforms are being prepared in Macedonia, Russia, Ukraine, and Romania.[26]

As noted above, the most iconoclastic pension reform, explicitly modelled on the Chilean[27] precedent, was implemented in Kazakhstan (1998). All Kazakh workers, regardless of their age, are required to contribute 10 per cent of their gross wage to one of the newly set-up pension funds.[28] Most countries in the region introduced a three-pillar structure, however. Argentine-style[29] partial pension privatization was implemented in Hungary (1998), Poland (1999), Latvia (2001), Bulgaria, Croatia, Estonia (2002), Lithuania (2004–5), and Slovakia (2005).[30] In these countries, the

[24] Only the Czech Republic and Slovenia have opted against mandatory prefunding so far: K. Müller, 'Beyond Privatisation: Pension Reform in the Czech Republic and Slovenia', *Journal of European Social Policy*, 12, 4 (2002), 293–306.

[25] The World Bank started propagating this model in its well known report, *Averting the Old Age Crisis: Policies to Protect the Old and Promote Growth* (Washington DC, 1994), and has only recently modified its approach. See Holzmann and Hinz, *Old Age Income Support in the 21st Century*, for the Bank's new position.

[26] H. von Gersdorff and M. Rutkowski, 'Pension Reforms: Security through Diversity', *Spectrum Magazine* (Summer 2004), 13–5.

[27] Chile was the first country in the world to privatize its pension system. In 1981, in the context of an anti-statist ideology and extraordinary powers of the Pinochet regime, the existing public PAYG system was replaced by a compulsory prefunded scheme run by private pension fund administrators.

[28] For further details on this reform, see R. P. Hinz, A. Zviniene, and A.-M. Vilamovska, 'The New Pensions in Kazakhstan: Challenges in Making the Transition', World Bank SP Discussion Paper 0537 (Washington DC, 2005).

[29] In 1994, Argentina was the first Latin American country to replicate the 'Chilean model' under a non-authoritarian regime. Fifteen months of political bargaining left their marks on reform design, however, and pension privatization was only partial. The reformed Argentine pension system adds a newly established prefunded tier, run by competing pension fund administrators, to the public PAYG tier. In the midst of economic collapse facing the country in late 2001, both pension tiers turned out to be extremely vulnerable.

[30] For further details on these reforms, see Müller, *Privatising Old-age Security*; OECD (ed.), *Pension Reform in the Baltic Countries* (Paris, 2004); P. Golias, 'Pension Reform in Slovakia', February 2004 (reviewed in May 2005), available at www.ineko.sk/reformy2003/menu_dochodky_paper_golias.pdf, accessed on 21 May 2006.

Table 15.1. Pension privatization in Eastern Europe and Central Asia.*

	Kazakhstan	Hungary	Poland	Latvia	Bulgaria	Croatia	Estonia	Lithuania	Slovakia
Public tier	Closed down	Traditional PAYG	NDC	NDC	Pension points	Pension points	Traditional PAYG	Traditional PAYG	Pension points
	–	Mandatory	Mandatory	Mandatory	Mandatory	Mandatory	Mandatory	Mandatory	Mandatory
Private tier	Prefunded	Prefunded	Prefunded	Prefunded	Prefunded	Prefunded	Prefunded	Prefunded	Prefunded
	Mandatory	Mandatory for new entrants to the labour market; optional for all others	Mandatory up to age 29; optional between ages 30 to 49	Mandatory up to age 29; optional between ages 30 to 49	Mandatory up to age 42	Mandatory up to age 39; optional between ages 40 and 49	Mandatory up to age 18; optional for all others	Optional for all insured	Mandatory for new entrants to the labour market; optional for all others
	10% individual contribution rate	8% individual contribution rate	9% individual contribution rate	Individual contribution rate will increase to 10%	Contribution rate will increase to 5% (including employer's share)	Individual contribution rate: 2.5% + employer's contribution: 2.5%	Individual contribution rate: 2% + employer's contribution: 4%	5% individual contribution rate	9% employer's contribution
	since 1998	since 1998	since 1999	since 2001	since 2002	since 2002	since 2002	since 2004	since 2005

* Age thresholds are indicated as of the year of reform introduction.

Source: Adapted from K. Müller, 'Las reformas de pensiones en los países ex socialistas', *Quaderns de Política Econòmica*, 9 (2005), 41–51.

post-reform pension system is of a mixed type, combining a mandatory public PAYG tier with a prefunded one, while there is also a voluntary third tier.

In the three-tier model, the first, PAYG tier is mandatory for all insured and covers acquired pension claims, to be topped up by post-reform pension claims if the insured decides to stick to the purely public pension option. The second tier is usually designed as a decentralized prefunded scheme, run by competing private pension funds in charge of account and asset management.[31] Upon retirement, the calculation of annuities is based on the total amount of accumulated funds and the remaining life expectancy of the insured.

The second tier is financed by a contribution rate of 2–10 per cent, to be diverted from the first tier.[32] Pension privatization usually implies that contributions to the newly created individual accounts are financed entirely by employees to strengthen the idea of individual responsibility for old-age provision. However, policy-makers in Estonia, Bulgaria, and Croatia have recently opted for a co-financing of both mandatory tiers by employers' and employees' contributions, and in Slovakia employers even pay the entire second-tier contribution.

Membership in the second tier is usually a question of age and/or choice. While Poles, Latvians, and Croats aged 50 and over were required to remain in the old system, Poles and Latvians under 30 and Croats under 40 years of age were obliged to join both mandatory tiers. Those between 30 and 49 (Poland, Latvia) or 40 and 49 (Croatia) could do the same or stay in the old public scheme. In Hungary and Slovakia, all new entrants to the labour market were obliged to join the new scheme, while all others who were not yet retired could choose the purely public or the mixed option. In Lithuania, all workers may opt to participate in the second tier, regardless of their age, but are not obliged to do so.[33] Contrary to this, all Bulgarians up to age 42 were required to participate in the second tier.

Currently, the new scheme thus offers a purely public as well as a mixed pension option on an optional, partially optional, or mandatory basis. However, given that the young and new entrants to the labour

[31] In Latvia, however, the Treasury acted as the sole asset manager for the first eighteen months, while private asset managers were admitted only afterwards and are now competing with the Treasury's conservative asset management.
[32] Only in Estonia an additional 2 per cent is to be paid to second-tier accounts by those insured that opted for membership.
[33] Interestingly, full optionality had also been a feature of Argentina's pension privatization a decade earlier: Müller, *Privatising Old-age Security*, pp. 25–32.

market are obliged to participate in the second tier, the future pension system will contain a mandatory prefunded component for all. Only in Lithuania can the future insured continue to choose the purely public option.

By the end of 2004—only a few years after the start of pension privatization in the region—between 39 and 89 per cent of the employed already participated in the second tier (see Table 15.2). With 11.3 million affiliates, the number of fund members was largest in Poland, one of the earliest reformers. In contrast, the number of affiliates was just about half a million in the three Baltic states (Estonia, Latvia, Lithuania). With US$13.8 million in assets or 4.5 per cent of GDP, populous Poland also came first in terms of the accumulated capital stock, followed by Hungary and Croatia. In Lithuania, Latvia, and Bulgaria, second-tier assets amounted to less than 1 per cent of GDP. In all three countries wage levels are particularly low. Moreover, in the latter two, contribution rates to the prefunded tier started at no more than 2.5 and 2 per cent respectively.

Advocates of a shift to prefunding claim that the move increases long-term saving and investment and boosts capital market development, resulting in greatly improved macroeconomic growth.[34] The strict actuarial relationship between contributions and benefits in prefunded schemes is thought to remove unfavourable incentives affecting labour supply and savings behaviour. Moreover, pension privatization is expected to restrict the role of the state in old-age security and to reduce public spending in

Table 15.2. Eastern Europe: affiliates and capital stock in the second tier (as of 31 December 2004).

	Affiliates to the second tier		Capital stock in the second tier	
	Thousands	% of employed persons	US$ million	% of GDP
Hungary	2,402	62	4,457	3.9
Poland	11,362	89	13,817	4.5
Latvia	634	62	93	0.6
Estonia	425	71	216	1.8
Bulgaria	2,005	69	166	0.6
Croatia	1,170	83	1,404	3.8
Lithuania	558	39	50	0.2

Source: Own research.

[34] World Bank, *Averting the Old Age Crisis*; G. Corsetti and K. Schmidt-Hebbel, 'Pension Reform and Growth', in S. Valdés-Prieto (ed.), *The Economics of Pensions: Principles, Policies, and International Experience* (Cambridge, 1997), pp. 127–59.

the long term. It is also considered attractive due to imputed rate of return differentials between private and public pension schemes.[35]

While the three-tier approach promises to diversify the risks inherent in both public PAYG schemes and private pension funds, it should be noted that economic and demographic risks are common to both types of scheme.[36] Moreover, future retirees may face considerable investment risks. Capital markets in transition countries are still in a development phase and are generally characterized by weak market capitalization, as well as insufficient listings, liquidity, and trading volumes. In a context of widespread state capture[37] they often lack adequate legal and supervisory frameworks. Moreover, informed choice between the public and the private pension option, as well as among pension funds, presupposes financial literacy.[38] This is a less than realistic assumption for the greater part of the population even in countries without a socialist past, such as the UK.[39]

Costs are also an issue here. Private pension funds usually charge high commissions, reflecting the costs created by numerous sales agents, substantial marketing expenses, and frequent fund-switching. The sum of these charges substantially reduces the share of contributions effectively credited to individual accounts. When internal rates of return were calculated for Poland, Hungary, and Latvia, these turned out to be negative.[40] Upon retirement, converting an account into a lifetime annuity generates additional costs.

The total fiscal burden caused by the transition to prefunding in CEE and the FSU will be considerable, since coverage was near-universal under the socialist retirement scheme. The induced burden is estimated in

[35] R. Disney, 'OECD Public Pension Programmes in Crisis: An Evaluation of the Reform Options', World Bank SP Discussion Paper 9921 (Washington DC, 1999).

[36] N. Barr, 'Reforming Pensions: Myths, Truths, and Policy Choices', IMF Working Paper WP/007139 (Washington DC, 2000).

[37] According to J. S. Hellman, G. Jones, and D. Kaufmann, '"Seize the State, Seize the Day": State Capture, Corruption, and Influence in Transition', World Bank Policy Research Working Paper 2444 (Washington DC, 2000), 2, '[s]tate capture is defined as shaping the formation of the basic rules of the game (i.e. laws, rules, decrees and regulations) through illicit and non-transparent private payments to public officials'.

[38] E. P. Davis, 'Policy Implementation Issues in Reforming Pension Systems', EBRD Working Paper 31 (London, 1998).

[39] E. Whitehouse, 'Pensions, Consumer Financial Literacy and Public Education: Lessons from the United Kingdom', in OECD, *Regulating Private Pension Schemes: Trends and Challenges* (Paris, 2002), pp. 289–313.

[40] UNFE, 'Informacja o stopie zwrotu', Superintendency for Pension Funds (Warsaw, 2001); M. Augusztinovics *et al.*, 'The Hungarian Pension System Before and After the 1998 Reform', in E. Fultz (ed.), *Pension Reform in Central and Eastern Europe*, vol. 1 (Budapest, 2002); I. Vanovska, 'Pension Reform in Latvia', paper commissioned by ILO-CEET (Riga, 2005).

the range of an annual 0.5–2 per cent of GDP for several decades.[41] As contributions are increasingly being drained away from the public pension system, '[t]he "unsustainability" thus may prove a self-fulfilling prophecy'.[42] Moreover, if the prefunded tier underperforms and guarantees are insufficient, governments will find themselves obliged to support the elderly. Hence, even when the pension system is formally contribution defined, the risk of old-age poverty is ultimately borne by the state, facing sizeable contingent liabilities.[43]

Concluding Remarks

Pension reformers in transition countries did not start from scratch. Rather, a more difficult task had to be tackled—the rebuilding of the existing institutional framework, largely comparable at the onset of transition. The number of CEE and FSU countries that have introduced far-reaching pension reforms is significant when compared with the difficulties facing more modest reform attempts in the west. CEE and FSU countries have thus proven their ability to modify radically existing retirement arrangements—a 'pension revolution', according to the World Bank.[44] However, a closer look at experience so far reveals that in the area of old-age security, a panacea is yet to be found. The previous sections have highlighted the limitations of both parametric and systemic reforms in the post-socialist world.

In most transition countries, the different approaches to pension reform share a basic feature: a deliberate move from a universalist–redistributive heritage to strongly differentiated, earnings-related benefits, with an emphasis on contributory financing, often accompanied by a shift from DB to DC. The reform paths outlined above were by no means mutually exclusive. Systemic reform was often accompanied or preceded by parametric reform, and two countries—Latvia and Poland—opted for both NDC and mandatory prefunding. Hence, the strengthening of the

[41] PragmaConsulting, *The Pension Issues in the New Member States* (Mechelen, 2005), p. 49.
[42] M. Augusztinovics, 'Pension Systems and Reforms in the Transition Economies', in Economic Commission for Europe (ed.), *Economic Survey of Europe 1999 No. 3* (New York and Geneva, 1999), p. 102.
[43] K. Müller, 'Public–Private Interaction in Structural Pension Reform', in OECD, *Regulating Private Pension Schemes*, pp. 105–16.
[44] World Bank, 'East Europe Banks on a Pension Revolution', News & Broadcast, 27 January 2005, available at http://web.worldbank.org/WBSITE/EXTERNAL/NEWS/0,,contentMDK:20289271~pagePK:34370~piPK:42768~theSitePK:4607,00.html, accessed on 21 May 2006.

contribution–benefit link often extended to more than one tier of the reformed pension system. In the context of the transitional economies, this policy—intended to improve horizontal equity and to strengthen contribution incentives—raises concerns on two grounds: coverage and benefit adequacy.

The dramatic erosion of coverage in CEE and FSU countries is a direct result of labour market dynamics in the post-socialist era. Crucially, plummeting formal employment is starting to translate into sharply decreasing coverage ratios. The unemployed face high and increasing poverty risk and are unable to make provisions for their old age, as are most informal sector workers. Thus, the differences in level and scope of old-age protection in the region have been widening dramatically, both within and among transition countries. It has now become clear that the current elderly generation will be the last to enjoy virtually universal pension coverage. An agenda limited to contributory approaches to old-age security—whether publicly or privately organized—is inadequate to tackle the erosion of coverage. Hence, the most pressing issue facing the pre-reform pension schemes has not been resolved so far.

Benefit adequacy, a core objective since the Laeken summit, may also be jeopardized by the policy of linking benefits closer to lifetime earnings. It is not only widening disparities between future pensioners, but also likely to result in benefits far below the pre-reform level for those insured featuring a discontinuous working life and lower-than-average salaries—such as many women. It should be noted that meagre female income replacement rates place the bulk of pensioners at a severe risk of poverty in old age: due to lower retirement ages and substantially higher longevity of women in many transition countries, nearly two-thirds of retirees are female. The new rules translate a shorter contribution period and more years spent in retirement into substantially lower benefits. In Poland, female replacement rates from both mandatory tiers were expected to drop from 50 to 30 per cent of the final salary, whereas in Kazakhstan, average female replacement rates were to reach a mere 15 per cent of final year's earnings.[45] These projections are contrary to the pre-reform rhetoric of a win–win scenario.[46]

[45] A. Chlon-Dominczak, 'The Polish Pension Reform of 1999', in E. Fultz (ed.), *Pension Reform in Central and Eastern Europe*, vol. 1 (Budapest, 2002), p. 128; Hinz, Zviniene, and Vilamovska, 'The New Pensions in Kazakhstan', 38. See also E. Fultz, M. Ruck, and S. Steinhilber (eds), *The Gender Dimensions of Social Security Reforms in Central and Eastern Europe: Case Studies of the Czech Republic, Hungary, and Poland* (Budapest, 2003).

[46] See, for example, Holzmann, 'On Economic Benefits and Fiscal Requirements', 3: 'Shifting to a funded scheme . . . allows for arguments that all can win, thus abandoning intractable zero-sum games.'

In the light of the shortcomings of the 'pension revolution' in terms of coverage and benefit adequacy, non-contributory benefits for the elderly may merit increased consideration.[47] Such benefits—variably known as demogrant, social pension, national pension, or old-age allowance—currently play a rather marginal role in the post-socialist world. Due to permanent funding constraints, these benefits are often so low that their poverty-reduction function is severely hampered.[48] The importance of non-contributory pensions will have to increase if large-scale old-age poverty is to be avoided in the future.

To sum up, seventeen years after the start of political and economic transformation, pension reform is still an unfinished task in most post-socialist countries. Pension reformers in the region will need to find answers beyond the large-scale move from state to market and from PAYG to prefunding that is currently taking place, and will need to embark on second and third rounds of pension reform. Yet, it will depend not only on the chosen reform design whether current and future elderly in the region will enjoy decent living conditions, but also on the economic and political context. State capacities—especially extractive and administrative capacities—clearly differ widely throughout the region. As noted by Nicholas Barr,[49] 'if government is ineffective, *any* pension scheme will be at risk'—whether private or public, contributory or non-contributory.

Bibliography

Alam, A. *et al.*, *Growth, Poverty, and Inequality: Eastern Europe and the Former Soviet Union* (Washington DC, 2005).

Augusztinovics, M., 'Pension Systems and Reforms in the Transition Economies', in Economic Commission for Europe (ed.), *Economic Survey of Europe 1999 No. 3* (New York and Geneva, 1999).

—— *et al.*, 'The Hungarian Pension System Before and After the 1998 Reform', in E. Fultz (ed.), *Pension Reform in Central and Eastern Europe*, vol. 1 (Budapest, 2002).

[47] Here, the distinction between contributory and non-contributory benefits is based on the definition in A. Barrientos and P. Lloyd-Sherlock, 'Non-contributory Pensions and Social Protection', ILO Issues in Social Protection Discussion Paper 12 (Geneva, 2002), 4: whether 'payroll contributions to social insurance schemes constitute a prerequisite for entitlement' or not.

[48] K. Müller, 'Post-socialist Pension Reform: Contributory and Non-contributory Approaches', *Public Finance and Management*, 5, 2 (2005). Available at www.spaef.com/PFM_PUB/, accessed on 12 January 2006.

[49] Barr, 'Reforming Pensions', 23.

Barr, N., 'Reforming Pensions: Myths, Truths, and Policy Choices', IMF Working Paper WP/007139 (Washington DC, 2000).
—— and M. Rutkowski, 'Pensions', in Barr (ed.), *Labor Markets and Social Policy in Central and Eastern Europe: The Accession and Beyond* (Washington DC, 2005).
Barrientos, A. and P. Lloyd-Sherlock, 'Non-contributory Pensions and Social Protection', ILO Issues in Social Protection Discussion Paper 12 (Geneva, 2002).
Bite, I. and V. Zagorskis, 'Country Study Latvia', in GVG (ed.), *Social Protection in the Candidate Countries—Country Studies Estonia, Latvia, Lithuania* (Berlin, 2003), pp. 1–138.
Braithwaite, J., C. Grootaert, and B. Milanovic, *Poverty and Social Assistance in Transition Countries* (New York, 2000).
Castel, P. and L. Fox, 'Gender Dimensions of Pension Reform in the Former Soviet Union', in R. Holzmann and J. E. Stiglitz (eds), *New Ideas about Old Age Security: Toward Sustainable Pension Systems in the 21st Century* (Washington DC, 2001), pp. 424–51.
Castello Branco, M. de, 'Pension Reform in the Baltics, Russia, and other Countries of the Former Soviet Union (BRO)', IMF Working Paper WP/98/11 (Washington DC, 1998).
Chlon-Dominczak, A., 'The Polish Pension Reform of 1999', in E. Fultz (ed.), *Pension Reform in Central and Eastern Europe*, vol. 1 (Budapest, 2002).
Cichon, M., 'Notional Defined-contribution Schemes: Old Wine in New Bottles?', *International Social Security Review*, 52, 4 (1999).
Corsetti, G. and K. Schmidt-Hebbel, 'Pension Reform and Growth', in S. Valdés-Prieto (ed.), *The Economics of Pensions: Principles, Policies, and International Experience* (Cambridge, 1997), pp. 127–59.
Davis, E. P., 'Policy Implementation Issues in Reforming Pension Systems', EBRD Working Paper 31 (London, 1998).
Disney, R., 'Notional Accounts as a Pension Reform Strategy: An Evaluation', World Bank SP Discussion Paper 9928 (Washington DC, 1999).
——, 'OECD Public Pension Programmes in Crisis: An Evaluation of the Reform Options', World Bank SP Discussion Paper 9921 (Washington DC, 1999).
Franco, D. and N. Sartor, 'Notional Defined Contribution in Italy: Unsatisfactory Present, Uncertain Future', paper for World Bank and RFV Conference on Notional Defined Contribution Pensions (Sandhamn, September 2003).
Fultz, E., 'Pension Reform in the EU Accession Countries: Challenges, Achievements and Pitfalls', *International Social Security Review*, 57, 2 (2004), 3–24.
——, M. Ruck, and S. Steinhilber (eds), *The Gender Dimensions of Social Security Reforms in Central and Eastern Europe: Case Studies of the Czech Republic, Hungary, and Poland* (Budapest, 2003).
Gersdorff, H. von and M. Rutkowski, 'Pension Reforms: Security through Diversity', *Spectrum Magazine* (Summer 2004), 13–5.
Golias, P., 'Pension Reform in Slovakia', February 2004 (reviewed in May 2005), available at www.ineko.sk/reformy2003/menu_dochodky_ paper_golias.pdf, accessed on 21 May 2006.

Hellman, J. S., G. Jones, and D. Kaufmann, '"Seize the State, Seize the Day": State Capture, Corruption, and Influence in Transition', World Bank Policy Research Working Paper 2444 (Washington DC, 2000).

Hinz, R. P., A. Zviniene, and A.-M. Vilamovska, 'The New Pensions in Kazakhstan: Challenges in Making the Transition', World Bank SP Discussion Paper 0537 (Washington DC, 2005).

Holzmann, R., 'On Economic Benefits and Fiscal Requirements of Moving from Unfunded to Funded Pensions', University of Saarland Forschungsbericht 9702 (Saarbrücken, 1997).

—— and R. Hinz, *Old Age Income Support in the 21st Century: An International Perspective on Pension Systems and Reform* (Washington DC, 2005), pp. 150–9.

—— and E. Palmer, *Pension Reform through NDCs: Issues and Prospects for Non-financial Defined Contribution Schemes* (Washington DC, forthcoming).

Kornai, J., 'Reforming the Welfare State in Postsocialist Societies', *World Development*, 25, 8 (1997).

Lindeman, D., M. Rutkowski, and O. Sluchynskyy, 'The Evolution of Pension Systems in Eastern Europe and Central Asia: Opportunities, Constraints, Dilemmas and Emerging Best Practices', mimeo., 2000.

Müller, K., *The Political Economy of Pension Reform in Central–Eastern Europe* (Cheltenham and Northampton MA, 1999).

——, 'Beyond Privatisation: Pension Reform in the Czech Republic and Slovenia', *Journal of European Social Policy*, 12, 4 (2002), 293–306.

——, 'Pension Reform Paths in Central–Eastern Europe and the Former Soviet Union', *Social Policy and Administration*, 36, 2 (2002), 156–75.

——, 'Old-age Security in the Baltics: Legacy, Early Reforms and Recent Trends', *Europe–Asia Studies*, 54, 5 (2002), 725–48.

——, 'Public–Private Interaction in Structural Pension Reform', in OECD (ed.), *Regulating Private Pension Schemes: Trends and Challenges* (Paris 2002), pp. 105–16.

——, 'Die Rentenreformen in den mittel- und osteuropäischen EU-Beitrittsländern', *Vierteljahreshefte zur Wirtschaftsforschung*, 72, 4 (2003), 551–64.

——, *Privatising Old-age Security: Latin America and Eastern Europe Compared* (Cheltenham and Northampton MA, 2003).

——, 'Post-socialist Pension Reform: Contributory and Non-contributory Approaches', *Public Finance and Management*, 5, 2 (2005), available at www.spaef.com/PFM_PUB/, accessed on 21 May 2006.

——, 'Las reformas de pensiones en los paises ex socialistas', *Quaderns de Política Econòmica*, 9 (2005), 41–51.

OECD (ed.), *Pension Reform in the Baltic Countries* (Paris, 2004).

PragmaConsulting, *The Pension Issues in the New Member States* (Mechelen, 2005).

UNFE, 'Informacja o stopie zwrotu', Superintendency for Pension Funds (Warsaw, 2001).

Vanovska, I., 'Pension Reform in Latvia', paper commissioned by ILO-CEET (Riga, 2005).

Werner, A. T., 'Poland: Individual Pension Accounts Prove to be Unpopular', *Pensions International*, 74 (October 2005), 9–11.

Whitehouse, E., 'Pensions, Consumer Financial Literacy and Public Education: Lessons from the United Kingdom', in OECD (ed.), *Regulating Private Pension Schemes: Trends and Challenges* (Paris 2002), pp. 289–313.

World Bank, *Averting the Old Age Crisis: Policies to Protect the Old and Promote Growth* (Washington DC, 1994).

——, 'East Europe Banks on a Pension Revolution', News & Broadcast, 27 January 2005, available at http://web.worldbank.org/WBSITE/EXTERNAL/NEWS/0,,contentMDK:20289271~pagePK:34370~piPK:42768~theSitePK:4607,00.html, accessed on 21 May 2006.

——, *Balancing Protection and Opportunity: A Strategy for Social Protection in Transition Economies* (Washington DC, 2000).

Zukowski, M., *Wielostopniowe systemy zabezpieczenia emerytalnego w Unii Europejskiej i w Polsce: Miedzy panstwem a rynkiem* (Poznan, 1997).

16.
Reforming Pensions in Germany and Sweden: New Pathways to a Better Future?

KARL HINRICHS

Introduction

The development of pension systems in Germany and Sweden shows several similarities. In both countries the decisive leap towards earnings-related public pensions took place at the end of the 1950s. The expanded public pension scheme became the cornerstone of the German *Sozialstaat* and the 'jewel in the crown' of the social democratic welfare state in Sweden.[1] Again, during the 1990s, Sweden and Germany turned away from established paradigms and introduced pension reforms that changed institutions in a path-breaking fashion. These reforms were initiated to make the respective pension systems fit for imminent population ageing, and they have clearly put both pension systems on a multi-pillar track. This chapter focuses on these recent developments—in particular, on innovative policy changes and the politics of pension reforms. After reviewing their course and content in the next two sections, selected features of the reform process and some potential outcomes are compared. Special attention is given to the issue of sustainability: in Germany and Sweden, this cannot be defined by long-term *financial* viability alone. Only if participants can trust in the financial viability of pension schemes *and* are assured of adequate pension security will the corresponding institutions be considered legitimate. It is therefore important to determine whether recently concluded policy changes have maintained *social* sustainability as well. Will both pension systems continue to protect older people from poverty, deliver appropriate earnings replacement when

[1] Urban Lundberg, *Juvelen i kronan: Socialdemokraterna och den allmänna pensionen* (Stockholm, 2003). Also Whiteside's contribution in this volume.

terminating employment, and assure that pensioners will not fall behind prevailing standards of living throughout their retirement? In comparison, in this and other respects, the reformed Swedish pension system is apparently doing better than its German counterpart, where the process of recalibration and cost-containment has turned into a never-ending story.

Germany: The Sad Decline of Earnings-related Public Pensions[2]

The result of the structural reform in Germany (1957) was that, at the end of a full career (and throughout retirement), the public scheme provided a real replacement of lifetime (not most recent) earnings of about 70 per cent. Despite much rhetoric about a 'three-pillar model', the reform actually meant the birth of a state-dominated 'one-pillar' approach; the high level of public benefits discouraged the development of occupational pensions, and voluntary private provision for old age was largely confined to the better-off. In general, no paid work was necessary after age 65 and status maintenance was not contingent upon private pensions.

In comparative perspective, the pension reform of 1989 that took effect in 1992 was an early response to imminent population ageing. It was also the product of corporatist incrementalism: a continuation of consensual pension politics involving the social partners and the major political parties. One element of the reform was the introduction of the 'fixed relative position' principle, i.e. post-tax wage indexing of new and current pensions, which had actually been applied by arbitrary tinkering with the adjustment formula since the late 1970s. Further, after a transitional period, all workers taking out a first pension before they reach the standard retirement age (65) would face a permanent reduction of their pension benefit (3.6 per cent pa) whereas, previously, fewer years of contributions had merely meant foregone entitlements. Federal subsidies to the public pension scheme were increased to 20 per cent of the scheme's total spending. Finally, credits for childcare (first recognized as an equivalent to waged work in 1986) were improved (three instead of one year for births after

[2] This section mainly draws on Karl Hinrichs, *Reforming the Public Pension Scheme in Germany: The End of the Traditional Consensus?*, Universität Bremen, Zentrum für Sozialpolitik, ZeS-Arbeitspapier 11/98 (Bremen, 1998), and Karl Hinrichs, 'New Century—New Paradigm: Pension Reforms in Germany', in Giuliano Bonoli and Toshimitsu Shinkawa (eds), *Ageing and Pension Reform Around the World: Evidence from Eleven Countries* (Cheltenham, 2005), pp. 47–73.

1991). The cumulative effect of the various reforms was to reduce the contribution rate to 26.9 per cent instead of a projected 36.4 per cent by 2030.[3] All political actors concurred that no substantial readjustments would be needed before 2010.

Until 2001, when a tacit consensus between the relevant political actors re-emerged and facilitated the introduction of a path-breaking reform, further changes in public pensions after 1989 were highly controversial. As numbers of elderly unemployed claiming an early retirement pension (at age 60) rose, the phasing-out of early retirement options without permanent deductions was accelerated in 1996. Various non-contributory entitlements were also reduced, thereby strengthening the link between contributions and benefits. These changes were a prelude for a more substantial reform legislated in 1997, again bitterly opposed by the Social Democrats and the labour unions. In particular, they resisted reductions in disability pensions and the inclusion of a demographic factor in the benefit formula (that would have led to a gradually declining replacement rate as longevity increased), but did not oppose improved childcare credits and higher federal subsidies (funded by a higher rate of VAT). After coming into office in 1998, the Red–Green government under Chancellor Schroeder suspended both of the 'social atrocities' and legislated a more moderate reform of disability pensions in 2000 instead. Moreover, it introduced (and subsequently raised) an energy tax (*Öko-steuer*), funnelling the revenues into the budget of the public pension scheme in order to ensure a lower contribution rate. Finally, the Red–Green government created a paradigmatic change when it introduced a reform package in 2001, involving three important innovations.

First, the reform replaced the principle of 'fixed relative position' with that of a 'fixed contribution rate'.[4] The contribution rate must not exceed 20 per cent by 2020 and 22 per cent by 2030. In order to keep to these targets, 'brake mechanisms' were included in the benefit formula, and the government was empowered to take further 'appropriate' action if necessary. Thus, the benefit level became the dependent variable (and revenues from predefined maximum contribution rates the independent one), and its expected decline meant a clear departure from the doctrine of status maintenance (after a complete full-time career) sustained by public pensions alone.

[3] 'Gutachten des Sozialbeirats zum Rentenversicherungsbericht 1998', in Bundesregierung, *Rentenversicherungsbericht 1998*, Deutscher Bundestag, Drucksache 13/11290, Bonn 1998, pp. 239–51 (p. 242).

[4] John Myles, 'A New Social Contract for the Elderly?', in Gösta Esping-Andersen *et al.*, *Why We Need a New Welfare State* (Oxford, 2002), pp. 130–72.

Second, the core of the 2001 reform was the institutionalization of the *Riester-Rente* that is designed to close the resulting pension gap. From 2002, voluntary take-up of certified savings plans was rewarded with direct subsidies or tax privileges, biased in favour of families raising children and high-income earners. These incentives (which also apply if a proportion of earnings is converted into contributions to an employer-sponsored occupational pension plan) are limited to savings of 4 per cent of earnings from 2008. This extension to retirement income policy has irrevocably put the German pension system on a multi-pillar track, replacing the public pension policy and a one-pillar approach that had been in place since 1957.

Less attention has been paid to a third innovation, designed to close another gap. Old-age (and disability) pensioners with insufficient resources are no longer referred to the general social assistance scheme, but, rather, are entitled to benefits from a special basic security scheme which are still means-tested and not higher than before. However, the obligation of adult children to financially support their elderly parents is removed. It is expected that this will increase the take-up rate, and non-stigmatized access to benefits under the new scheme will make the combined effects of 'new risks' in the labour market (less regular full-time employment) and of past and future pension retrenchments socially more bearable.

The 2001 reform gained a majority in the *Bundestag* after the labour unions and the traditionalists within the SPD were won over by some (symbolic) concessions.[5] A tacit inter-party consensus emerged after further concessions were granted to the opposition CDU/CSU; the party abandoned determined efforts to close ranks in the *Bundesrat* and no unified bloc of states with the CDU in power obstructed the reform package. A similar pattern of conflict and, ultimately, of conflict resolution occurred in 2004. Based on recommendations of two reform commissions, new proposals included a shift in pension taxation (gradually, contributions will be tax-exempt; correspondingly, benefits are taxed upon receipt) and another change in the benefit formula. Calculations made prior to the 2001 reform had turned out to be overly optimistic. In order not to miss the contribution targets, a so-called 'sustainability factor', taking account of the changing numerical relation of pensioners and contributors, was included in the benefit formula which will create a further decline in the

[5] Christine Trampusch, 'Sequenzorientierte Policy-Analyse: Warum die Rentenreform von Walter Riester nicht an Reformblockaden scheiterte', *Berliner Journal für Soziologie*, 16, 1 (2006), 55–76; Hinrichs, 'New Century', pp. 62–5.

replacement rate. If the change in taxation is also taken into account the *net* standard replacement rate is going to drop from about 69 per cent in 2000 to about 52 per cent in 2030.[6]

Since this decline will materialize only if annual wage growth is large enough to kick start all brake mechanisms in the benefit formula, the current Black–Red government plans to introduce a 'make-up' factor that allows for a prolonged non-indexing of benefits until the replacement rate attains the 'correct' level. Furthermore, the government decided to raise the standard retirement age by two years (to age 67) between 2012 and 2029. This measure implies lower benefits for workers who (have to) claim their public pension at an earlier age (at age 62 at earliest). Finally, the contribution rate will rise from 19.5 to 19.9 per cent in 2007 to avoid a deficit resulting from the decline in covered employment.

Sweden: Transferring Risks to Future Pensioners

The political conflict about how to universalize access to earnings-related pensions during the late 1950s developed into one of the fiercest in Swedish history. The central controversy between two political blocs (the bourgeois parties versus the Social Democrats and the blue-collar unions) was about accumulating funds in a state-run scheme since, during a long period of maturation, incoming contributions would exceed pension outlays. Placing these surpluses in public buffer funds provided the government with enormous power to control the economy ('pension fund socialism'). In the end, the Social Democrats prevailed over the opposition of the bourgeois parties, and in 1959 a public earnings-related pension scheme (ATP) was enacted.[7]

In the early 1990s, when a parliamentary commission on pensions presented its final report, Sweden entered into a deep economic crisis. The commission emphasized that the costs of the ATP scheme were strongly dependent on economic growth and vulnerable to further increases in longevity. Moreover, the report showed (again) the unfairness of the 15/30 rule (a full pension was earned after thirty years of employment based on the fifteen best earning years) to workers with a flat earnings profile, blue-collar workers of both sexes in particular. Finally, the

[6] Winfried Hain, Albert Lohmann, and Eckhard Lübke, 'Veränderungen bei der Rentenanpassung durch das "RV-Nachhaltigkeitsgesetz"', *Deutsche Rentenversicherung*, 59, 6–7 (2004), 333–49, at 344.

[7] Hugh Heclo, *Modern Social Policies in Britain and Sweden: From Relief to Income Maintenance* (New Haven CT, 1974), pp. 232–52.

depletion of the ATP funds in future would endanger an adequate national savings rate. These undeniable problems and the inability of the commission members to agree upon remedies stimulated the creation by the new right-wing government of a pension reform group in 1991. This included experts from all seven parties in parliament but not from the social partners or other interest groups. Although the institutional changes that emanated from the reform group's work were at least as radical as the state pension system created thirty years before, it was incomparably less controversial. From the beginning, it was agreed that, even in the long run, a reformed pension system should not become more costly than it was in the early 1990s when the total contribution rate stood at about 18.5 per cent. Additionally, to make a reformed system politically stable, all parties agreeing to the reform in the first place would support future refinements and amendments as well.[8] The *Riksdag* approved the framework legislation, based on a compromise between the four non-socialist parties and the Social Democrats, in June 1994. In a now renamed 'implementation group', representatives from the five parties supporting the reform (with external experts) continued working on the technical details. It was finally legislated in June 1998 after the reform coalition had fended off criticism, particularly from the labour unions; the Social Democratic leadership successfully coped with protests from rank-and-file members.[9]

A central feature of the new system was the transition of the ATP scheme into a so-called notional defined-contribution plan (NDC). This version of a pay-as-you-go (PAYG) scheme almost perfectly mimics a fully funded pension plan (FDC) and provides nearly as much choice for the participants (with regard to sharing pension rights between spouses, retirement age, or withdrawal options), but also contains a number of its risks. The new scheme is based on individual lifetime accounts, with benefits explicitly linked to contributions paid so that the accumulation of entitlements becomes transparent, thus creating stronger property rights as well as a sense of actuarial fairness. While it strengthens incentives to

[8] Anders Lindbom, 'De borgerliga partierna och pensionsreformen', in Joakim Palme (ed.), *Hur blev den stora kompromissen möjlig? Politiken bakom den svenska pensionsreformen* (Stockholm, 2001), pp. 50–87.

[9] Karen Anderson and Traute Meyer, 'Social Democracy, Unions, and Pension Politics in Germany and Sweden', *Journal of Public Policy*, 23, 1 (2003), 23–54; Urban Lundberg, *Social Democracy Lost: The Social Democratic Party in Sweden and the Politics of Pension Reform, 1978–1998*, Institutet för Framtidsstudier, Arbetsrapport 2005:1 (Stockholm, 2005); Joakim Palme, 'Pension Reform in Sweden and the Changing Boundaries between Public and Private', in Gordon L. Clark and Noel Whiteside (eds), *Pension Security in the 21st Century: Redrawing the Public–Private Debate* (Oxford, 2003), pp. 144–67.

work and minimizes distortions, NDC pensions become less predictable: contributions yield an interest corresponding to the growth of per capita income. When the accumulated (notional) pension wealth is converted into an annuity at the end of the working life, the actual replacement ratio depends on that cohort's life expectancy at age 65. Finally, the new NDC scheme is designed to operate at a stable contribution rate of 16 per cent. If this target becomes endangered an 'automatic balance mechanism' is triggered by which NDC pension wealth as well as actual pensions are temporarily indexed at a lower rate.[10] In this way violating (notional) 'property rights' may possibly become the Achilles' heel of the NDC scheme.

In addition, 2.5 percentage points of the total contribution rate are channelled into individual prefunded accounts for a premium pension. This partial privatization of the mandatory pension system was its most controversial aspect. Calculations showed that a contribution rate of 16 per cent to the NDC scheme would suffice to honour all earned entitlements, but future benefits were lower than hitherto provided by the ATP scheme. The right-wing parties proposed a compulsory rate not higher than 16 per cent, leaving to individuals the decision of whether to invest in an additional personal pension. The Social Democrats wanted to retain the current 18.5 per cent rate, which would have meant an additional build-up of collective funds. The political compromise was a mandatory layer of funded pensions assuring adequate wage replacement; this satisfied the Social Democrats and served right-wing interests by securing private ownership and individual choice. The result was a highly regulated but not very cost-efficient arrangement that allows maximum choice. Individuals may choose up to a maximum of five from among over 700 managed funds (and to move accounts between them without extra charge) or not to choose, in which case the contributions are transferred to a publicly managed default fund. This part of the mandatory system offers a wide spectrum of options regarding the timing and form of withdrawal, but ultimately pension wealth has to be annuitized (in a flexible or fixed variant regarding annual adjustment).

Due to the age-related conversion factor (continually adjusted to cohort life expectancy) applied in both parts of the mandatory system, no minimum retirement age is really required any more. The potential retiree enjoys extended freedom of choice and always pays an actuarial 'price' for their decision when to claim the pension: whether to take it in full, or

[10] Ole Settergren, 'The Automatic Balance Mechanism of the Swedish Pension System: A Non-technical Introduction', *Wirtschaftspolitische Blätter*, 38, 4 (2001), 339–49.

to combine employment with a partial benefit, or to take out the NDC and the premium pension at different times. However, in order not to impede economic growth due to mass early exit from the labour force, both pension benefits can be claimed at age 61 at earliest, but there is no upper limit for acquiring further entitlements from employment. Moreover, the right to remain in one's job was raised from 65 to 67 years of age. Age 65 nevertheless remains a central chronological marker since contractual pensions are still related to it; disability pensions, which have been moved to the health insurance system and financed separately, are converted into old-age pensions at this age. Furthermore, the guaranteed (partially means-tested) pension that replaced the universal flat-rate basic pension cannot be claimed before age 65 in order to prevent self-inflicted eligibility, when one retires earlier with too low entitlements from the NDC and premium pension scheme.

With the new public system phasing in after the year 2000, contractual schemes (covering about 90 per cent of employees) and individual savings for retirement become more relevant, since public earnings-related benefits will be lower (unless one defers retirement beyond age 65) and less predictable in future. The pensionable income ceiling for the NDC scheme amounts to only 144 per cent of the median wage of the working population. Contributions to private (unit-linked) insurance and individual retirement saving accounts are tax-deductible up to a ceiling. Withdrawals have to be phased over at least five years and must not start before the age of 55. Particularly among women and older workers, these savings contracts have spread enormously since 1990: in that year about 17 per cent of the working-age population invested in private pensions, while in 2003 about 40 per cent did so, and many more have entered other saving arrangements.[11] The steep rise is partly due to the fact that the NDC scheme pays no widow's benefits for persons born after 1944, but it also shows a spontaneous reaction to anxieties about future lower levels of public pensions.

In summary, the reformed Swedish pension system offers much transparency for the participants. Annual statements explicitly show the return of contributions to the individual NDC and premium pension accounts. The reform implies an almost complete transition towards defined-contribution (DC) pensions (including all contractual pension schemes except for private white-collar workers so far). Concomitant features are a clear

[11] Joakim Palme *et al.*, *A Welfare Balance Sheet for the 1990s: Final Report of the Swedish Welfare Commission*, Scandinavian Journal of Public Health 31, Supplement 60 (Basingstoke, 2003), p. 67, and own calculations with database of Statistics Sweden.

trend towards a higher degree of prefunding and expanded private components within a now advanced multi-pillar approach. As a consequence, all risks incorporated in the respective plan (wage growth, performance of capital markets, increased life expectancy, etc.) are inevitably shifted to the future retiree, whereas the previous defined-benefit (DB) approach left all risks with the plan's sponsor.

'And the winner is . . .'

After 2001 the German and Swedish pension systems show a similar institutional structure. On top of a basic security layer there is a public PAYG earnings-related tier that is less generous than before. Newly created fully funded components have been added to the respective systems in both countries and will change the public–private mix in retirement income. Since new privately managed components perform social policy functions, the regulatory role of the state has been extended. Although the distance between the two systems has narrowed it can be argued that the reformed Swedish system will better protect financial security in old age and also maintain social sustainability.

In Sweden, the universal basic pension was changed into a guaranteed pension that is solely tested against pensions paid out through the statutory system (NDC and FDC pensions) with a 48 per cent withdrawal rate in the upper part of the taper interval so as to maintain incentives to work and to save. Since the guaranteed pension is indexed to consumer prices and employees—in particular females—increasingly attain entitlements from complete contribution records, it will diminish in importance. In contrast, the receipt of basic security benefits in Germany, like Britain, is contingent upon a complete means test. More German pensioners will become eligible for means testing as provisions that hitherto guaranteed socially adequate public pensions have been removed from the scheme, and pension benefits will not rise (in nominal terms) to compensate fully for inflation. Moreover, if they can afford to save at all, additional voluntary provision for old age is not attractive for low-wage workers as accruing benefits will be taxed at a 100 per cent rate. In this respect, the reformed German system is confronted with problems similar to those facing the British government in the late 1990s: how to persuade the low-earner to save, a dilemma tackled, albeit unsuccessfully, by New Labour with the introduction of Pension Credit.

In Sweden, benefits from the NDC pillar will be lower than from the old ATP scheme, and they will decline further (in relative terms) if, in future, the automatic stabilization mechanism is triggered for demographic or economic reasons. In Germany, however, the replacement ratio will definitely become much lower due to the brakes built into the benefit formula. Due to the life expectancy factor in Sweden and raising the standard retirement age in Germany, in both countries the scheduled benefit level can be attained only when working beyond the age of 65. The possibility of doing so is considerably better in Sweden than in Germany because the employment rate of people aged 55–64 and the average age of exit from paid work are already significantly higher. Moreover, the inclusion of increasing cohort longevity in the age-related factor that converts accumulated (notional) pension wealth into an income stream elegantly circumvents political controversies about raising the 'official' retirement age. In Germany, as also in France or Austria, there is much resistance against such attempts; a culture of early retirement has developed and leaving the labour market before reaching age 65 is regarded as a vested right. If older workers have to internalize the costs of their retirement decisions, early exit is discouraged. It remains to be seen whether the incentives are strong enough to actually make Swedish employees work longer in order to avoid lower benefits since the preference for early exit is no less pronounced there than elsewhere.[12]

The *Riester-Rente* in Germany and the *premiepension* in Sweden are meant to compensate for lower benefits from the PAYG schemes and thus to facilitate status maintenance in old age. This objective will probably be attained more fully in Sweden than in Germany as, being part of the statutory system, participation is mandatory and contributions to both schemes are also paid during periods of non-employment (education, military service, first years of parenthood, unemployment, sickness). Furthermore, collective agreements supply about 90 per cent of Swedish employees with contractual pensions from their employers that add about 10 per cent of the former wage to the retirement income (substantially more for workers with above-average earnings). Although the German government has constantly repeated the message that public pensions alone will no longer provide an adequate wage replacement, at the end of 2005, only 5.6 million employees had taken up a *Riester-Rente* contract and another 3 million had opted for its substitute, namely to contribute to (more cost-efficient) occupational pension plans.[13] This amounts

[12] Ingrid Esser, *Continued Work or Retirement? Preferred Exit-age in Western European Countries*, Institutet för Framtidsstudier, Arbetsrapport 2005:9 (Stockholm, 2005).

[13] The total number of workers covered by occupational pensions is higher. In 2003 the figure was 15.3 million; or 57 per cent of all employees liable to social insurance contributions. See Bundesregierung, *Nationaler Strategiebericht Alterssicherung*, Deutscher Bundestag, Drucksache 15/5571, Berlin 2005, p. 6.

to a total of about 20 per cent of eligible workers. Thus, coverage with supplementary pensions is on the rise but far from complete; this objective will not be attained on a voluntary basis. Whatever the reasons for widespread abstention—low understanding of the true impact of the cumulative reforms,[14] no money available to be set aside, or simple myopia—this situation will leave an increasing number of future pensioners without an accustomed level of wage replacement or even at the margins of poverty on retirement. Nor will contributions be paid without interruptions (e.g. during unemployment) or always at the recommended rate of 4 per cent. As the Pensions Commission in Britain has noted in its second report, the problem of persistence is daunting for voluntary schemes.

A larger share of private, fully funded components in the retirement income mix of future pensioners in Sweden and Germany means a greater exposure to financial market risks. On the one hand, as in Britain, the presence of such risks requires strict state regulation of the private pension market in order to protect pension savers' interests. Therefore, the suppliers of *Riester-Rente* products, among others, have to guarantee at least the return of the contributions paid in nominal terms and to provide transparent information of their administrative costs. On the other hand, state regulation cannot eliminate financial market risks completely (almost all holders of *premiepension* accounts suffered considerable losses between 2001 and 2003). Thus, pension savers have to be given ample choice to cope with risks according to the individual degree of risk aversion. This puts new demands on employees as pension savers. Pensions are complex products; choice is time-consuming and presupposes a certain degree of financial literacy as bad choices are costly to revise. In Germany, the complexity of the protective regulation and the variety of products on offer caused many employees not to opt for a *Riester-Rente* in the first place and this contributed to the low take-up rate. Since participation in the premium pension scheme is mandatory, Swedish workers have no such option. If they procrastinate or do not care, their contributions are placed in the state-run default fund. This has become by far the largest fund manager (administering about one-third of all assets at the end of 2004) because 33 per cent of the individuals made no active choice

[14] A rough indicator of the combined impact of labour market changes and pension reforms is the decrease of the *average* pension paid to newly retired *men* as a percentage of the 'standard pension' between 1990 and 2004 from 94.5 per cent to 75.4 per cent (figures for West Germany, calculated from Deutsche Rentenversicherung Bund, *Rentenversicherung in Zeitreihen. Ausgabe 2005*, DRV-Schriften Bd. 22 (Berlin: DRV, 2005), pp. 88 and 233.

during the initial round in 2000. Among new entrants the share had increased to more than 90 per cent in 2004.[15]

In Sweden, the right-wing parties demanded the funded pension component (FDC) mainly for ideological reasons (strengthening ownership and freedom of choice). It is historically ironic that it was exactly the accumulated assets in the earlier ATP buffer funds (in 1995, about five times annual pension expenditure) the political right vigorously opposed during the late 1950s that facilitated a painless carving-out of a 2.5 per cent contribution rate for the premium pension while still keeping the NDC scheme going at a lower rate (and somewhat lower benefits). In contrast, the German public pension scheme operates with a very small contingency reserve. Therefore, contributions to the supplementary (but actually compensatory) *Riester-Rente* come on top of those to the public pension scheme, so that employees who follow the recommendation to take out a contract for the *Riester-Rente* are burdened with additional contributions. These are collectively actually higher than the contribution would have been in 2030, had the public pension scheme continued to provide status maintenance. This reflects the well known double-payment problem when a PAYG system is changed to partial prefunding. In this way, the employees pay half of the cost of the public scheme and the full contribution (4 per cent minus the subsidies received) to the *Riester-Rente*. The employers are guaranteed a maximum rate of 11 per cent until 2030 in order to keep their statutory (non-wage) labour costs in check.

At first glance, the Swedish and German pension systems operate on a comparable cost level (18.5 versus 19.5 per cent contribution rate to the mandatory system). Additionally, in Sweden the government is financially responsible for the guaranteed pension (as is the German government for its basic security scheme). Apart from contributions, the Swedish government pays for participants who are temporarily not in employment (and in education, military service, or childcare), but the mandatory system receives no subsidies out of general tax revenues. This contrasts with the situation in Germany. At present, payments out of the federal budget (including contributions for childcare credits, currently facilitating a lower rate levied on earnings) amount to about 33 per cent of the annual expenditure of an apparently contribution-financed public pension scheme, whereas in 1992 they covered only 21 per cent. Pension subsidies

[15] Statens offentliga utredningar, *Svårnavigerat? Premiepensionssparande på rätt kurs*, SOU 2005:87 (Stockholm, 2005), pp. 78–80.

amounted to 42 per cent of the federal tax revenues in 2004.[16] Tax expenditure on the *Riester-Rente* is additional to these figures. These enormous transfers make the German pension system vulnerable to budget decisions designed to reduce federal deficits. If a rise of the contribution rate beyond the 20/22 per cent targets is prevented to maintain the competitiveness of German employers, the threat of further cuts to entitlements will continue. This leads to the last argument.

When looking at the mode of pension reform in both countries, the Swedish way has definitely led to less insecurity among the public and rebuilt trust in the system more successfully. At the beginning of the 1990s there was an almost unanimous and general perception of crisis in Sweden which was not limited to pensions. Although the reform projects of the two political blocs clearly differed, the crisis perception and the tradition of deliberative policy-making helped to build a broad inter-party consensus for a large systemic reform and to keep the issue out of election campaigns in 1994 and 1998.[17] Probably not part of an intentional obsfucation strategy, such a complex reform package had the political advantage that it was individually difficult to ascertain whether one would be a loser or a winner and how one compared to others. Although more than ten years passed from appointing a reform commission until the final elements were implemented in 2003, this was a 'one-shot' reform; no substantial amendments are conceived for the future.[18] In principle, that was also the idea of the German pension reform introduced in 1989. However, internal challenges (reunification, decline of covered employment, more pessimistic demographic projections) and external pressures (EMU criteria) have led to a series of further policy changes. As such, every step was small and incremental but added up to a paradigmatic change—the 2001 reform denoting the turning point—and turned pension reform in Germany into a never-ending story.[19] The issue of containing pension

[16] Bundesrechnungshof, *Bemerkungen des Bundesrechnungshofes 2004 zur Haushalts- und Wirtschaftsführung*, Deutscher Bundestag, Drucksache 15/4200, Berlin 2004, pp. 63–5.

[17] Lundberg, *Social Democracy Lost*.

[18] A committee that evaluated the *premiepension* system came forward with a number of proposals in October 2005 (see Statens offentliga utredningar, *Svårnavigerat?*). Their implementation would not touch the basic design of the system. In particular, the committee focused on reducing the bewildering range of over 700 fund management alternatives, improving guidance for largely ignorant participants to encourage active and better choice, transforming the default fund into a safer generation fund that reduces portfolio risks as participants get older, and lowering administrative charges.

[19] Karl Hinrichs and Olli Kangas, 'When Is a Change Big Enough to Be a System Shift? Small System-shifting Changes in German and Finnish Pension Policies', *Social Policy and Administration*, 37, 6 (2003), 573–91.

expenditure being permanently on the political agenda has had public repercussions. Compared to the Swedes, Germans are less optimistic about retirement and think more about it, and they are considerably less confident in government's ability to pay public pensions to current as well as to future retirees. Moreover, nearly 40 per cent of Germans believe that an average retiree will live 'not at all comfortably' on public benefits while in Sweden only 20 per cent believe so.[20]

Conclusion

Past generations of pensioners in both Sweden and Germany enjoyed a higher degree of income security than will be the case for future generations, exposed to greater risks. In both countries these risks stem from financial markets. Prefunded privately managed provision for old age is gaining in importance. Greater emphasis is put on individual equity—in Sweden due to an almost complete transition to defined-contribution pensions, in Germany to ridding the benefit formula of elements ensuring socially adequate public pensions. Risk increases, as the ability to produce a complete employment career even beyond age 65 is a precondition for attaining a status maintenance pension. In Germany, as in Britain, individual failure to engage in supplementary pension saving will have grave consequences. Further, Germans of employable age and some present pensioners as well, face political risks since pension reform is still an unfinished project. Low confidence in the public scheme in particular reflects repeated political failure to credibly attain financial sustainability and generational equity. However, constant or even growing pension insecurity hampers the restoration of social sustainability. In this respect at least, Germany may be heading down the track that Britain has trodden in recent years.

Bibliography

Anderson. K. and Traute Meyer, 'Social Democracy, Unions, and Pension Politics in Germany and Sweden', *Journal of Public Policy*, 23, 1 (2003), 23–54.

Esser, I., *Continued Work or Retirement? Preferred Exit-age in Western European Countries*, Institutet för Framtidsstudier, Arbetsrapport 2005:9 (Stockholm, 2005).

[20] Harris Interactive and American Association of Retired Persons, *International Retirement Security Survey* (Washington DC, 2005), pp. 30, 33, 89, and 91.

Hain, W., Albert Lohmann, and Eckhard Lübke, 'Veränderungen bei der Rentenanpassung durch das "RV-Nachhaltigkeitsgesetz"', *Deutsche Rentenversicherung*, 59, 6–7 (2004), 333–49.

Harris Interactive and American Association of Retired Persons, *International Retirement Security Survey* (Washington DC, 2005).

Heclo, H., *Modern Social Policies in Britain and Sweden: From Relief to Income Maintenance* (New Haven CT, 1974).

Hinrichs, K., *Reforming the Public Pension Scheme in Germany: The End of the Traditional Consensus?*, Universität Bremen, Zentrum für Sozialpolitik, ZeS-Arbeitspapier 11/98 (Bremen, 1998).

——, 'New Century—New Paradigm: Pension Reforms in Germany', in Giuliano Bonoli and Toshimitsu Shinkawa (eds), *Ageing and Pension Reform Around the World: Evidence from Eleven Countries* (Cheltenham, 2005), pp. 47–73.

—— and Olli Kangas, 'When Is a Change Big Enough to Be a System Shift? Small System-shifting Changes in German and Finnish Pension Policies', *Social Policy and Administration*, 37, 6 (2003), 573–91.

Lindbom, A., 'De borgerliga partierna och pensionsreformen', in Joakim Palme (ed.), *Hur blev den stora kompromissen möjlig? Politiken bakom den svenska pensionsreformen* (Stockholm, 2001).

Lundberg, U., *Juvelen i kronan: Socialdemokraterna och den allmänna pensionen* (Stockholm, 2003).

——, *Social Democracy Lost: The Social Democratic Party in Sweden and the Politics of Pension Reform, 1978–1998*, Institutet för Framtidsstudier, Arbetsrapport 2005:1 (Stockholm, 2005).

Myles, J., 'A New Social Contract for the Elderly?', in Gösta Esping-Andersen *et al., Why We Need a New Welfare State* (Oxford, 2002), pp. 130–72.

Palme, J., 'Pension Reform in Sweden and the Changing Boundaries between Public and Private', in Gordon L. Clark and Noel Whiteside (eds), *Pension Security in the 21st Century: Redrawing the Public–Private Debate* (Oxford, 2003), pp. 144–67.

—— *et al., A Welfare Balance Sheet for the 1990s: Final Report of the Swedish Welfare Commission*, Scandinavian Journal of Public Health 31, Supplement 60 (Basingstoke, 2003).

Settergren, O., 'The Automatic Balance Mechanism of the Swedish Pension System: A Non-technical Introduction', *Wirtschaftspolitische Blätter*, 38, 4 (2001), 339–49.

Trampusch, C., 'Sequenzorientierte Policy-Analyse: Warum die Rentenreform von Walter Riester nicht an Reformblockaden scheiterte', *Berliner Journal für Soziologie*, 16, 1 (2006), 55–76.

17. Epilogue

HUGH PEMBERTON, PAT THANE, AND NOEL WHITESIDE

The message found in many of our chapters is that radical change in pensions policy is possible. The reforms proposed by Lord Turner's Pensions Commission were certainly radical, although perhaps not as radical as they might have been. Still, they offered an important step towards greater transparency by cutting through some of the complexity that has bedevilled British pensions in the past.

How well did the government rise to the challenge posed by the Pensions Commission? In the months leading up to the white paper, a major battle raged in Whitehall. Although interpreted (as is common in the British media) through the prism of conflict between Tony Blair and Gordon Brown, in fact a very familiar and traditional pattern of British pension policy-making was unfolding, with the Treasury fighting to contain spending commitments on pensions over the long term. It was arguably only the potentially expensive prospect of over 70 per cent of pensioners being able to claim means-tested Pension Credit by the middle of the century that has forced a recalibration of the present system. We suspect that Treasury consideration of the Pensions Commission's proposals depended on their potential for containing this future liability. Treasury objectives have partly been secured by moderating the timescales envisaged by Turner for the introduction of proposed reforms.

A few details demonstrate how the Commission's recommendations have been modified to secure this end. The most heavily trailed of the white paper's proposals is the relinking of the basic state pension (BSP) to average earnings rather than prices. This represents a welcome and significant break with the policy of all but six (1976–82) of the previous sixty years. However, the government intends to introduce the measure from 2012, not 2010 as recommended by the Commission. The change is promised only 'subject to affordability and the fiscal position'; this clearly leaves scope for a future government to backtrack on this commitment. The delay generates savings over the long term (as the link will be restored at a lower percentage of average earnings than would otherwise have been the case). It also condemns a larger number of people to means-tested assistance than the Pensions Commission envisaged and a large number to poverty because they will fail to claim, as routinely occurs when benefits are means tested. Indeed, in introducing the white paper in the House of Commons, the Minister for Work and Pensions stated that about one-third of pensioners would still be claiming Pension Credit in 2050. As just over 40 per cent of pensioners are eligible for Pension Credit today, this hardly represents a radical improvement in the circumstances of the poorer section of the pensioner population.

The government, predictably, endorsed the Pensions Commission's proposed raising of the state pension age. Here again, the hand of the Treasury is visible. The rise from 65 to 66 is brought forward to 2024 (rather than 2030 as proposed by the Pensions Commission), with further rises to 67 in 2034 and 68 in 2044. Thus the state pension age will rise sooner and faster than proposed by the Commission. This makes sense, as the white paper argues, given the rate at which expectation of healthy life is extending. Indeed, as the Pensions Commission noted, it could reasonably rise further, to at least 69 by 2050. Such proposals will generate significant savings on top of those following the rises in women's state pension age which are already in the pipeline. That the state pension age should rise at all represents a significant break with half a century of an assumed male retirement age of 65. But it looks rather less radical when compared to the five-year increase in women's state pension age, set to rise from 60 to 65, which created little public concern when it was introduced by the Conservative government in 1995. This affects all women born after April 1950 and will reduce the pensioner population by 2.2 million in the 2020s. Initial public resistance to the current proposed delays in the retirement age has been somewhat more vocal, but hardly overwhelming. We think more ambitious targets for raising the state pension age, possibly incorporating partial retirement, could have raised more funds to help the poorest pensioners, who will otherwise remain liable for means tests as noted above. Instead, the Treasury is directing proposed savings to restricting public liability for rising pension expenditure. Although the proposals in the white paper add 0.9 per cent of gross domestic product to state expenditure on pensions by 2020, savings elsewhere, chiefly gleaned from changes in women's state pension age, will allow overall pension spending to be kept at the present level of 5.2 per cent.[1]

[1] Thereafter, it is predicted to rise to approx. 5.9 per cent in 2030, 6.5 per cent in 2040, and 6.7 per cent in 2050.

In the white paper the government advertises its intention 'radically [to] reform the contributory principle' in pensions. It proposes to reduce the number of contributing years needed to qualify for the BSP from forty-four for men and thirty-nine for women to thirty for all those reaching state pension age from 2010. A weekly National Insurance credit will be paid for those caring for children under 12, rather than the less flexible annual Home Responsibilities Protection (HRP). Provision for those caring for the disabled is improved as credits will be available for those caring for twenty hours per week as opposed to the current thirty-five. Finally, the government also proposes to follow the Pensions Commission recommendation to change the earnings-related state second pension into a flat-rate top-up payable to all contributors to National Insurance. This, however, was already official policy before the Pensions Commission's final report. As the white paper notes:

> The pensions system we have today is rooted in the society of the 1940s. Society has moved on and, unless we act now, women and carers retiring in the next two decades will continue to suffer the effects of the system of contributions which applied during their working lives.[2]

In this context, the government's proposals seem welcome. However, we are entering a hall of mirrors, and appearances are deceptive.

For current pensioners, the white paper actually offers very little. Women and carers have been ill-served by the British pensions system ever since it was introduced in 1946, as our volume points out. The proposals put forward by the government do nothing to address the present problems of the very large number of people, mainly women, with existing histories of disrupted past contributions and low earnings. The government, although it proposes to mitigate some of its worst effects, plans to continue relating pension entitlements to labour market participation. Pension entitlement will not shift to a residency qualification as recommended by the Pensions Commission. The government argues that there 'is no established system for recording residence retrospectively outside those under the existing tax and benefit systems'.[3] And these reforms will not be backdated. The problem of large numbers of women with poor contribution records and little or no entitlement to the BSP will continue.

But will matters improve in the future under the white paper's proposals? If we take into account pension reforms already in place that came into effect in 2002 and 2006, the real advances apparently offered by the

[2] Department for Work and Pensions, *Security in Retirement: Towards a New Pensions System* (London, 2006), p. 12.

[3] Department for Work and Pensions, *Security in Retirement*, p. 126.

white paper dissolve before our eyes. A higher full state pension of £135 per week (at current prices) will be available in 2050 for those fulfilling the thirty-year contributory requirement.[4] However, first recall that HRP is available today for all receiving Child Benefit, covering children up to 16 years old (an age limit that the white paper proposes to reduce to 12 years). Credits for caring currently cover contributions, at the lowest rate, to the state second pension (S2P), offering roughly £1 top-up per week for each year covered, as well as to the basic state pension. Add to this the additional state pension now offered to those who defer their claim beyond the state pension age, which works out at roughly 10.4 per cent for each year delayed.[5] Today, any woman able to claim (through credits and contributions to both the basic state pension and S2P) £100 per week combined state pension could, if she chose to defer her state pension until 65, be awarded £152 per week under current regulations. This is substantially more than the pension proposed by the white paper for 2050 and more than this woman would receive in 2020, when the universal retirement age of 65 applies to men and women alike. By then, all those with established rights to £100 per week who delay drawing a state pension until 68 (as will be required by 2044) could claim £131.20 if the current system remains unchanged. Not much (if any) improvement there, particularly when we consider that by 2044 most retirees will have paid three years' additional contributions. Through complex changes in regulation and the modification of established concessions, the Treasury's scheme offers an illusory impression of improvement. It may be affordable, but it is palpably socially unjust.

The fourth major plank of the white paper is its endorsement of the Pensions Commission's proposal for a new National Pensions Savings Scheme (NPSS), although very few details appear in print. In outline, the white paper's scheme differs little from that proposed by the Commission. Employees would contribute a minimum of 4 per cent of a band of earnings between approximately £5,000 and £33,000 per year; employers would be obliged to contribute 3 per cent; and a further 1 per cent would be paid by the state through tax relief. Enrolment would be automatic, with an option for individuals to opt out and for companies sustaining defined-contribution plans to do the same. Voluntary enrolment by the

[4] The white paper is actually entirely vague about the date from which a pension of £135 per week will be paid but 2050 is the date referred to by John Hutton in his statement to the House of Commons. See *House of Commons Debates*, vol. 446, no. 158, 25 May 2006, col. 1649, www.publications.parliament.uk.

[5] A lump sum of approx. £4,670 for each year of postponed claim can be claimed instead. The Pension Service, *Your Introduction to State Pension Deferral*, leaflet, May 2006.

unemployed and self-employed would be encouraged. The only notable change is that a barrage of complaints from small business has pushed the government into phasing in the employer contribution over three years, with a possible extension in the transition period if this is deemed necessary.

In fact, there is a worrying lack of detail in this part of the white paper's proposals: but we should note a change in language from the Commission's 'National Pensions Savings Scheme' to the white paper's 'personal savings accounts'. Here the battles within Whitehall over pensions reform were perhaps most evident. The white paper notes:

> Initial analysis suggests that the best delivery model for the personal accounts scheme is that proposed by the Pensions Commission, but the Government will conduct further analysis of this, and industry alternatives, in order to strike the right balance between value for money for the taxpayer and value for money for the saver.[6]

This opens the way for a radical recasting of Lord Turner's NPSS proposals in favour of the private sector. This will be no surprise to anyone who has studied the history of state earnings-related pensions in Britain. In the wake of the Pensions Commission's second report the scale of opposition to its NPSS proposals became evident. It vividly recalled the reaction to a similar scheme proposed by Labour in 1957. The Treasury, then as now, remained averse to a state-run scheme with funds invested in stock and bond markets because of fears that the government would be expected to stand as guarantor in the event of a collapse in asset values. In the 1950s, as today, occupational pension scheme members feared that employers might 'level down' their own pension contributions to the 3 per cent minimum required by the NPSS. The City worried in the 1950s, as it worries now, about the impact on investment markets of a large state-run (or state-sponsored) pension fund. The white paper estimates a membership of between 6 and 10 million (which seems quite pessimistic) but based on these figures one might expect, on quite conservative assumptions about the level of NPSS contributors' average earnings and about investment returns, to see the NPSS fund worth between £200 billion and £335 billion after 20 years—a very large fund indeed. And the industry in the 1950s opposed, as it opposes today, a scheme whose low costs threatened its existing and future business. If history is any guide, those opposing a state-run scheme will seek to channel the proposal in a direction more congenial to private-sector interests, or perhaps to scupper it altogether.

[6] Department for Work and Pensions, *Security in Retirement*, p. 17.

If administration is placed in the hands of the private sector, however, we are being offered a second version of stakeholder pensions, with increased compulsion and retaining full exposure of the contributor to the risks of provider or market failure.

In their introductions to the white paper both the Prime Minister and the Secretary of State for Work and Pensions identify the need to simplify the pensions system as one of their key aims. In this respect, the white paper offers little. Simplification, it appears, is to be achieved through changes that restore incentives to save and by somewhat vague proposals to change the rules on contracting-out, and to rewrite pensions legislation in readily understandable English. The government is deluding itself. A substantial proportion of future pensioners will remain reliant on means-tested assistance; the incentive problem posed by Pensions Credit will remain as problematic in the future as it is today. Almost all of the complex, ramshackle apparatus of the system built up over the past half-century will remain in place and to this will be added the new personal savings accounts, whose administration promises to be highly complex. As Baroness Hollis points out in her chapter, procedures for crediting carers with National Insurance contributions to shape a state pension entitlement further complicates an already dauntingly complex system of administration.

When compared with the reformed schemes created by other developed nations, the white paper's proposals do little to raise the desperately inadequate state pensions on offer to Britain's citizens. Historically, continental pensions have proved more durable, popular, and sustainable than British state pensions have ever been. Even in the USA, social security provides a pension set at around 40 per cent of median earnings, well above the level New Labour aims to achieve in about forty-five years time. As the comparative chapters in our volume show, high unemployment, early retirement, rising contributions, and an ageing population, combined in Germany with the effects of reunification, have all recently forced continental nations to take stock of their established pension commitments. Yet, even following reform, state pensions in Italy, Germany, and Sweden will all remain well above anything to be found in Britain, either now or in the future. In spite of the bitter conflicts and debates witnessed recently in continental Europe, future pensioners will still receive a pension in excess of 50 per cent of previous earnings.

Continental and Scandinavian systems have long differed from the British on three key points. First, they retain a basic commitment to keep state pension benefits above the level of means-tested assistance. In France, Germany, and elsewhere, the state subsidizes earnings-related schemes on behalf of the unemployed as well as those caring for children and the incapacitated. This creates popular support (and fierce opposition to political meddling with pension rights). It also sustains an incentive to save. In Germany, contributions to private occupational plans, offset against tax, have boomed since the cuts in state pensions were introduced. Numbers covered exploded from 167,000 in December 2001 to 1.127 million by March 2003—an increase of 575 per cent in 15 months. Second, representatives of the insured have long governed continental pension systems. Any alteration in pension rights has to be a negotiated process, necessarily entailing public deliberation and debate. This runs quite counter to British traditions where policy is created behind closed doors by economists in the Treasury working on precepts dominated by the principles of rational choice and the assumed superiority of the private sector. Finally, recent continental pension reforms have established notional defined-contribution schemes to replace earlier pay-as-you-go defined-benefit systems. Pioneered in Sweden and Latvia, such systems—described in this volume by Hinrichs, Ferrera, and Müller—align pension benefits to the individual contributory record. The Pensions Commission recommended a funded system but, by advocating a single national scheme under NPSS, removed those risks associated with the collapse or financial failure of private providers and radically lowered administration costs. The white paper, as noted above, appears set to establish private-sector management of individual accounts and thus to raise likely costs of administration and load the contributor with the consequences of provider failure.[7] The Beveridge Report of 1942 forcefully criticized the involvement of commercial agencies in the delivery of state social security. Both historical and more recent evidence here and in the USA has demonstrated how right Beveridge was.

When contrasted with continental pension systems and continental pension policy-making, the weaknesses of Britain's proposed pension settlement become clear. The white paper does not address what Howard Glennerster refers to in his chapter as 'the perverse political dynamics of

[7] The Treasury has already acknowledged that, following its invitation to the industry to put forward alternatives to the Pensions Commission's NPSS, all the proposals submitted included administration costs above the 0.3 per cent level envisaged by Lord Turner (these costs ranged from 0.4 per cent in the National Association of Pension Funds scheme to 0.75 per cent in the Association of British Insurers' proposals). See 'Joint Memorandum from HM Treasury and the Department of Work and Pensions' in House of Commons Treasury Committee, *The Design of a National Pensions Savings Scheme and the Role of Financial Services Regulation, Vol. II: Oral and Written Evidence*, 18 May 2006, pp. 125–8, www.publications.parliament.uk/pa/cm/cmtreasy.htm.

UK pensions'. The white paper implies that a consensus for reform has been constructed by the Pensions Commission on which the present government can build; that those reforms deemed necessary can be enacted; and that we will then all live happily ever after. This volume shows that such optimism is misplaced. British pension policy has historically been made with short-term electoral horizons in mind. The compromises evident in the white paper make clear that nothing has changed. Policy since 1946 has been highly unstable (much more so than in continental Europe)—a consequence of alterations in policy as governments came and went. It has been dominated by powerful vested interests who willingly colluded in ignoring the long-term consequences of their actions. Neither consensus-building nor the long-term health of the system has ever been high on the agenda. The failure to create any inter-party agreement on the long-term future of pensions suggests that priorities have not changed. The Pensions Commission has been the exception that proves the rule. But the Pensions Commission is no more. It is highly regrettable that the white paper ignores the need to create an independent standing commission to mediate between interests and between generations, to build and sustain a lasting consensus on pensions. Instead, the white paper offers a hall of mirrors, giving an illusion of improvement that does not stand up to close examination and is highly unlikely to be sustained.

Conventions. These [illegible] implies that a consensus for reform has
been constructed by the Pentagon [illegible] mission on which the present government can build, that the rationale [illegible] necessary can be [illegible]
and that [illegible] over time. The volume [illegible]
[illegible] displaced [illegible] external policy has historically been
made [illegible] a second [illegible]. The components
[illegible] whatever [illegible] that nothing has changed [illegible]
since 1948 [illegible] highly [illegible] continue to
[illegible] concept [illegible]
and [illegible] dominated by powerful vested interests [illegible]
[illegible] their actions.
Neither [illegible] of the system has
ever been high on the agenda [illegible]
[illegible]
[illegible]
[illegible]
[illegible] lead [illegible]
[illegible]
[illegible]
[illegible]
[illegible]

Index